blue
rider
press

e x o d u s

ALSO BY DEBORAH FELDMAN

Unorthodox

exodus

(יציאה)

a memoir

DEBORAH FELDMAN

BLUE RIDER PRESS
a member of Penguin Group (USA)
New York

blue
rider
press

Published by the Penguin Group
Penguin Group (USA) LLC
375 Hudson Street
New York, New York 10014

USA · Canada · UK · Ireland · Australia
New Zealand · India · South Africa · China

penguin.com
A Penguin Random House Company

Grateful acknowledgment is made to reprint the excerpt from "My Tribe Speaks," by
Anna Margolin, in *With Everything We've Got: A Personal Anthology of Yiddish Poetry*,
edited and translated by Richard J. Fein, Host Publications, 2009.

Library of Congress Cataloging-in-Publication Data

Feldman, Deborah, date.
Exodus : a memoir / by Deborah Feldman.
p.   cm.
ISBN 978-0-399-16277-0
1 Feldman, Deborah, 1986–   2. Jews—New York (State)—New York—Biography.
3. Jews—New York (State)—New York—Identity.   4. New York (N.Y.)—Biography.   I. Title.
F128.9.J5F524   2014   2013046263
974.7—dc23

Printed in the United States of America
1   3   5   7   9   10   8   6   4   2

Book design by Meighan Cavanaugh

*Penguin is committed to publishing works of quality and integrity.
In that spirit, we are proud to offer this book to our readers;
however, the story, the experiences, and the words
are the author's alone.*

To Pearl, my grandmother,

who was my first light along this path

אלע זיי, מיין שטאם,

בלוט פון מיין בלוט

און פלאם פון מיין פלאם,

טויט און לעבעדיק אויסגעמישט,

טרויעריק, גראטעסק און גרויס

טראמפלען דורך מיר ווי דורך א טונקל הויז.

טראמפלען מיט תפילות און קללות און קלאג,

טרייסלען מיין הארץ ווי א קופערנעם גלאק,

עס ווארפט זיך מיין צונג,

איך דערקען ניט מיין קול –

מיין שטאם רעדט.

All of them—my tribe,
Blood of my blood,
Flame of my flame,
The dead and the living mixed;
Sad, grotesque, large,
They tramp through me as through a dark house,
Tramp with prayers and curses and laments.
They shake my heart like a copper bell,
My tongue quivering.
I don't recognize my own voice—
My tribe speaks.

—Anna Margolin, "My Tribe Speaks"

I

מחילה

forgiveness

There she is, just across the street, sulking on the stoop. Seven years old, skin pale almost to the point of translucence, lips pursed into a sullen pout. She stares gloomily at the silver Mary Janes on her feet, the tips of which catch the last rays of sunlight quickly fading behind the three-story brownstone.

She has been scrubbed and primped in preparation for Passover, soon to arrive. Her hair hurts where it's been pulled too tight into a bun at the top of her head. She feels each strand stretching from its inflamed follicle, especially at the nape of her neck, where an early-spring breeze raises goose bumps on the exposed skin. Her hands are folded into the lap of her brand-new purple dress, with peonies and violets splashed wildly on the fabric, smocking at the chest, and a sash tied around the waist. There are new white tights stretched over her thin legs.

This little side street in Williamsburg, Brooklyn, usually bustling with black-clad men carrying prayer books, is momentarily silent and empty, its residents indoors making preparations for the evening. The little girl has managed to sneak away in the rush, to sit alone across from the young pear tree the neighbors planted a few years ago after carving out a square of beige dirt in the stretch of lifeless asphalt. Now it flowers gently, bulbous white blossoms dangling precariously from its boughs.

I cross the street toward her. No cars come. The silence is magnificent, enormous. She doesn't seem to notice me approaching, nor does she look up when I sit down next to her on the stoop. I look at her face and know instantly, with the pain of a punch to the gut, exactly how long it's been since there was a smile on it.

I put my arm around her shoulder, ever so gently, as if she might break from the weight, and I whisper into her ear, "Everything is going to be fine."

She turns and looks at me for the first time, her face a mask of distrust.

"It's going to be just fine. I promise."

Snap. The hypnotherapist wakes me by clicking her fingers together in a classic stage move.

"You did good," she says. "Go home and try to have sex tonight. Let me know what happens. I have a feeling we've fixed the problem. Not completely, but enough for now."

I get out of the chair, feeling dizzy and disoriented. The little girl in the purple dress recedes rapidly from my memory, even as I grasp for her in my wakeful state. What did we talk about? I can't remember. Did she tell us anything? Does the doctor know something about my past now, something that I don't?

Never mind. The important thing is, did it really work?

It's been a year since my husband and I crossed the threshold into our new home and our new life, only to discover that our most important purpose as a couple could not be fulfilled: procreation. Repeated attempts and numerous medical opinions have only served to confuse us further; it's as if a wall has been erected inside me. Could this be the miracle cure I've been waiting for? Will I really be able to go home tonight and finally consummate my marriage?

I often wonder why I went back to that day, when the hypnotherapist instructed me to find some version of my childhood self to reassure. It's always the child lurking within us that rebels, that sulks, that angrily demands our attention. On that day, however, I was quiet and internal. Everyone around me was caught up in their work, and I was allowed to move about, feeling temporarily forgotten. It was not a moment of great injury.

But someone had photographed me earlier. I remember posing in the garden, being coaxed and prodded into a portrait of pleasantness. I saw the photo some years later, and in it I was cringing as if afraid. My brow was furrowed and my shoulders were raised in a guarded posture. It seemed as if there was a person on the other side of the camera making a threat.

The hypnotherapist had asked me to go back as far as I could, and that's where I went, to the moment the flash went off and I was temporarily blinded, unable to see the person behind the camera, unable to recall that person later. But I could not approach her there, in the garden, while she was being watched, so I waited for that quiet, private moment that I knew would follow, so that I could pass on the information as instructed.

The exercise was supposed to heal the wound that had been inflicted so long ago, the one that had eaten so deep into my subconscious that it had managed to seep into my muscles themselves, sealing them shut. Which particular injury had caused the damage I did not know, but the therapist had assured me that all I needed to do was find my wounded self and console her, and the rest would take care of itself.

All these years later, even though I've left my marriage and my community and am raising my own child far away from Brooklyn, I still go back to that little girl. I have so much more to share with her now.

I ask her, "Did you ever think this is where we'd be?"

I'd always dreamed of living by the water. I had glimpsed the ocean only a few times during my urban, closeted childhood in the Satmar community in Williamsburg. My days were spent on asphalt, which would swell in the heat of summer and give off an acrid odor. Trucks would rattle over potholes patched with metal plates, their exhaust poisoning the air. The serenity of the ocean seemed remote, when in fact the sea split into brooding gray serpents that snaked around us from all sides.

I often painted elaborate fairy-tale endings for myself in my mind, inserting myself into grand, ramshackle beach houses, secluded island retreats, houses on stilts with rivers flowing beneath them. Not once during my daydreams did I place my future self in the tenement apartment I was most likely to end up in. The memory of those delightful visions returned to me in the summer of

2012, as I searched for the first place that would truly be my home and suddenly realized that those dreams weren't so unrealistic anymore.

Yet proximity to water wasn't on the short list of requirements I presented to my broker, who specialized in the unique corner of rural New England I was scouting, an area where three states converged, yet which seemed to boast very little of each of them in terms of identity. The area was partly occupied by urbanites who kept a place in the country and embraced by the parents who had moved there for the private schools. After a tumultuous three-year period in Manhattan, during which I had struggled to get my divorce and establish a custody agreement, this seemed like a place to do that which needed doing, the raising of a child, the healing of one's wounds.

The broker, John, picked me up in his old converted Rover; the windows and roof had been removed, and only the supports, wrapped in padded leather fabric, remained. I climbed up into the passenger seat and gripped the roof frame while we jostled along country roads. A field of sunflowers appeared on the right as we drove up a steep hill, only to gaze down an even greater drop on the other side, clear to a river and the verdant mountains beyond. We turned a corner and passed a meadow upon which strange-looking cows were grazing. They had shaggy straight hair, which spilled over their eyes in tufts, and looked almost like sheep in need of a shearing.

"Those are Scottish Highlanders," John informed me. "They're the hardiest of all cows; they can plow any field. No territory is too harsh for them. Great for beginners," he joked. "You should try raising some up here."

This then, was the place for me, I thought, a place where the hardiest of species could thrive on the rockiest of foundations, a place for beginners.

I looked at a few houses; each had some flaw or another. Then we drove down a dead-end street near town, to the very last drive-way, which swung up and around a grove of evergreens, and there it was: a modestly sized contemporary house on a hill overlooking a large lake. It was one of those moments in life when you just know. I went through the motions; the broker insisted it wasn't a sure thing, but I knew it was.

The most powerful thing about living on the water, I would soon learn, is that one is forced into a perpetual relationship with a mirror—a reflective surface in some way quite literal and in many other ways deeply spiritual. Contemplating water somehow has the effect of forcing one to contemplate oneself. A good thing, if one's self needs fixing.

We moved in over the summer. It was a glorious time. Isaac, then six years old, swam in the lake every day. We lay on the dock and peered over the edge to see the sunfish and perch sheltering beneath. He collected snail shells, he tried to skip rocks but rarely succeeded, he spied on rabbits making short work of leafy plants. Every evening the sun would set in magnificent colors over the water, the lake would seem stiller somehow, and the world would get very quiet. I watched, pretzel-legged on the grass, as the last of the pink glow faded, and the crickets assumed their nightly rou-tine. The madness of Manhattan seemed very far away.

This sense of quiet in my life was very new and, as yet, out of character. My friend Heather used to remark, back when we at-tended Sarah Lawrence together, that I drove like a bat out of hell. It wasn't that my aggressive maneuvering around New York traffic bothered her; it was just her way of describing, rather endearingly, my general approach to life after a reckless escape from an arranged marriage in a sheltered community. I was constantly shooting off in every direction, arriving at every destination as if I had a trail of cartoon dust clouds behind me.

I thought a lot about that expression, "bat out of hell," in the early days after making the big move to the country. Growing up we had a similar saying in Yiddish that essentially translates to "a cow out of the stall." It was used to describe a Hasidic Jew who had left the community, likening the person's behavior to that of a cow suddenly let loose after a lifetime of imprisonment. It was believed that such cows were most likely to charge madcap down a hill to their deaths. Hasidic rebels reportedly indulged in wild, drug-abusing lifestyles that inevitably ended in ruin, similar to the cow's doomed trajectory. Freedom posed an especial danger, the adage emphasized, to those who had never previously experienced it.

This saying, scornfully evoked when the conversation turned to the subject of the few known rebels in our society, irritated me greatly as a child. Didn't the phrase do more to point out the failings of life in a stall than the dangers of freedom? Wasn't it clear that the cow would have been better off grazing freely in the first place?

Never mind. If I were a cow out of a stall, then I would be a Scottish Highlander, capable of making it even in the most dangerous terrain, I told myself. There would be no fatal fall for me, no catapulting off a cliff.

I will admit that people like me do go a little overboard immediately after leaving. We do it for many reasons. For one, we don't know any better. It's like we never learned how to move around at all, having been stuck in one place for so long that we can't get our sea legs. We can't quite master a steady gait. Another reason: You know after World War II, when the concentration camps were liberated, how some people gorged on food and died from shock? Deprivation can make you crazy, desperate. I walked around with that post-deprivation feeling for a long time, gorging inappropriately on every experience with the underlying fear that it would be snatched from me before I could get my fill. But the truth is, even without those reasons, we still run from our stalls as fast as we can, just because we can. Because the feeling of being free is so incredible, so intoxicating, we don't want to meander our way through it. We want to race down that mountain, wind whipping past our ears, whooping loudly in triumph.

Leaving, to me, felt like climbing a tremendous hill, one of those steep inclines that becomes almost treacherous in that the more momentum you build while racing down it, the more difficult it becomes to stop safely. If you've ever biked up a hill only to zip freakishly fast down the other side of it, which I did for the first time the summer my son and I moved to the country, you'll understand what I mean. The wonderful thing about it is the natural leveling of the ground that occurs at the bottom. And eventually, we all do hit bottom, and not in the way of the cliché, which I've always disliked. (The bottom is a good thing. Who decided otherwise?)

When you hit bottom, and your bicycle tires spin more slowly, or your awkward, close-together steps become longer and looser, you've hit your stride. You've found your gait. And everything is A-OK. You get a silly smile on your face at the memory of how you felt flying down the hill, and you think, man, I am awesome for doing that.

Let me be clear: my life, right now, is amazing. I have everything I ever dreamed of, and I never forget just how lucky I am to have achieved it. But my feelings have been failing to catch on to the changes in my life; in some ways my brain is still stuck in the past. When I finally went to a psychiatrist to receive a formal diagnosis on the list of mental illnesses I was so sure I suffered from, the verdict of post-traumatic stress disorder seemed almost anticlimactic.

It might not even be that, the psychiatrist said, recommending talk therapy and nothing else. It could just be an adjustment disorder. Those things go away in six months, he said.

And yet, I was having bad dreams every night, waking up each morning enveloped by feelings of dread, and I panicked secretly when in groups or crowds. None of this was consistent with the calm and fulfilling existence I had begun living.

How to describe this feeling? A form of displacement, like being unable to see yourself in a photograph of a scene you remember being part of, or looking at the spot on the map where you know you live but being unable to find the street. Somehow you've been erased, as if it were all a dream. I had begun, since leaving, to see life as an enormous grid, a cross-section of human connections. Every man and woman appeared as a plotted point on an intricate map, lines drawn between them and close family members, longer lines waiting to rush through open tunnels on the grid to anchor friends, neighbors, lovers, even acquaintances. Wherever I looked, I saw the invisible threads that connected people; every person seemed to have their grid firmly and inextricably in place. And I thought of that saying "No man is an island" and wondered how long I'd survive without a grid of my own, and if it was even possible to rebuild one from scratch.

Maybe my residual angst is actually predicated on a real experience, not just leftover trauma. Is it the experience of being dislodged from the grid? Funny, since I can't ever remember having been securely fixed on it, and I have a niggling fear that my birth was a mistake, like a computer glitch that left me permanently disconnected, smack in the middle of a no-man's-land between points, with no ability to form real and lasting connections. The system that everyone else uses seems closed off to me.

I suspect I'm not the average loner. For my entire life I have occupied an enclosed mental space that no one has managed to penetrate. I have grown "close" to people in the sense that we have been in each other's proximity, but never close enough for those walls to come down. Ask people who know me and they will confirm that in a whole manner of ways. Is it just a coincidence, I wonder, that many of my most beloved friends live in different states, or that the meaningful romances in my life have been long-distance relationships?

Perhaps I've chosen loneliness because it is my language. I don't want it to be, but it's the only condition that feels familiar to me, and somehow safe. Of course I'd like to earn my rightful place on that grid, no matter how poorly plotted my location, because this feeling of placement that I'm searching for—well, that's a basic human right. So I'm going to try to figure out how to fight my way in, even though I've been thoroughly trained to fear being a fully realized part of the outside world with every fiber of my being. I don't yet know where I'll end up—in fact I'm starting to realize that the process may be more complex and time-consuming than

I'd suspected—but if there's something I'm sure of, it's that the process itself is worth it. Sometimes it's only through pain that we feel alive; better to have that than no sensation at all.

I had gone six months without a full night's sleep when I stopped into my favorite coffee shop one morning in March of 2013 to perk myself up with a soy latte before I picked Isaac up from school. It felt like I hadn't slept in years; I had been struggling with middle-of-the-night insomnia. As I sat down to wait for my coffee, I recognized an acquaintance, Robert, a local naturopath.

"You look a bit under the weather," he remarked.

"I haven't been sleeping," I said. "I really need to see someone about this."

"You should meet my friend Ed," he said, pointing to the white-bearded man sitting next to him. "Ed's a renowned sleep specialist."

What a crazy coincidence, I thought. I reached out to shake Ed's hand. "Hi, I'm Deborah."

After he introduced himself, I jumped right in. "Have you seen the article in the *New Yorker* this week about that woman who went to a sleep clinic?"

"I did." Ed nodded his head sagely.

"I loved what she said about larks and owls," I said, referring to the article's differentiation between two genetic types of sleeping patterns: early sleepers and risers were larks, and late ones were owls. "I had never heard that before, but it totally makes sense. I'm such a lark."

"That information has been around for a while. But the article really offered very little in the way of a solution to insomnia. Even the woman's insomnia wasn't cured by going to the clinic—it was just more finely diagnosed."

"That's the thing about doctors, isn't it?" I laughed. "They're really good at telling you what your problem is, but not so good at fixing it."

"Very often that's the case, yes."

"Do you think you can help me?" I asked. "According to the article, I'm an MOTN, or middle-of-the-night, insomniac. I fall asleep somewhat easily but wake up on schedule a few hours later, and then I can't fall asleep again until dawn."

"That doesn't work for you, having two sleep periods a night?" Ed asked.

The article had said it was normal, and I'd read the research: middle-of-the-night wakefulness had, until the industrial revolution, been accepted as a normal period in one's daily routine.

"I have to get my son to school at 7:45, though. Then it becomes stressful, knowing I won't get the sleep I need. I'm starting to be afraid of nighttime. I've always been a good sleeper too, before this year, so I can't understand why it's happening."

Ed fumbled around in his tote bag. "I don't seem to have any business cards at the moment, but here, take my personal one." He handed me a card with his name and email address on it, and the word "Shaman" printed on the top right corner.

"Shaman?" I asked.

"Long story," he said, smiling. "That's who I am in my personal life."

"Well, *that's* who I want to see. Not the sleep doctor! Shamanize me!"

Ed bowed his head and smiled. "Why don't you come by next week?"

We made a date for the next Tuesday.

"Just one thing," he said. "Between now and then, keep an eye out. Any new animals cross your path, anything out of the ordinary at all, take note of it. You'll tell me about it when we see each other."

I agreed to keep an eye out for any strange encounters, but nothing special crossed my path in the following days. I did notice one thing as I was driving around a curve late one night: a strangely positioned waning crescent moon, looking like a prim smile in the black sky. I had never seen the underside of the moon lit up in that way. It seemed to me that crescents should be upright, not lying on their backs as if they were cradling something.

I arrived at Ed's farmhouse on a cold day in late March. We had just experienced what would be our last snowstorm, and the land was blanketed in a fresh layer of white powder. Yet the birds seemed to know that despite the snow, it was spring after all, and they flitted from frozen tree branch to frozen tree branch, chirping merrily.

I parked in front of the barn turned garage and walked past the enormous pile of wood to the front door, where Ed greeted me. I left my yellow galoshes on the doormat and followed him in my socks to the sunroom at the back of the house, a light-filled space framed on three sides by floor-to-ceiling windows. What looked like a massage table draped in Navajo-themed fabrics was on the right. On the left was a chair and a table, on which sat a bowl of different colored crystals.

"Pick a stone," Ed instructed me.

I selected a smooth black one, which looked to me like obsidian.

"Interesting choice," he said.

"I have a dark side," I joked. It was then I noticed the pretty but unassuming rose quartz I'd overlooked.

"Why don't you sit there on the bed?" he said, motioning toward the massage table.

I did, shifting until I found a comfortable spot.

"Do you know why you haven't been sleeping?"

"Stress, I guess. I have a lot of anxiety. I'm very neurotic—if you define 'neurotic' as having a fear of life." I smiled sheepishly. "I'm afraid of everything. It's embarrassing."

"Blow it into the stone."

"What?"

"Cup the stone in your hand and blow your anxiety into it, as hard as you can."

I did it, feeling foolish. Snow had started to fall again, a thick curtain coming down around us.

"Now you can watch as I prepare a sacred space for us."

He pulled a hooded brown cape over his head and turned to me wielding a wooden rattle and a bottle of vanilla-scented water. I listened to his chants, which he addressed to each wind, claiming their qualities and asking them to assist in the healing process.

"South Wind, great serpent, wrap your coils of light around us, teach us to shed the past the way you shed your skin, to walk softly on the earth, OH!" He paused, shook the rattle, blew over the top of the bottle to make a soft whistling sound, then swished some of the water in his mouth and blew it out into a furious, blooming spray. I was caught completely off guard and jerked backward away from the spit.

"West Wind, mother jaguar, protect our medicine space, teach us the way of peace, to live impeccably, show us the way beyond death, OH!" Again, Ed performed the same routine of rattle, whistle, spit. I tried to appear unperturbed. "North Wind, hummingbird, grandmothers and grandfathers, ancient ones, come and warm your hands by our fires, whisper to us, we honor you who have come before us, and you who will come after us, our children's children, OH!" Rattle, whistle, spit.

"East Wind, great eagle, come to us from the place of the rising sun, keep us under your wing, show us the mountains we only dare to dream of, teach us to fly wing to wing with the Great Spirit, OH!"

Ed crouched to tap the wide wooden floor planks with his rattle.

"Mother Earth! We've gathered for the healing of all your children, the Stone People, the Plant People, the four-legged, the two-legged, the creepy crawlers, the finned, the furred, and the winged ones. All our relations, OH!"

His chant was fast, practiced. The words sped up and blurred into one another at this point. I stopped concentrating and gazed off into the distance beyond him, out the window to the field covered in snow. A squirrel hopped nervously toward the wooded edge that cut off my vision.

It's probably not real, I thought. *All this show, what is it really going to accomplish? Why am I here?* And a voice in my head responded: *Who cares? Since when do you say no to the possibility of something just because it strikes you as strange? What happened to your adventurous spirit? Give it a chance!*

Back in the room, Ed was looking up toward the ceiling now. "Father Sun, Grandmother Moon! Great Spirit, you who are known by a thousand names and you who are the unnamable One, thank you for bringing us together and allowing us to sing the song of life, OH!" The ceremony concluded with one last great spit in my direction, and Ed lifted his hands over his head as though clearing the air above us.

"Now you can lie down, and I'm going to explore your chakras, see where the energy is blocked."

I eased cautiously onto the bed, resting my head on the small hard pillow that Ed had placed underneath. He dangled a string with a small weight at the end of it, making circular movements over my body as he worked his way up. He stopped at my solar plexus. Somehow I wasn't surprised.

"Your two most blocked chakras are the root chakra and the heart chakra," he said. "But the root is the most injured. So I will put the stone you chose right there." He laid a folded cloth on my pelvis and put the stone in the middle. Then he moved behind me and placed his index fingers on what he called "certain pressure points" behind my head.

"Now I'm going to ask you to do some work. If at any point it gets to be too much and you need to stop, just let me know, okay? I don't want to push you too far."

"I'll be fine," I assured him, grinning. "I'm not known for backing away from a challenge."

"Close your eyes."

I did as I was told.

"I need you to go back to your earliest memory of the fear and anxiety you described to me before. As far back as you possibly can. Where did all this start for you?"

I searched the recesses of my mind. It seemed that my entire childhood was like a sack of memories in which a stain of worry and dread had spread, tingeing everything a deep crimson color, but somehow it was difficult to pick the memory that started it all.

Ed said, "Take as long as you want."

"Ah!" I'd come up with something.

"Don't tell me. Just think about it."

I have lost something important. I lie about it because I am afraid of being punished for losing the object, but instead I am beaten for lying.

"Feel it," Ed urged. "Go deep into the pain."

The more I focused on the image of my childhood self cowering in a corner as the blows fell, the more my body seemed to fill with the physical sensation of that experience in the present. I began to tremble slightly. My breathing quickened. A tear fell out of each eye and rolled down into my hair.

"Good," Ed murmured. "Good work."

It struck me suddenly why this whole shamanic healing thing could actually work. I had recently learned about a psychotherapeutic technique called eye movement desensitization and reprocessing (EMDR), which was designed to help people struggling with post-traumatic stress disorder. In a treatment session, a patient recalled traumatic memories while being distracted by visual and sensory stimulation. The stimulation causes the recall process to use different neurological pathways and connections, thereby sidestepping the usual associations of anxiety and dread that are attached to the memory. The psychologist who pioneered the treatment had discovered that when a traumatic or distressing experience occurs, it can overwhelm normal cognitive and neurological coping mechanisms. The memory and associated stimuli are inadequately processed and stored in an isolated memory network. The goal of EMDR therapy, therefore, is to *re*-process these distressing memories, reducing their lingering effects and allowing patients to develop more adaptive coping mechanisms.

What Ed was doing wasn't too far off from an EMDR session. Distract the client with visually stimulating displays, apply pressure to sensory points, and there you have it—the forced recall of traumatic memories travel along alternate neurological routes.

And so, with this realization, I resolved to fully commit myself to the effort.

"Now, go back to the first time you felt angry," Ed said.

"Angry?" I asked dubiously. "I'm not really a very angry person."

"That just means you have to go deeper. Try to find the place where the anger is."

I genuinely did try. I traced delicately over the map of my childhood memories, as if holding a pendulum of my own, waiting for it to find true north. Where, oh where, was the anger? Sadness there was plenty of. Loneliness, despair, and self-loathing I could find, but no anger.

Here was the little girl who wore hand-me-downs from the seventies, not because her family was poor, but because nobody cared enough to buy her new clothes. She watched as her cousins were lavished with cashmere sweaters, velvet hair ribbons, and lacy stockings, and so deduced that they were more worthy of love than she was. Here was the adolescent living in her grandparents' empty nest, a house that resonated with the booming silence of deflated and abandoned dreams. She sat on sofas covered in plastic, watching the flickering candle commemorating her murdered relatives burn through the years, and wondered how to find happiness in a world that seemed to admonish against it so strongly.

This was a girl who was considered a black sheep in her family long before she broke any rules. A product of a destroyed marriage in a community that placed all value on the health of the family unit, she was the daughter of the mentally retarded man whose condition had caused all of his siblings difficulties in finding a match, and birthed by a woman who had dreams of education and a life that was unacceptable to the Hasidic world. She was doomed before she could even talk in her own defense.

Although the Hasidic community hates me for rejecting the way of life I was taught to hold sacred, in actuality I was rejected by those same people before I'd ever even entertained the slightest thought of rebellion. Rejection was my fate, to be an outcast was my destiny. What was asked of me, then, was acceptance of God's will, the grace to live under the burdens I had been doomed to shoulder without complaint.

Until recently, I couldn't remember much about my early childhood. Now, the occasional beating stands out: the time when I was standing on a chair and someone tipped it over just so I would fall; when a vacuum cleaner was thrown at me so hard that I developed enormous purple bruises. Abuse was common in the world I grew up in. Parents hit their children, teachers hit their students, and rabbis claimed that the Talmud made it right. You could count yourself lucky if you went through life and didn't once suffer at the hands of a parent, spouse, sibling, or teacher. The Satmar Hasidic community in New York is a culture of violence, not necessarily because its members fetishize it, but because the group's only inheritance is the violence of European anti-Semitism that culminated in the Second World War. Authority and discipline are seen as necessary, as much to preempt divine punishment as to self-flagellate for the sin of surviving a tragedy that wiped out most of our ancestors. I do not remember ever feeling victimized when a blow fell; rather, it was such an event that gave me a form of equality among my peers. Like some grand initiation into the postwar Hasidic identity, suffering brought us closer to that first generation of survivors, and it compensated somehow for all those who had died horribly, and in whose stead we now existed.

It wasn't until I hit the very last year of my childhood, when my seventeen-year-old self detected a small spark of something that seemed like it could be—wait, was it? Yes, there it was: a small, hard kernel of anger, wrapped tightly into a ball, packed into the very core of my inner self like some seed waiting to sprout and bear fruit.

"I found it," I said triumphantly.

"Good, where is it?"

"I'm seventeen. I'm getting married."

"There's nothing earlier?" Ed asked searchingly.

"No, this is where it is."

"Okay then. Breathe deep. Be in the anger. Experience the memory."

I went back to that time, the days and weeks after my wedding.

Perhaps it was reasonable for my aunt Chaya to see an early, arranged marriage as the ultimate solution to the problem I presented. There were hardly any other options for a young girl. I remember it was discussed whether I should be allowed to travel abroad to a seminary for girls, considered a haven for those from a troubled background. But it was decided that the stigma would only make it more difficult to marry me off when I returned. I was very disappointed when my dreams of traveling abroad on my own were dashed.

I wonder now what prompted Chaya's choice of husband for me. She knew me well enough to understand that a little bit of freedom and understanding from a spouse might have been enough to keep me in my place. But instead, she chose a man from one of the most fanatical families in our community, more extreme than any of our relatives. Was she trying to quell my obvious independence by trapping me in a repressive marriage? How ironic then, because I surely believe that was a major catalyst to my break from the community. Take everything people value away from them, and they have nothing left to lose—but give them some of what they want, and they may be too afraid to let go of the little that they have. In the end, I did not feel like I was losing much.

When I did get married, it was with as much hope as Chaya must have harbored. To her, my husband represented legitimacy; she assured me that if I succeeded at building a family with him, it would redeem the shame of my past. I may never have fit in with my blood relatives, but this new family would be rightly mine, she reminded me. I would be the head of it; there would be no chance of being an outcast within my own home.

Sadly, my marriage was doomed from the moment my husband and I entered our new apartment for the first time and found ourselves unable to consummate the arrangement. This was unacceptable according to Jewish law, and Chaya's plans for me. "A man must be a king in the bedroom," she told me the next morning, when Eli had absconded to the synagogue for prayers. I will never forget that particular aphorism she shared with me, although I could list many others as disturbing. In that moment, she tried to reveal her secret, her means to gain the power she so craved. Satisfy a man in the bedroom, she implied, and you will be ruler everywhere else.

I could not make my husband a king in the bedroom, no matter how much I wanted to, just to get everyone off my back. Rabbis, religious counselors, my in-laws—everyone put pressure on me to achieve intercourse, as if all it could possibly take were the right words, just threatening enough, or just cajoling enough. In the end, it took a year of fruitless doctor's visits to figure out what was wrong with me and try to fix it. In the process, my husband's family mutinied and tried to convince him to divorce me, which he almost did. Only when I finally got pregnant was I left in peace.

Three years later, it was Chaya who informed me over the phone of the messages that had been discovered by my uncle Jacob. They had been exchanged between his youngest unmarried daughter and my husband and had begun in our first year of marriage. Chaya didn't say anything as to their content, but she didn't have to. Eli and I had not received an invitation to Jacob's eldest daughter's wedding. It was clear that my entire family knew, or would know soon enough, that Eli had crossed the line.

Chaya expected me to be enraged, I could tell. She reacted with discomfited surprise when I responded calmly to her news. This was her problem, not mine, I thought. She had so forcefully arranged my marriage to Eli. She had chosen him for whatever qualities she had seen. If he had failed her, that was a reflection on her judgment, not mine.

All this I thought about before I said anything to her. I knew I already had one foot out the door of my marriage, and my world. She had always wanted to control everything, and I realized how angry she must be that she hadn't been able to control this particular event. Surely, she would want to control it now.

"Well, what would you like to do?" I asked her. There was no rage, only matter-of-factness, in my tone. Her will would be done regardless. I heard a pause at the other end of the line, barely a beat, but Chaya was not one to pause before she expressed her opinion or intent. I had rattled her.

"I'll make sure you get invited to the wedding," she assured me. "And I'll have my husband talk with Eli, make sure he knows he can't ever do this again. That we'll have our eye on him."

"Whatever you say, Chaya," I replied. "I have to finish folding the laundry right now, but I'll talk to you later."

I showed up at the wedding with straight shoulders and a firm jaw, but spoke to no one. It wasn't that I was ashamed. No, I felt only a vague sense of triumph. It seemed to me that they had all failed, that the circumstances were a product of their mistakes. Finally the tables were turned. I was no longer the one at fault; instead, I was the blameless white sheep in a sea of black ones.

I watched them approach me delicately, not knowing how to act. I saw only mortification on their faces, and a particular squirming guilt on the face of the cousin who had been the seductress. Her eyes could not meet mine. But I bore no resentment toward her.

It was only after I had been separated from my husband for three weeks that I received another call from Chaya. Eli had asked her to entreat me to return to his house. Ironically, back when I had been unable to perform sexually for a year, he had also asked her to tell me he wanted a divorce. How she had yelled and abused me then. I listened to her voicemail. Her voice was coated, practically dripping, in false kindness.

"Whatever happens," she said, "blood is thicker than water. We're your family and we will always support you."

I took the message for what it was: an effort to play to my vulnerabilities and engage me in conversation. She was saying the words she thought would melt me, remembering me as the child who above all wanted nothing more than to be accepted. She dangled the promise of a newly loving family in order to manipulate me into conversation, where surely, she must have reasoned, I could be bribed and threatened into my rightful place.

I didn't call back. I changed my number. And when her condemnations of me were published in the newspaper a few years later, I remembered her message with a sense of bittersweet satisfaction. "Whatever happens . . . we will always support you."

The *New York Post* printed an interview with my family after I had suddenly attained notoriety in my community, and my uncle, the same one who regularly sent me poorly spelled death threats and insults, often in emails cc'd to my entire extended family, said to the reporter that, in essence, all of this had always been *my* problem, because I had simply "lacked happiness." This, despite all my family had done for me, he said. They had arranged a marriage to a good man, he said, spent thousands on a wedding—clearly I was abnormal if, even after all that, I lacked happiness.

Certainly this attack was less vicious than the ones my uncle lobbed at me in assumed privacy. Phrases like "ugly horse-face" should have stung more, but it was the "lacked happiness" comment that eventually led me to my first real therapist; it had hit that deep and sensitive nerve in me that had always throbbed with the fear that in some undeniable way I was marked for unhappiness from the beginning.

Some people speak of inherited Holocaust guilt. The children of survivors repress their feelings and squash their own dreams, I'd read. The Hasidic sect I grew up in was a community living with a pooled inheritance of residual trauma. Although I was reminded of that every time I thought to even feel resentful or deprived, I came away from childhood with the knowledge that nothing would ever be as bad as it could really get. I knew that even at my lowest point, I would still have a lot.

At the very core of my character, underneath the abuse and self-hate that came later, is the legacy I inherited from the people who raised me. As sure as if it were etched in stone, I know I am a survivor. This is the primary identity I inherited from my war-ravaged grandparents, from my ancestors who survived centuries of persecution in Europe, from my people, who wandered in exile for millennia. This is how I think of myself, first and foremost. Yet how was I to access that reserve of strength from underneath the weighty pile of emotional garbage heaped on top of it?

"What are you angry about?" Ed asked.

For a moment, it didn't come to me. My mind drew a temporary blank. Then it filled suddenly, with one giant, pulsing word.

"Sex."

Ed's fingers dug deeper into my skull. "Good," he said. "Now blow it out."

I tried, but I was shaking too hard to breathe normally. My torso lifted jerkily off the table as I convulsed with the memory of betrayal and powerlessness. I never thought I could feel this enraged. I was filled to the brim with the kind of rage that you could use to set the world on fire, to simply explode everything. It scared me.

"Just blow it out," Ed said. "You're doing great. Do you want to stop?"

I shook my head no; I couldn't speak at first. My eyes were screwed shut, my jaw tense.

"I'm seeing red," I finally said.

"That's protection," Ed said.

No, that's pressure on my cornea, I thought.

I started to cry, the tears coming faster and faster, beyond my control. I didn't want to cry; I wanted to be a woman who didn't fall apart when confronted with the force of her own emotions. I couldn't believe all that anger was in me all this time, waiting for permission to come to the surface. I had been too busy trying to survive to process what I had been through—until now.

I remember thinking that it would be a good thing, getting married. I would finally have my independence. I didn't know that I had a defunct vagina or that sex would become the new tool of oppression in my life. Eli and I were married for one year before we achieved successful intercourse. I call it successful because there was partial penetration. After what felt like unbearable pressure from my family and Eli's family, despite the fact that every muscle in me screamed no, despite the fact that even the barest attempt felt excruciatingly painful, I gave in. It was August 2005. His family was threatening me with a divorce if I didn't cooperate. My family had made it clear to me that such an event would render me homeless, without support. Eli had disappeared; he wasn't answering his phone. It was clear he was letting his family do the talking. I was out of options.

Eli came home in the end, all apologies, and I promised to try harder. I visited a hypnotherapist, once, and then we tried again according to her instructions. I clenched my teeth and swallowed my screams. It felt like a hot poker was rubbing against my insides. But it was happening. However reluctantly, my vagina had opened just far enough, grudgingly, bitterly, to allow for penetration.

When it was finished, that first time, I cried silently, my body trembling from the effort of trying to withhold a display of pain. Eli looked at me then, and I smiled and tried to make it seem as if they were tears of happiness. He cried too and hugged me, and the sensation of his body on top of mine felt like a cement block.

A week later, we were pregnant. I thought I was off the hook. His mother had only wanted grandbabies, after all. She exclaimed all manner of thanks to the lord when she heard the news. But then Eli wanted sex all the time. After a few tries, I could tell he realized that it was still painful for me, but that I was trying to hide it. And yet, it didn't seem to bother him. Suddenly he became a man who didn't mind forcing himself on someone, who felt that sex with me was his unquestionable right. We slept in separate beds, as did all Hasidic couples, but he still asked to come into mine, and refusing him felt dangerous. Each time he covered me with his body, I felt like I was a machine he was using for his pleasure. I waited until he fell asleep across the room and then cried silently into my sheets.

After my son was born, sex became an incrementally less painful but no less humiliating experience. I became panicky during sex, unable to rein in my emotions. I often started crying before

Eli had even withdrawn, which then meant I had to halfheartedly convince him that it wasn't about the sex. I didn't have the energy to try to explain to him how I felt. I was so sure he wouldn't understand, and even if he did, what good could come of it? I would still always be obligated to have sex with him. I didn't see a way we could work out this problem of my hating the experience of sex; I was sure I could never learn to feel it differently. I wanted desperately to escape, even through death, but I couldn't bear the thought of my son being alone in the world without a defender.

I had a strange guilty feeling, lying on Ed's table and admitting this, as if somehow it was not okay to complain about being forced into sex when you're married, because that's the expectation. You were married, you had bad sex, welcome to the club. I know I'm not a special case. But where did this come from, this feeling that I didn't even have a right to claim that pain? From the community that told me my desires were invalid, my emotions irrelevant?

"Blow it out," Ed urged me. "Breathe deep."

I still couldn't calm down enough to take a complete breath, but the tears had slowed.

I'm seven months pregnant, my belly already enormous against a figure rendered slight from the weight loss that occurred during my stressful first year of marriage. I'm kneeling on the floor, washing my husband's feet in a basin of soapy water. I'm massaging the soles as he leans back and enjoys the relief. He's worked hard all day.

It's as if I am seeing myself from above.

I'm so diminished. What kind of woman have I become? I'm pregnant and kneeling at the feet of my husband. My belly hurts, my knees are burning from the bedroom carpet embedded in my skin. I'm aware that somewhere out there pregnant women are getting their feet rubbed by their husbands. Somehow, I know I don't deserve that.

During the day, when Eli is at work, I lie on the sofa. I am hopeless and depressed. I touch my stomach a lot, feeling for elbows and feet, wondering what's going to happen to this irredeemable child growing in me. There's a little bump that I keep touching behind my belly button, which I swear feels like one of the baby's fingers. I touch it with my own index finger, pushing it in, around in circles, until it becomes a habit.

At one of my doctor's appointments, my gynecologist informs me that it's not the baby's finger after all. It's an umbilical hernia, common in pregnant women, a result of my abdominal muscles separating.

"You'll have to take care of that before you have another child," she warns me.

I can't imagine having another child. I hope I die in childbirth. I hope the hernia kills me. More than anything, I hope I don't live to see my own unhappiness passed on to another human being because of my actions. It may not have been my choice to become pregnant, but somehow my body made a home for this baby even when I didn't want it, even when I was so frightened and horrified at the thought. It went ahead and made a child, and in the end, I'm accountable for that. Because I still think I could have stopped it. Just like my pelvis clamped shut to protect me from sex, why couldn't my uterus have shut down to prevent a pregnancy?

"All right now," Ed said soothingly, as my breathing slowed and fell back into a rhythm. "Let's wrap this up for today. We can work on this some more when you come back."

"I have surgery in three days," I said.

Seven years later, and that old umbilical hernia, which I'd almost forgotten about, was back. Obstructed, this time, between the slowly tightening walls of my abdominal muscles. I could feel it squeezed just under my belly button, and it felt sore and tender, like someone had punched me in the stomach a few days ago. My doctor said it would be a simple procedure. The hernia would be repaired and the separated abdominal muscles would be sutured together.

"I can schedule another session when I'm recovered, I think."

"Before that," Ed said, "I need you to start a ritual. When you go home, go out into nature and create a circle somewhere, with anything you can find on the ground. It can be any sort of circle. Then I want you to visit it every day until your surgery."

I promised to heed his instructions.

At home I walked down the hill to the frozen lake, my galoshes leaving deep footprints in the layers of crusty snow. At the foot of the hill, just before the start of the lake perimeter, I drew a deep circle in the snow with a twig and placed some fir limbs in the center. I stamped on the snow in the circle until it was packed hard—a clear, round depression like a coin in the snowbank.

I came back to it the next day and nothing had changed. Nor had it the next. But on the very last day before my surgery, there it was. A slim, curved crescent on the underside of the circle where the snow had melted, leaving a smile of brown earth like the crescent moon I had seen earlier. How had that one sliver of snow melted when the weather had been below freezing, and there wasn't a patch of earth visible for miles?

I went in for surgery that morning and walked out of the clinic that same afternoon. My recovery was remarkably anticlimactic. It felt very similar to my recovery from labor and delivery. I lay on the sofa and cradled my stomach, and it brought back those memories of lying on the sofa all those years ago, feeling my baby flail his limbs against the wall of my belly. Whatever had gone wrong in my body during that time had now been corrected. I had been, in a very technical way, made whole again.

What was it about seven years? I tried to remember . . . then it hit me—the *Shmita* year, or in English, the Sabbath year. In the ancient Jewish tradition of agricultural cycles regarding the holy land of Israel, the land was supposed to lie fallow every seven years. As a child, I had learned that among other commandments, the fallow year had involved such prohibitions as no planting, pruning, or gathering of fallen fruit. At the time, it had struck me as wasteful. Now I regarded the memory of the phenomenon almost reverentially. A Sabbath year: a year of rest, a time to allow the land to replenish its reserves and restore itself to full strength.

Was this my Sabbath year? Seven years after I became a mother, during which time I struggled to raise myself as I raised my child, is this the milepost on which I can lean and take a breath?

II

רחמנות

mercy

The goal, the reason for moving, for starting a new life, was to heal and recover, but being a parent made the matter more urgent than abstract. I worried I'd never be the mother my son deserved if I didn't fix what was wrong with me. No matter how much I gave my son, he would always have to deal with a mother who was anxious and overwhelmed. What were his chances, then, of developing a healthy approach to living?

A few months after we moved, I was driving Isaac to school, and we came up over the hill that leads to an old college campus, an assortment of dignified buildings gracing an enormous slope of land behind our lake. The sun was just rising behind the buildings on the left, golden rays melting into the illuminated treetops.

"Mom, why do you always say to eat my breakfast because the kids in Africa are starving? If I eat it, how does the food get to

Africa? I don't understand," he said from the backseat. I glanced in the rearview mirror and saw the thoughtful expression on his face.

"It's an expression, Isaac," I said. "I'm trying to teach you not to take food for granted, or waste it, because there is hunger in other parts of the world. It's bad behavior to waste food when there are others who need it desperately."

"But, Mom, why don't they have enough food in Africa?"

"Because they're poor."

"But why? Why is America not poor?"

I tried to explain to him the differences between first- and third-world countries, but nothing I said seemed to satisfy him. He started coming up with ideas about how we could make Africa wealthy.

"Mom, what if we opened businesses in Africa? What if we opened restaurants? Why can't we just go and bring them food from here?"

I told him about some of the issues that were preventing progress from being made in Africa. There was tribal violence, lack of education, lack of safety, lack of cleanliness and health care. I tried to summarize delicately; I wanted to educate, not traumatize.

He still wrinkled his forehead, as if determined to solve world hunger in our brief conversation, before he was dropped off at school for the day. As if he wanted to approach his studies with an unburdened conscience.

"Hey, I have an idea for you," I said. "You know there are already some people who are making a big difference in developing countries all over the world. Those people are effective because they're very educated; they know what they're doing and how to do it. If you keep doing well in school like you already are, someday you'll get to go to a great college, and while you're there, I bet you can figure out the solution to world hunger. That's the amazing thing about getting an education," I said, "the more you know, the more you'll be able to accomplish."

"Okay," Isaac said, "but it will be a lot of years until I go to college."

I dropped him off in front of the school building and drove away smiling. I had this feeling that somehow my sacrifice had already paid off. My son was already embarking on a journey of education that could take him anywhere. Every door in the world might open for him, if he chose to knock on it. If I continued to nurture his curiosity and courage, he would never feel the sensation of walls closing in on him the way I do all the time. Wasn't this enough for now?

One morning soon after that conversation, as we were driving down the same roads, my son told me about waking up in his father's car and finding himself alone. After waiting for a while, he proceeded to open the car door, cross the street by himself, and wander around a few shops to see if his father was in one of them. Eventually Eli came out of the fish market and saw that the car was empty, at which point he went back to look for Isaac. He found him, looking lost, at the cash registers of a supermarket.

"I was very scared," Isaac told me. "I waited for Dad, but he didn't come back."

My fists clenched tightly around the steering wheel as Isaac told me this.

That night Isaac had a bad dream.

"I was on a ship with my dad, and it was sinking, and I was afraid I would never see you again."

He crawled into my bed and huddled close to me, his body trembling. I put my arm around him and blinked back tears. Only too vividly did I remember my own dreams of abandonment as a child. Would it be like that for Isaac? Would he never be granted the security of knowing that someone would always be there? I had never left him unattended, nor would I, but repeated attempts to convince Eli to do the same had failed. I couldn't bear to see my son endure even the smallest part of the fear and anxiety I had grown up with.

It seemed so clear to me what that dream meant. I had to send him off most weekends to be with his dad, while I remained help-less at a distance. I had not been able to save him when he was abandoned in that car; I had not been there to advocate for him. I could only be in control of his life with me. It was terrifying to consider that things would always be this way. That I would never be there when his father lost his temper, or simply his judgment, that Isaac would have to navigate those situations for himself.

Eli expressed no remorse for his decision to leave Isaac in the car on his own. He reacted angrily when I asked him to sign an agreement saying he wouldn't leave his son unattended again. I was beginning to understand that the fight was far from over. I would be battling for my son until he became an adult, until he could decide for himself. I was forever tied to the man I had not chosen, to the fate my family and community had chosen for me. I would always be only half-free. This knowledge drove me wild with frustration and anger. How could it have come to this, after so much struggling? Would I always be dragging my chains around, swallowing the bitter remorse surrounding the irrevocable decisions that had been made for me in my youth?

What was it they said about that heedless charge down the hill to freedom? That it would inevitably end in destruction. The price I seemed to have paid for my escape still didn't seem as high as the one I would have paid if I'd stayed, but I struggled now with a new enemy: perpetual exhaustion of the spirit. I wondered if I'd emptied an unrenewable resource in my dash toward freedom, if I'd somehow exhausted a store of psychic capital designed to last me for a lifetime.

It might have seemed to some that I'd whittled my life down to the bare minimum, but for me, it became just enough. Living in the middle of nowhere was what I wanted. I needed a life that reflected what I felt on the inside: a profound sense of alienation from the society of my origins and the society I had transplanted into, a sense of being in limbo and therefore of being nowhere.

Ironically, I'd found myself unable to create a sense of home, or identity, in the city where I'd been born and raised. Now, here I was, in a place that seemed just quiet and empty enough for the outline of my spirit to take shape. Here I might become visible, the way a cul-de-sac might merit a spot on a map of a barren locale. And even if it could do nothing for me in the end, certainly it was the place for Isaac to figure out who he was and what kind of person he might want to grow into.

A month after my surgery, we celebrated Isaac's seventh birthday. The weather was unseasonably warm that week; we planned to have a shindig at our house so the kids could all run around outdoors. My mother took the regional train up from New York, loaded with party favors and balloons she'd found in a 99-cent store. I bought the snacks and cupcakes.

The day of Isaac's birthday happened to be Grandparents' Day at his school, so I dropped them both off in the morning and returned home to blow up the balloons. When I picked them up at lunchtime, they'd created a wreath together, Isaac being the designer and my mom wielding the glue gun. They got along well with each other, having none of the baggage that my mom and I grew up taking for granted when it came to our families. To Isaac, she's just my mom. She's another person who loves him, and it's uncomplicated.

Isaac knows that my mom didn't raise me, but he's never asked why. I would like for him to be able to take for granted that a mother is always there for her child, but I can already tell, by the way he clings to me, that he doesn't see me as the immovable caregiver most children see their parents as. He already senses that I come from an unstable, secret world, and this makes his world seem somehow less certain.

In many ways, I am a repeat of my mother's life. Perhaps that is why I've always struggled with feelings of anxiety and fear when I'm around her. Am I doomed to simply relive her life experience and pass it on to the next generation in an unstoppable cycle of misery? Her marriage was also arranged when she was a teenager. She too was forced to have sex, to have a baby, with a man she didn't love. While I was being raised mostly by my grandparents, she was working menial jobs to put herself through college, an act that constituted her final rejection of our family and community. My father had presented three wives with a religious divorce by the time she was able to obtain her legal one.

My mom and I can't talk about these things—it's too painful for both of us—but talking about books is our safe conversation, the one thing that binds us together. She tells me how she, too, used to sneak out to the library as a child, filling her days with books by British authors, like the Malory Towers series by Enid Blyton. She was a child of divorce as well, a symbol of scandal among her peers. What made her feel most isolated, though, was her intelligence. She felt perpetually surrounded by the unintelligent, much like the characters in Roald Dahl's books did, including the one I identified with so much as a child: Matilda.

I have no doubt my mother is happy. Her life began as mine did, it progressed as mine did, and yet here she is today, accomplished, educated, and independent. She's also single, and I worry about that. My mother and I both acknowledge that we have enormous difficulty trusting others because of our experiences in the Hasidic community. If she hasn't managed to get over it by her late forties, I can't help having that sinking feeling in my heart that I, too, may never learn to trust someone. Is this then the ultimate risk that we take when we escape the only world we've ever known: the possibility that we'll never truly be moored in a new one?

My mother designated herself the photographer at Isaac's birthday party. I set my bulky Canon to automatic so it didn't feel too complicated for her. The event was a huge success. That particular early-spring afternoon was very hot, and the kids arrived in bathing suits ready to jump into the lake. We distributed water balloons and challenged them all to stay dry for the duration of the throwing contest.

I watched Isaac running around, cupcake icing smeared around his mouth, looking gloriously happy to be the center of attention. I knew how special it felt to him, to have everyone here to celebrate. We'd never been entrenched in a place or community as we were now; it was the first time he could feel a sense of permanence and security. I wished that, in the process of providing that for him, I could have figured out how to provide it for myself simultaneously, but this didn't seem to be enough. There never seemed to be a simple answer to what was missing in my life.

When I'd fully recovered from the hernia surgery, I returned to Ed's sunlit room. This time around, I chose a smooth white crystal with crimson veins.

"Maybe this time we can go inside and find something good?" I asked.

"Yes," Ed said with confidence. "Let's go looking in the underworld."

I lay down, and Ed shook the rattle feverishly over my body, his eyes squinted tightly shut while he performed energy-clearing motions for about fifteen minutes. He told me to imagine myself going deep into the earth, to the still waters underneath, and having everything washed away. "Only the purest self is left behind," he said.

I tried to visualize it. *I'm lying in a stream and the water is washing over me. I'm part of the earth, the flowers, the animals; it's all one. I'm integrating.*

"Step into the circle," a woman whispers. "You need to care for everything around you in order for it to care for you in return. If you want to be included, just step in."

I couldn't decide whether the voice was a memory of someone who once spoke to me or a presence outside myself. As soon as it stopped, it was almost like I had never heard it.

Ed stopped shaking the rattle abruptly and told me to sit up.

"What did you find?"

I told him what I'd heard.

"That's very good," he said approvingly. "What you just learned is what we shamans call *ayni*, or 'being in relationship.' It's about being aware of how everything is working around you and with you. You're in the circle of life."

"What were you doing while you were performing the ritual? What did you see?"

"I went looking for the parts of your soul that had chosen to leave for whatever reason. We all have that—the soul has four chambers, and one chamber is for the wound. That's when a part of you can split off."

"So what was the wound?"

"Well," Ed said, hesitating for a moment before going on, "I saw something metallic, an object. At first I couldn't quite tell if I was seeing it right. It was a bicycle. I think that's what it was."

"The wound is a bicycle?"

"That's what I saw when I went looking for the thing that made your strongest, purest self peel away from you. There must have been a moment when you gave up and decided to just be a good girl and suppress your true self, and somehow it's connected to a bicycle."

Suddenly, out of nowhere, I remember it vividly: *I'm sitting on the stoop, eyeing the neighborhood boys as they zoom by on their two-wheelers. I tentatively approach the bicycle when I think no one is looking. I put my feet on the pedals and the next thing I know, I feel like I'm flying . . . pedaling faster and faster until I'm almost around the block. And then I hear them come up behind me, a gang of boys on bikes. They knock me over to the ground, and their leader slaps me on the face, saying, "Girls don't ride bikes."*

And I never did again, until this year.

"Well, there you have it," Ed said. "That was the moment when you figured out it was safer if you buried the part of you that thought for yourself, that was unafraid. And eventually she gave up trying to come back."

I started riding last summer, after we moved to the lake house. My college friend's dad had patiently taught me to ride his wife's bike. The first time I pushed down on the pedals and coasted on my own momentum felt like a miracle. I rode the trails and the roads, planning different routes for myself each time. Some days I'd struggle up a hill only to discover a whole new world on the other side, a stretch of mountainside, a lake collecting in a valley, horses meandering in a meadow.

In *Zen and the Art of Motorcycle Maintenance*, Robert Pirsig describes the distinction between traveling by car versus by bike. The car window serves to frame the scene one is passing, he explains, making it similar to seeing it through a television or computer screen; the driver is removed and insulated from that which he is viewing. On a bike, however, the traveler is immersed in the world through which he traverses. There is no frame but the perimeters of his vision.

So it feels to be on a bike again for the first time since that childhood incident—fully immersed in the world, alive to its noises and colors, susceptible to its movements. How different it is from the sheltering of my childhood, the limits that were constantly placed on where I could go, and for how long, and with whom.

I had my first inevitable accident sometime in autumn, after a summer of triumphant journeys, of forty-mile days, of hills beaten and declines fearlessly embraced. They say a cyclist must fall, as soon as possible, if only to understand the physics of it. There is a right way to fall, and once you do it, the fear of falling no longer holds you in its grasp.

It was a beautiful, crisp day. The leaves were only just starting to curl at the ends; deciduous trees were lit up in fiery halos of red and orange. I climbed up a cracked, ill-maintained shoulder of a main road, and as I approached the crest, I heard the noise of an oncoming car behind me, a shrieking honk, and I panicked. I didn't have time to look behind me to see the red Jeep barreling my way; I simply aimed my body away from the road and lost control as the bike spun in the gravelly ditch and toppled me to the ground.

I had the wind knocked out of me for what felt like a few minutes, and then I righted myself, preparing to get back on my bike and head for home. When I looked down, I noticed bright rivulets of red running down my legs, from holes in the flesh where the sharp scrape and gouge of pebbles had done their work.

I experienced what felt like a slow pulling away, a detachment from the scene. Somewhere outside my body, an eye winked and a voice said, *Good, that's good. That's what you deserve, isn't it?* And the sound of that cruel statement echoing in my mind was so devastating to me that I started to cry, because who would say such a horrible thing about someone, and moreover, who would be generating that voice but myself, the lone traveler left on this road?

I limped home, rolling the bike along with me. I couldn't feel the sting where it should have been, in the wounds in my legs and palms, only the horror of satisfaction at my own injury.

In my bathroom I scrubbed aggressively at the blood, remembering the moment when my friend Heather had shown me the bandage she used to cover the place where she cut herself. I shouldn't have been feeling this frightening thrill, this enthusiastic response to the sight of bloody lacerations marking a trail on my legs.

I had never cut myself. I had heard that cutting was a practice in search of feeling, and feeling had never been an area in which I sensed a lack. To hurt oneself because one loathed oneself, that I understood, but surely I had grown up and past that terrible voice, the one that said my existence was a burden on everyone around me, and I should do them all a favor and die.

I am ten years old, looking at the full bottle of thyroid medication in my drawer and wondering what would happen if I stop taking the medication that had been prescribed to me since birth. It seems that I can no longer nurture any reasonable hope of gaining the approval of my family; will this, then, earn me the title of "good girl"?

I put the bottle back in its drawer without taking a pill, and don't look at it again for months. In the spring I become flattened with a tremendous fatigue. I climb into bed and stay there for three weeks, floating in and out of wakefulness, but never once leaving the bed. It takes a long time for someone to notice how ill I am. The next thing I know, I'm eating farina my grandmother has prepared and wearing some new hand-me-downs for school. I am back on the medication. I feel thwarted. How can I cease to be a blight on my family and community if all my efforts are defeated?

I used to dream about being in the concentration camps with my grandmother. Always I awoke knowing with certainty that I had died, or was about to die, and that this was somehow proof that I still wasn't strong enough, or special enough, to survive what my grandmother had endured. Compared with her, I was a whiny weakling.

I would stand in front of the gilded, oxidized mirror in my grandmother's bedroom when she was away and stare at myself for hours, trying to imagine what I would have looked like on the brink of death, my skin clinging to my bones, my eyes sunken into my skull. What was different about her that she was able to emerge from the pit of human despair that surely would have swallowed me whole? Did she believe in her inalienable right to life in a way I could never hope to?

III

ירושה

inheritance

Sometimes, when the house was empty and quiet, I would root through my grandmother's drawers, looking for clues. It was difficult to learn anything about her otherwise. I asked many questions, but my grandmother was almost never in the mood to talk. Therefore I gathered frayed documents and sepia photographs obsessively, sneaking into my grandfather's office to use the color copy machine before putting the found treasures back in their original hiding places. I kept a folder under my mattress stuffed with facsimiles of postcards, letters, and documents. I also kept detailed notes, jotting down names every time I heard them, documenting anecdotes whenever I was lucky enough to be in earshot. I was trying, surreptitiously, to put together a family tree of my ancestors, one as detailed as possible. I did not know why I felt so driven to color in the vague outlines of my past at the time, but I remember that the folder was one of the few items I took with me when I eventually left my community. I abandoned years of diaries and journals and personal photographs, but for some reason I rescued that folder from the musty basement where it had lain untouched for years. Those documents were my only connection to my roots, not the shallow ones that had been planted in New York, but roots that went far back into the earth on the other side of the ocean. They were roots I could never really shake off, nor did I want to.

Was it the incessant secrecy, the silence that shrouded our household, that incited my insatiable curiosity to know more about my family's past? The more my questions were met with dead air, the hungrier I became to fill up those spaces with images and words. Even though no one told me the story behind the photographs or explained the letters written in incomprehensible languages, I savored those mementos under my bed for years, feeling that my imagination told the best story anyway.

Once, I found an old brown envelope, tattered at the edges, reinforced with brown tape, tucked between the Hungarian down comforters my grandmother stacked in the old wooden crib that still sat in the corner of her bedroom, despite the fact that her youngest child was in his thirties. There was an old passport, with a photo of her as a young girl, thick, dark hair waving as if there were a breeze, pinned by a clip on the side where it was thickest. She had a tired smile on her face, like someone who had just completed a Herculean task, a long hike or swim. The date said 1947, so that task would have been an arduous recovery from typhus. She would have had to gain the weight lost in the concentration camp, grow back the hair, come to terms with the loss of everything.

My grandmother's passport did not have a shiny leather cover like mine does now. It was a simple folded sheet of card stock. It was temporary. It said STATELESS in bold black letters. It was the passport issued to her after the war, when Hungary didn't want to recognize her as its citizen anymore, and no country wanted to step up in its place. Until her American naturalization, my grandmother used that declaration of categorical homelessness as her ticket across borders and oceans. She was, for many years, a displaced person who relied on the sporadic generosity of host countries and international relief organizations.

In the story of the Jews, we are technically all displaced persons. The last time we had a home was before the Second Temple was destroyed in AD 70. Then God punished us by sending us into exile, or *galus*, as we call it, and the diaspora happened. We were cursed with wandering; we moved from region to region, from country to country. Every time we settled into a comfortable routine, something would come along and shake the earth from beneath us. Crusades, Cossacks, Tatars, Nazis. The earth shook in 1944, and a few years later my grandmother came to America with her stateless passport.

Enclosed in the brown envelope was all the correspondence between her and the bureaucratic government agency in charge of her naturalization. She was addressed as DP3159057. At the time, she told me, she was working as a secretary in Williamsburg. She didn't mention the company she worked for, or what she did exactly, as a secretary, but she did mention that she shared an apartment with roommates on Hooper Street and that at night she was awakened by the cries they emitted in their terrible dreams. Everybody around her was haunted in the same way. So she gave her information to a matchmaker.

"I'm ready to start a new life," she had said. She wanted to have many children. She had just gotten her period for the first time at twenty-four years old, and she was relieved. She had lost ten siblings in the war. She would ultimately give birth to eleven children.

She did not raise her kids with the same traditions with which her parents had raised her. It was a postwar generation, and if you hadn't given up on God completely, you were well on your way to the other end of the spectrum. She had married an avid follower of what was beginning to be an extremist movement. My grandfather, while educated and successful at a young age, was the only man she had met who insisted on keeping his traditional beard in the New World. Later, their sons and daughters would grow up in a self-imposed ghetto led by rabbis who were trying to make sense of the Holocaust and appease the angry God that had razed the European Jewish population.

Over the years, my grandmother paid little notice to the winds of fanaticism blowing around her home. At times when the community was in its grips and my grandfather brought news of tightening restrictions into his home, my grandmother waved it away and sang a little tune as she carefully frosted a hazelnut torte. I remember that the little things made her very happy. She prepared such beautiful and tasty food, food the likes of which I found only when I traveled to Europe or ate in very old-style establishments. It was regal and classic in the way people rarely cook anymore in the United States.

To my grandmother I attached ineffable elegance. There was no elegance in Hasidic life, but there was elegance in her, in her origins, in her story, and in her inimitable cooking. My grandmother was European, and though I could not fully grasp what that meant, I imagined that it was something wonderful and otherworldly. I cherished the photos taken of her as a young woman in gorgeous hand-sewn dresses with rows of tiny cloth buttons. I loved the way her slim ankles looked in delicate T-strap shoes. There was something spectacular about her loveliness and poise, which stood in sharp contrast to a photograph I had found in her drawer, one of her being carried out from Bergen-Belsen on a stretcher by the British Red Cross. To embody beauty after you had endured the ugliest of assaults, that was magic to me. I surmised that there was something very powerful at the core of my grandmother's spirit.

My grandmother's passport gave her name as Irenka, Hungarian for Irene. It was not a name I ever heard her called, but then no one called me by the name on my birth certificate either. It was custom to have a secular name, to make it easier for the outsiders to relate to us. Better that than they should resent us for having to break their teeth over our Hebrew names. My grandmother's religious name was Pearl, a beautiful name that I thought I might give my daughter someday, except that, I reasoned, I would have a daughter too early for that. We didn't name our children after the living, like Sephardic Jews do. It would have to be my granddaughter's name.

Of all the passive and submissive women in the Bible I could have been named after, somehow Deborah ended up on my birth certificate. No one in my family had ever been named that, and Ashkenazi Jews never give their children random names. The custom is always to name a child after a dead relative.

Indeed, I was given two names at my Kiddish, the Jewish equivalent of a christening for girls: Sarah and Deborah. I was called Sarah growing up. There were plenty of dead Sarahs in my family.

Deborah was an afterthought, rarely mentioned. I never heard any tales told about an ancestor with that name. When I scoured the family tree I had managed to assemble through careful sleuthing, no one by that name showed up, even when I went back seven generations. Why Deborah?

In the book of Judges, Deborah is introduced with the words "*eshes lapidus*." It's common in the Bible for people to be tagged in such a way, with descriptions following their names. Wife of, son of—that's how they were identified in those days. The weird thing is, if the words *eshes lapidus*, or "woman of Lapidus," are to mean that Deborah is a wife, why is Lapidus never identified separately in the scripture? Why isn't he given a patronym? In the Bible, all male figures are identified by the names of their fathers, sometimes even their grandfathers and great-grandfathers, too.

Lapidus is a Hebrew word for torch, or fire. It is not the mundane term, but a literary word, a term with elevated connotations. It is an unlikely name for a person. Educated people infer that the description of Deborah therefore translates to "woman of the torch," or "fiery woman," as opposed to wife of anyone.

Woman of fire.

Nothing was beyond the scope of Deborah's achievement. She is undoubtedly the most empowered woman in Jewish history. She was a judge, a leader, a military strategist and commander, a prophetess, and an icon. The Greeks later put her effigy on a coin. She was revered for her beauty, her wisdom, and most of all, her strength. Men tried to marry her, rabbis surmise, but she refused. So she was given the ambiguous affixation—*eshes lapidus*.

When I first applied to college, needing a legal name for documents, I discovered that my birth certificate said only Deborah, and from then on, the Sarah was dropped. To me, Sarah was my old name, a name for a passive girl. Deborah would be my future.

Deborah, woman of fire.

Centuries after Deborah's rule, Jews were still talking about her, but not necessarily politely. The group of rabbis who sat around a table in a synagogue and argued with one another about every word in the Bible, and who had the minutes of their meetings transcribed into a collection of work that would become the Talmud, made a point of belittling, with a pernicious determination, the few women who had made it into biblical history. They focused on Deborah with unreserved vitriol, for of the paltry group of women who received positive mentions in scripture, she is truly the only threat. Not just a holy woman, neither a mother nor a wife, Deborah broke every rule in the book by occupying a position that had only ever been held by men and would never again be held by a woman. She died untamed, although surely there were those who wanted her retired into a convenient marriage to sink behind the name of her husband into obscurity.

There is a particularly memorable passage in the Talmud that records a conversation in which rabbis compete with one another to mock the names of the female prophets. By happenstance, some of the women were named after animals, names designed to denote industriousness, a cherished quality in a Jewish woman. *Deborah* is the Hebrew term for bee, a hardworking creature. The rabbis poke fun at Deborah by attacking her name as vulgar and unsophisticated.

But Hebrew, as a language, works in a particularly interesting way. Words are composed of three-letter roots, which have altered meanings based on suffixes, prefixes, and vowels stuck in between.

The root of *Deborah* consists of the Hebrew equivalents for *D*, *B*, and *R*. This is the root word for speech. The Hebrew version of *H*, tacked on to the end of an action word, usually denotes feminine gender. Therefore, *DeBoRaH* would literally deconstruct as "she speaks."

These sorts of language gymnastics are a beloved sport of Talmudic rabbis. They spend countless pages indulging in a game called *gematria*, in which they use a code that assigns numerical values to Hebrew letters to draw connections between different words by showing their sums to be equal. The acrobatics involved to draw these complex conclusions are necessary because too frequently they are cited as the only evidence to support a rabbi's claim. Hasidic Jews still donate to charity in multiples of eighteen because that is the numerical value for the word *chai*, or life. In this way, they feel that their generosity will buy them life, because it is in the right numerical form.

Hebrew is certainly a language that invites the obsessive codecracker. It is very layered, packing meaning upon meaning. Words often have dual or triple uses. The poetic nature of Hebrew scripture has allowed for centuries of conjecture and deconstruction not unlike that which I experienced in a poetry class in college. The difference is that all of us in that class knew that no matter how many assumptions we made about the meaning, and how cogently we supported our theses, we were never granted any certainty about the true intent of the poet, or the message behind his or her words. Ultimately, the poem remained unsolved.

My grandfather understood this concept. He often warned me that, although we were living our lives according to a strict rabbinical interpretation of the Torah, there was a distinct possibility that we had a lot of it wrong. He was the first person to explain the concept of a metaphor to me. That's the thing about the Hebrew language, he said. You never know if you've picked the right meaning. It could be literal or figurative. The language could be deliberately obscure, designed to cloak a meaning that only someone with the right code could access. And codes can go wrong. You could be using the wrong key to crack it and get an entirely mixed-up result.

Deborah = Bee.

Deborah = She who speaks.

Deborah = Woman of fire.

My grandfather was confident in his rabbi nonetheless. He reminded me that faith in the righteous was our insurance against error. If we had the right intentions in hand, it was ensured that God would modify his wishes to align with those of the saints leading us. Such reverence was there in heaven for our holy rabbis. The same holy rabbis who had mocked Deborah, who had been chosen by God to lead the Jewish nation to extraordinary victory, who had been blessed with a reign of unparalleled peace and prosperity, and most important, who had been beloved by her subjects and fondly remembered by them.

The author of the book of Deborah was clearly of a very different mind than the fastidious group who chronicled their highly subjective opinions in the Talmud.

"And Deborah rose, a mother in Israel, and spoke."

This is how Deborah is introduced. Why a mother if she was childless? Could there be a more loving description of her? She was a mother to a nation. She rose to power not as a woman who abandoned her femininity but as one who harnessed its most glorious qualities to lead her people to triumph. Reading this reminds me that, unlike what was taught to me, there is room for rule breaking in the Jewish tradition. God approves of a little feminism once in a while.

In the story of Deborah came my first opportunity to find a positive reflection in the Judaic mirror. In those early years after leaving, everywhere I went, someone or something wanted to show me an acquired perception of Jewish culture. A stereotype, a joke, a Woody Allen reference, countless such instances of a projected identity I had never been aware of, at least not as aware as I was of my existence within the framework of Jewishness I had grown up in.

No one had ever mentioned Deborah to me, except in passing. The stories of Moses, David, and Solomon were told and retold gloriously, but somehow the women slipped from collective memory, and only their shadows remained.

The anesthesiologist who had put me to sleep before my hernia surgery was Hungarian.

"When did you come over to America?" I asked as he hooked up my IV bag.

"In 1988."

"A year before communism fell!" I said.

He laughed. "How was I supposed to know that then?"

"I want to go there someday," I said, slurring a little as the drugs kicked in.

"Why?" he asked.

"Because my grandparents are Hungarian."

"Which part of Hungary are they from?" he asked.

"Nyíregyháza," I answered, pronouncing it correctly (*Nyir-ed-huza*).

"That's crazy," he said. "That's where I'm from. If you go, let me know. I'll introduce you to some of my friends."

"That'd be nice," I said as I drifted off.

It's hard to explain why I started to feel closer to my grandmother in the years after we last saw each other than at any moment during the time we spent together in my childhood. I had once stood alongside her in the kitchen and mixed bowls of cake batter and meringue, and perhaps we had talked of this and that, but even then I was yearning to know the person she had once been.

By the time I came along, my grandmother's life had been greatly diminished. I never knew her in her heyday, when she was raising a family of eleven with aplomb, sewing her children's clothes by hand according to the latest fashions she spied at Saks. She could look at a dress and instantly know how to make it; she didn't even need a pattern. Neighbors whispered that her rich husband gave her free rein, but they didn't know that the opposite was true. Despite his financial success, my grandfather didn't believe in spending money on material things. So she slaved away instead, and they kept up appearances. But this was only something I'd heard, you see—from an aunt or an older cousin who had heard it from somewhere else. The stories were all gone by the time I lived in that house—only their echoes remained.

My grandmother was almost a ghost to me then. Perhaps for that reason, her spirit seemed to accompany me on my way out. I did not feel the separation so keenly because I had always been attached to the memory of her, and that would never fade, no matter how far I traveled. Instead, by freeing myself from the bounds imposed on relationships by the Hasidic community, I was finally able to explore the person my grandmother had been. I opened that folder stuffed full of photographs and documents and started to piece together as much as I could, assembling a chronology of dates, places, and people. Yet there were so many missing elements, and I knew I had to start at the beginning if I was ever going to get the full story.

Three months after my surgery, in the midst of an early-summer 2013 heat wave, I emerged from the airport into the humid haze of Budapest. The anesthesiologist's friend, who had turned out to be the president of Nyíregyháza's only college, led me to the spot where his chauffeured Mercedes was waiting. A Hungarian novelist and poet, Zoltán had started studying English only a year ago.

It was painful for him, he said to me in German, that, with the mind of a novelist and the desire to convey all things beautifully, he could not communicate effectively with me. Although we understood each other just fine, I could feel his frustration. For a writer, it would always rankle to be hampered by a limited vocabulary. My German was then still heavily influenced by my native Yiddish, but luckily Zoltán had grown up around Yiddish speakers, and my odd turns of phrase and archaic grammar did not stump him.

"The second language in Hungary used to be German," he said, "but now it's mostly Russian. English isn't even on the table. Don't expect to be able to communicate with anyone directly," he warned me. He had found me an interpreter, someone who worked at the college but who had studied in America for a year. I was relieved to hear that.

We took a brief walking tour around the city. The banks of the Danube were inaccessible then, because of all the flooding—across central Europe, train lines were submerged and low regions turned into stagnant ponds. The Hungarian Parliament building, normally the architectural pride of the capital, was covered in scaffolding; only its imposing white spires could be seen amid the extensive renovation effort. We retreated from the noisy dump trucks and worker crews and walked down Andrássy út toward the famous Heroes' Square. Zoltán had a story for everything; he knew every sculpture and statue. He'd mention them by name and ask me if I'd ever heard of this person or that, but all the names sounded equally foreign to me. Famous Hungarian poet, he'd point out, famous Hungarian artist, famous king, famous general, and famous writer. So many famous Hungarians, he seemed to be saying. I wondered if any of them were famous outside Hungary.

My first glimpse of Budapest—so different from Europe's other capitals in that it lacks both contemporary chic and the varnished grandiosity of antique glamour—was jarring. Immediately I sensed just how influenced my childhood milieu was by the Old World aesthetic I saw around me. The voluminous block buildings, their facades cracked and darkened with age, reminded me of the impressive synagogues that rose between the tenement buildings of Williamsburg; I especially noticed the various flyers posted at eye level, some of them new, others rotted to strips and pieces by time and weather. Williamsburg, too, had been covered with such posters, called *pashkevillin*; because we had no radio or TV, we resorted to more old-fashioned means of communication and advertising.

In old Buda, the pastel-colored buildings, Bavarian in structure, Mediterranean in dress, seemed fake, like they were part of a movie set or theme park. Their doors and windows were tightly shuttered, and the small side streets baked silently in the midday sun. The cobblestones seemed manufactured and touristy. Only in the main square near the Fisherman's Bastion did we find a crowd milling, which thinned out as soon as we retreated from the riverbank.

We sat in an outdoor café in the blistering heat and drank some chilled Tokaji. Zoltán taught me how to toast in Hungarian. "*Egészségedre*," he enunciated slowly—meaning, "To your health!" Later I would constantly ask him to repeat it for me, because invariably I would invert the syllables or contort the pronunciation. None of the Hungarian I had heard as a child seemed to have stuck with me. "*Paprikajancsi*," my grandfather had sometimes called me when I was being particularly mischievous. Although it literally translated to "pepper jack," Zoltán said, it was actually the name of a classical clown character similar to Punchinello. Neither of my grandparents had wanted any of us to learn their native language. Hungarian was used only when secrets needed to be kept or in heated conversations had behind closed doors. It was the language of the past, to which we were not allowed any access. We were the future, and the future spoke only Yiddish.

We had a three-hour drive ahead of us to the great northern plain bordered by Romania to the east and Ukraine and Slovakia to the north, in which Nyíregyháza was only a small city. Zoltán planned to stop for dinner at a guesthouse he knew on the way, about forty miles from Budapest. I was starving. On the way out of the city there was heavy traffic, a result of one of the ubiquitous film crews that was using the highway ramp for a crash scene. Most of the big American blockbusters, Zoltán informed me, were at least partially filmed in Budapest. A stunted and incongruous economy combined with a complacent government allowed the city's streets to be bought for cheap.

As we drove, dense clouds piled up in the sky, and by the time we arrived at the little guesthouse just off the highway, they had spread out across the flat plain and seemed to sag just above us like a structure about to collapse. I had the inexplicable thought that if Europe lived under a uniform sky—as if sharing a communal roof—Hungary, at its center, was somehow more vulnerable to its failure. Upon exiting the car, I felt a stiff wind and noticed the reeds that grew by the side of the road whipping back and forth.

Inside the simple cafeteria-style restaurant, the shelves along the wall boasted tall glass jars of pickled vegetable salads—what my grandmother had called *savanyu*, Hungarian for sour. She, too, had pickled cauliflowers and peppers and cucumbers, anything really, and served them alongside various dishes throughout the year. I asked Zoltán if the jars were for sale or simply decorative. "Both," the shopkeeper answered, looking nonplussed at the question. There was no menu, because what was on offer here was apparently on offer at every guesthouse in the region, which rarely received ignorant visitors. I played it safe and went for the goulash, my first taste of the stew since I was a child. It arrived, smelling powerfully familiar, in all its brown and soupy glory, a large dollop of paprika jelly on the side. It felt like the first wholesome, truly nourishing meal I had eaten since my childhood. I devoured the entire bowl.

When we got back on the road, light rain was starting to fall. It became torrents as we raced along the flat, unchanging territory. Disheveled myrtles swayed precariously in the onslaught. Here and there the sun would streak through a tear in the clouds. Finally, we emerged into a sun-dappled mist, and an enormous, per-fectly formed rainbow arced over the road in front of us.

"Look, a rainbow," I exclaimed in German.

"Ah! A good sign, no?"

"When I was a child, I was taught that the rainbow was a gift from God to Noah. He promised never to unleash his rage onto the world again like he had in the great flood, but instead would send a warning sign for the people to repent. The rainbow is sup-posed to be a warning—if you see one, you're supposed to take it as a sign to repent for your sins."

Zoltán seemed perplexed. "But doesn't it make more sense for the rainbow to be a symbol for hope?"

"I guess we'll see," I said to myself in English, wondering if I'd look back at this moment as portentous.

We entered the Szatmár-Bereg region, an area that had once been part of Transylvania, now a poor and rural place. By the time we arrived in Nyíregyháza, whatever cooling-off the rain had pro-vided was gone. Only a few damp spots remained on concrete structures, and steam rose from the asphalt. Once upon a time, gracious town houses and courtyard apartments had lined these orderly boulevards, but no sign remained of the former elegance that my grandmother had described. Nyíregyháza seemed eco-nomically depressed, barely recovered from the communist regime that had fallen more than twenty years past. There had been no revolution here, no revival—the city seemed to have satisfied itself with a few new coats of paint.

"For the young people who grow up in this region, Nyíregyhá-za's college is the only opportunity to broaden one's horizons, to learn a field or skill that can expand the number of possibilities in their future," Zoltán said.

The center of Nyíregyháza featured a smattering of stucco houses with clay-pot roofs, but mostly there were the ever-present communist apartment blocks, their cracked concrete facades now done up in cheerful Mediterranean colors as if in rebellion.

Zoltán told me that the college campus had been awarded a prize for excellence from a global architectural foundation in 2009. And yet, its buildings, although new, had been erected in a similar Spartan style. It was as if the aesthetic here had been permanently altered by the communist regime; the buildings were squat, functional squares around a voluminous courtyard.

"So, do many people come through here?" I asked as we pulled up alongside the campus.

"Not as many as we would like. And even the ones who do, they don't all graduate. Perhaps it's a problem with laziness"—and then he corrected his vocabulary—"no, I mean, motivation."

"But why would they not be motivated?" I asked. "Especially if this is the only way to something better."

"A lot of the students who do very well here don't know what to do with their education once they've finished. Some of them are lucky and get jobs, but there aren't enough jobs for everyone, and they are competing with students from bigger cities. It's even harder to get work outside of Hungary, unless they're brought into the factories in Austria and Slovakia to provide cheap labor, as they work for forints. Those employers take advantage of the poor exchange rate and pay Hungarians according to the income scale here, whereas the other employees make three or four times as much."

We stopped in front of the college guesthouse, and then I checked in with the receptionist in the lobby.

"If you get hungry or thirsty, there are vending machines

through that corridor," Zoltán said, pointing. "Otherwise, Angelika, the interpreter, will come get you from your room first thing in the morning."

I wrote my name and passport number on the sheet the receptionist handed to me, and she gave me a key card. I entered my room and appraised the two twin beds and their standard hospital sheeting with relief. I hadn't been sure what to expect. The air conditioner failed to circulate anything other than hot air, but a shower room complete with multiple jets and spouts that had to be manipulated with a remote control surprised me. I might have preferred a working air conditioner, and managed even with a French bathtub arrangement—the one where you shower by using a trickling hose extension from the tub's faucet. I threw open the large windows that looked out into the main courtyard of the campus. Tall, sturdy-looking trees with thick boughs obscured my view of the ground, but I could hear the idle chatter of students floating up toward me. The air seemed to enter the room almost reluctantly, bringing with it the faint odor of cigarette smoke and damp concrete.

I slept the sleep of the dead, regardless of the heat. I was awakened by a mourning dove burbling outside my window. For a moment before I opened my eyes, I thought I was back in Brooklyn. I recalled waking up early on July mornings in my grandparents' house to that same sound of mourning doves cooing in the tree limbs level to my window, the last refreshing breeze of the night wafting into my room. Then I squinted into the bright early light, remembering where I was. I sat up immediately, walking over to the open windows to glimpse the foreign world in which I'd arrived and confirm it was still real.

The quad was empty except for a gardener who was trimming grass that had grown into the walkways. I could hear the faint buzzing sound of his electric cutter. I decided to explore the grounds while it was still quiet, before Angelika came to get me, so I took a shower and put on shorts and a T-shirt. In the antiseptic lobby I found a vending machine that served up every kind of Italian coffee drink for ninety forints, the approximate equivalent of forty cents. I could control the amount of sugar, the ratio of milk, and the potency of the espresso shot. My cappuccino dispensed itself in an individual plastic cup that popped out of a spout, followed by a plastic stirrer that dropped down into the hot foaming liquid. I lifted the cup to my nose and inhaled deeply. Coffee did not smell like this in the States, with that faint underlying note of almost-burnt caramel.

"*Jó reggelt*," I said to the guards as I passed them in the corridor. They smiled and replied with "Good morning," nodding their heads in an old-fashioned gesture of respect. I could feel their curious gaze follow me out the door. I had gathered by now that American visitors were rare in this part of the country. Before I left, I had tried to find a travel guide, but the one book I'd found that covered all of Hungary and not just Budapest had skimmed over this region, implying that it was impoverished and seamy, unsafe for the average tourist. I was lucky to be the recipient of the college's hospitality; now I was keenly aware of how lost I would have been here on my own.

It was a humid morning, the kind that started out just bearable and turned positively ovenlike by 8 a.m. The sky reminded me of the clouds in classical paintings; it was as if someone had taken a paintbrush and dipped it into the fresh white paint on the canvas, blurring the edges of the clouds into off-white and pale gray smears. They were not like American clouds, which was the first thing I had noticed about Hungary. It had an old, classical sky.

We had humid summers in Brooklyn, too, although it usually didn't get quite so bad in June. My grandmother had always been particularly good at handling the heat, refusing to turn on our air-conditioning units until it became positively unbearable. It was not until I reached Nyíregyháza that I understood why she was so unfazed. It felt like the muggy haze of a thousand summers had been trapped here on the plains, the mist collecting in layers.

Outside, two ancient gingko trees flanked the entrance to the building. Up close, their leaves weighed tremulously under drops of dew the size of nickels. Every so often, a branch would shake in the breeze, and the dewdrops would quiver and slide along the surface of the leaves, righting themselves eventually when the breeze died. Along the paths carved out between the lush gardens and lawns were the acacia trees my grandmother had spoken of to me so fondly, their dainty, fernlike leaves gently filtering the sun so that it dappled the grass beneath in lacy patterns.

Here were all the plants of her childhood, some of which she had tried to cultivate in our little backyard garden, and as I walked around the campus, I began to recognize some shrubs and flowers with joy. These were no English gardens at the college. These were the kind of gardens you might imagine had grown wild here and only been tamed, just barely, as an afterthought. Bushes and plants grew riotously into one another's territory, and the grass in between was twice as tall as grass was usually allowed to grow in America. Willows and poplars competed for space, fat lavender shrubs lined the pathway, and tendrils of creeping fig wound their way around them. I heard a mourning dove gurgle throatily on the branch above me. The atmosphere was lush and fragrant, the sun was already hot on my skin; I closed my eyes and inhaled deeply, trying to preserve the moment into an individually packaged memory, complete with vivid sensory details. It seems funny now, how we are never really in control of the moments that do stand out later, with their smells and sounds so immediate and evocative. I recalled another moment then, instead—one that I had made no effort to retain.

My grandmother may have grown the only real garden in prehipster Brooklyn. It was the early 1990s, and most people had cemented over their backyards to keep away the weeds. She had made an agreement with the neighbors on either side of us: she would take care of the little plots of land behind their houses if they, the owners, allowed her to plant whatever she desired there. And so she did, growing strawberries in the damp, rich soil that lay just under the thick refuge of ivy filtering all that wonderful light that hit the back of our brownstone in the afternoons. She planted fat pink climbing roses so that they used the chain-link fence marking the perimeter of the yard as a trellis; the thorny stems climbed higher each year, inextricably intertwined with the metal. Crocuses and daffodils came up in late winter, and gorgeously colored tulips popped up in clusters in early spring, followed closely by brilliant blue irises and delicate lilies of the valley.

She had a real eye for landscaping—it wasn't just haphazard with her. The garden was divided into three rectangular sections, each delineated by carefully trimmed white-edged Swedish ivy and bordered on the corners with broad-leafed hostas. Slabs of rock were laid in between the sections and at the borders to create a walking path, and little tufts of moss grew between the rocks. It was a magical place, so well cared for that it gave back generously and graciously each year. I had read Frances Hodgson Burnett's classic by then, and begun to pretend that it was my own secret garden. When I stood among the rustling leaves and smelled the delicate fragrance of the flowers, the incongruent urban cacophony was muted and remote, the sounds of honking cars and droning airplanes softened by wind-tossed stems and whispering petals. The ivy beds were like cushions that absorbed and suffocated the ugly sound of the city. In my imagination, it was as if invisible walls had gone up around the garden, and I had fallen, like Alice in Wonderland, into another plane of existence.

Every year, catalogs would arrive from Holland, offering nothing but tulip bulbs, and my grandmother and I would pore over the varieties and talk about which ones we might like to try. We'd survey the potted African violets on the windowsill to see if they were ready to be transplanted, but we'd leave the geranium cuttings until summer. There were always exciting plans to be made in the spring, and a summer of surprise growth to look forward to.

One morning in 1999, my grandmother and I went downstairs to check on the plants, and I watched as she fingered a strong-looking sapling that had sprung from the middle of the garden, just past the line of shade cast by the porch overhead.

"What is it?" I asked, thinking it was something she had planted last year, wondering if perhaps we could expect another rosebush.

"I made a mistake," she said, looking crestfallen. "I thought it was just a weed."

"What is it?" I asked again, more curious this time.

"It's a loganberry tree," she said. "I don't know how I missed it. I was surrounded by them as a child. I should have recognized it instantly."

Immediately I understood her consternation. It was too late to do anything about it now—she might have been able to tear it out when it had still been a shoot, but a tree that gave fruit could not be cut or pruned. It is against Jewish law to hinder a fruit tree's growth in any way.

She had to let it take over her garden, and as the years went by, it did so, growing so big and tall that it towered over our second-story porch and dropped purple splats of berries for three years, until it became permissible to pick and eat them. As the tree grew, it stole nutrients from the soil and light from the sky, becoming the hungriest, greediest thing in the garden. Year by year, the other plants began to die. The tulips grew fewer and fewer in number; the irises disappeared completely. My grandmother saw this, and although she never said anything, I watched her make fewer and fewer trips to that garden she had once cherished. Eventually, the ivy became so neglected it grew over those carefully laid paths, and weeds began to crowd the borders and infiltrate the center of the garden. These were no mild breed either, they were the thick, broad-leafed stalks indigenous to Brooklyn, hardy plants that hardly needed any time at all, it seemed, to grow as tall as trees and drown the garden completely in darkness. When I saw that the weeds would not be addressed, I went downstairs to rip them out myself. I had no knowledge of gardening; my grandmother had taught me only to love flowers, not how to take care of them. With bare fingers I pulled and tugged on each insidious weed, feeling with every success that there were already new ones growing to replace those that had been excised. My grandmother came out onto the porch and watched me work, thinking I was doing it to please her.

"You don't have do that for me, little lamb," she said, using her traditional term of endearment. But I wasn't doing it for her. I was desperately trying to rescue the only realized fantasy of my childhood, the one beautiful thing that had marked my upbringing in this otherwise godforsaken corner of Brooklyn. I pulled furiously, my vision blurred by pollen irritation, my nose stinging from the pungent odor of weed juice spilling onto the earth. I finished the whole backyard, and when I was done, the garden looked as if a massacre had taken place there; the weeds had left gaping holes and depressions in the ground. Never mind, I thought, those would fill. I would buy weed killer. I would keep pulling them out if it killed me. I was older by then, making money of my own from babysitting; I could plant new things in the holes to replace the weeds. Hydrangeas would be nice, perhaps some bleeding heart.

I made my way over to some young climbing roses, shriveled and drooping sadly where the twine had come loose. I found the rusted edge of metal tie used to affix the bush to the fence and tried to force the stems back into their original upright position, to no avail. The tie snapped back, its jagged edge tearing into the skin of my palm. Blood sprang from the gash, but I bit back my instinctual scream so that my grandmother wouldn't notice. I hadn't thought to ask for gardening gloves.

How I wanted her to come down then and work alongside me, just as we had always done. They seemed gone forever, those times. No matter how hard I worked to fix it all, I knew my grandmother had given up on the garden, and my grandmother did not change her mind about things she had given up on. She had learned to detach from the things she loved because she had experienced so much loss in her life already.

It was from her that I must have inherited that deep-rooted ability to detach. It hurt to love things now, I discovered, even though I wanted to love without being afraid of disappointment. I wanted to be able to invest my energies over and over again but what was easy, what was familiar, was the act of cutting—cutting off, cutting out, cutting away. When would I be able to stop trimming at the edges of my life, gnawing it down to the bone, and start building on it?

I had already begun to miss my grandmother then. Even as I stood next to her while she cooked and scrubbed and sang tremulous tunes I longed desperately for the woman she had been before loss and tragedy had sanded her down. After I left, it felt as if she had already died, and her spirit hovered over me like a guardian angel.

I finally had permission to dredge up her past. She was the ultimate model of displacement for me. Her story of exile and wandering was more real to me than the story of how she had settled into her new life in America, the only life I had known her in. As I experienced my own exile, and as I wandered around the world looking for a new identity, there was no one I could feel closer to than the memory of her young self, traversing rivers and oceans in search of a place to call home.

I was here now, in the world she had come from. These were her childhood smells and sounds.

These trees had been witnesses, and this sun had warmed her

on summer days like this one. I hadn't thought about how it would feel to be walking on ground she might have walked on, under a sky so distinctly different from the one that had seemed so far away in dusty, honking Brooklyn. My eyes filled at the realization, but the sun dried my tears before they could roll down my cheeks. Somewhere, a lawn mower started, and the sound of it made me open my eyes. A magpie strutted by, a starling pecked at a crevice between the paving stones.

This might have been me. That thought now formed itself like a sentence on a blackboard in my mind.

Of course, not the me I was now, but the hypothetical me, two generations descended from my grandmother. If she'd never had her world turned upside down by war, but had stayed here, tending her garden, feeding the birds, baking her strudels and pies, I'd have been some young peasant woman working on a farm perhaps, speaking only Hungarian and Yiddish, the rest of the world an abstract idea I'd never encounter in reality.

Although American culture had reached the rest of Western Europe and certainly parts of Budapest, Nyíregyháza had no billboards for American films and no American music playing on its radio stations. The fashions here did not seem influenced by the French, the Germans, or the Russians, but more so by the unself-consciousness of a culture that didn't have to suffer the burden of comparison.

Students had started to arrive on campus, clutching worn leather book bags to their chests, dressed in faded jeans and cotton tees. They glanced at me curiously, and I knew there was something about me that screamed *different* to them, but I couldn't quite put my finger on what that might be. Was it my hair, with its layered cut from a salon in New York, or my shorts, with their American logo on the back pockets? I was inclined to think it was something they could smell as they walked by, a sort of perfume of foreignness.

Back at the guesthouse I saw a petite young woman in high-heeled slingbacks knocking on my door. She reached down to smooth her red pencil skirt over impossibly slender thighs, then straightened up nervously to wait for the door to open.

"I'm here!" I called out from the other end of the corridor.

She turned and squinted, then smiled and proceeded to clack her heels down the hall toward me. I indicated I would come to her.

Angelika had the kind of distinct Transylvanian looks that would be very popular in an American TV show about vampires. Her hair was pitch-black and curled around her shoulders in long waves. Her eyes were the color of liquid amber and framed by long dark lashes and defined brows. She had a pert upturned nose and a smile that revealed two rows of braces encased in red rubbers. She was my age, with two children from a previous marriage. It was the first time I had met another woman of my age who was also a mom. This was the Old World, I reminded myself.

"I will take you to Zoltán's office, okay?"

"Do you know what the plan is for today?" I asked.

"No, Zoltán is the one in charge," she said, laughing. "I just follow instructions."

"Thank you for doing this for me," I said. "I'm sure you have more important work you could be doing."

"Are you kidding?" she said. "This is probably the most exciting thing I've ever done for my job. It's such a refreshing change from sitting behind my computer all day."

Zoltán suggested that I put on something more professional than shorts, as we were set to meet the mayor of Kántorjánosi, who had already been informed about our visit.

"You have to impress these people," Angelika said, "if you want them to get anything done for you. They have to feel that this important New York writer is coming to visit their small town, with a whole entourage. You will give them a story they will be telling for years!"

I hadn't thought of it that way.

"I'll meet you at the car," I said, and raced back to my room to put on a skirt and heels.

"Much better," Zoltán said when I teetered into the parking lot.

"*Nagyon szép?*" I asked, recalling a bit of Hungarian from my childhood.

"Yes, very pretty."

On the way to Kántorjánosi, a blink-and-you-miss-it village twenty-five miles from Nyíregyháza, I was largely silent as Angelika and Zoltán conversed. In my hand I held an old photograph of my grandmother's childhood home, which had been taken by one of my uncles on a 1988 visit. I had scavenged it during a childhood treasure hunt. Of course, I did not know the exact address, so my plan had been to drive through the village and see if any of the houses matched the picture taken twenty-five years earlier.

Not the most ironclad plan, I realized, as we drove past cornfields, apple orchards, and carefully tended vineyards. The land here was very flat, and stretched for miles around us. Every field was full of enormous, healthy crops, seemingly impervious to the unforgiving heat of summer. Had I been crazy to think I could just show up with a few photographs and my grandmother's past would magically materialize before me? Now that I had actually made it, something I never really believed would happen, it seemed silly, and I was scared to fail after having come all this way.

I wanted to accomplish something on this trip, something along the lines of closure. If I could piece together the journey my grandmother had taken before she landed in the lap of the Satmar Hasids, somehow I could put into context my own journey out and back into the larger world she had once inhabited. In a sense, I would be able to clarify my own displacement only in the context of hers. If I came home empty-handed, I worried, I'd never achieve context for my own life. We are, sometimes, simply reduced to where we come from—if not in the most immediate sense, then in an ancestral one. I was convinced that the angst that flowed in my veins was a result of more than just my childhood, that it was part of a greater composite inheritance that I was only a fragmentary part of.

Kántorjánosi had one main street, which split into two smaller streets after the town square, and a few dead-end roads. We drove through it so quickly, thinking it was bigger, that we had to turn around and go back once we realized there were no more houses. I scanned every house, looking in particular for the unique ironwork in the gate in my photograph, but all the houses looked similar, with stucco sides painted various shades of beige and sloping clay-pot roofs. They were all gated and had their own gardens.

"I don't see it! Do you see it?" I showed them the photograph. I had a panicky feeling that I had come all this way for nothing, that we would never be able to identify the exact house, that it was probably long gone by now.

"Is it that one?" Angelika asked, pointing as we coasted by a decrepit house, its gate rusted and warped. I turned back to look, trying to compare it with the one in the photo.

"They all look the same!" I said. "How can I be sure?"

"Never mind," Zoltán said. "Let's go talk to the mayor and see what he was able to find out."

The mayor's office was in a modest but new building that flanked the town square. Inside, some people were lined up in the hallway. They had dark skin and were missing teeth. "Gypsies," Angelika said. They seemed to be waiting for some form of assistance or welfare.

The mayor's secretary seemed unnerved by our presence. I could imagine how she might be put off by the idea that I was some big-shot American expecting them to drop everything and help me. She instructed us to enter the mayor's office and wait there for his arrival.

Inside we sat at a small table that was covered in a crocheted tablecloth like the ones my grandmother had used for her dining room table. She had told me stories of women who started preparing their own trousseaus from a young age, knitting and sewing their own linens. I wondered who had crocheted this tablecloth.

The mayor was a soft-spoken man who seemed a bit taken aback by all the fuss. I could tell that this town didn't get many visitors. He had found my grandmother's house, he told us—there was an old woman living there now who, he said, was quite popular in the town. She sat on a bench outside her house every day and talked to everyone who passed by. She claimed to remember some things about my family, even though she was in her nineties.

"Does she remember my grandmother?" I asked Angelika to ask the mayor.

"Perhaps," the mayor answered. "She's a bit fuzzy, but she says she remembers some things. Shall we go to her?"

We walked a little ways down the main street, named after the Hungarian poet Arany János, all of us in a group, and neighbors watched from behind their gates, openmouthed at the sight. The mayor talked to Zoltán about his plans for the city, and Angelika whispered the translations to me as we followed. The economy here was farm-based, he said, but somehow the Gypsy population accumulated enough money to furnish their homes quite lavishly. The mayor estimated that the region was now at least 50 percent Gypsy.

A woman with flared nostrils and hair dyed orange crossed the street in front of us, pushing a stroller loaded with black plastic bags. She paused on the other side of the road and gave us a blank stare as we passed.

Soon we came to a stop in front of the decrepit house that Angelika had pointed to earlier. Now I looked at the photograph in my hand again and saw that it was indeed the right house, but very neglected. The house was actually two buildings: a living area in the front and a separate kitchen in the back. The front building had a badly rusted tin roof, and lichens had coated the terra-cotta roof behind it. Both roofs seemed as if they might slide off on either side at any moment.

Outside the gate, an ancient-looking woman with only one tooth sat on a bench, her arm resting on a cane. She was wearing a loose flowery dress that buttoned down the front, and although her exposed skin was leathery and dark from the sun, the bits that showed through the gaps between the buttons were stark white. She grinned at us as we approached.

I'm not the first one to come visit her, she told Angelika as soon as we were within earshot. She remembered a tall young man many years ago who had asked her some questions.

"That was my uncle," I said. "He took this picture."

I showed her the photograph, and she apologized for the condition of the house, explaining that she had not been able to do any necessary repairs. Yet the garden behind her was bursting with color, and I remarked on it. There were numerous carefully pruned rosebushes and lilacs poking through the rusted curlicues in the gate. In particular, a bench lined with potted geraniums caught my eye.

"Tell her my grandmother used to do that," I said to Angelika. "She used to replant the cuttings. She would have been really happy to see this garden."

Angelika related the information, and the old woman smiled and responded eagerly.

"She used to have more things growing," Angelika said. "But now she is too old."

"Can you ask her what those enormous white, bell-shaped flowers are called, the ones growing by the door?"

"She doesn't know. She grows them to keep the flies away. Let me ask her what she knows about your family."

Angelika leaned in and started a conversation in Hungarian. I looked past them at the house. I couldn't believe this was where my grandmother spent her childhood, in this tiny little village.

The fashionable, cosmopolitan woman I knew couldn't possibly have come from such a far-flung, barren smattering of dwellings.

"So, she remembers an older woman who lived here," Angelika said, interrupting my reverie, "who was a midwife. She had five children, and one of the daughters was named Laura."

"That's my great-grandmother Leah," I said. "Does she remember her daughter Irenka?"

Angelika asked her and then told me, "She's not sure."

"Does she remember that they used to pump seltzer from the ground and sell it?"

"Yes. She said they had a little general store in the front room of the house."

"I remember my grandmother telling me that."

Angelika turned to listen to something the old woman was saying.

"Also, she says she bought the house after the war from a man named Schwartz."

"That would be Laura's father," I said, "but that's impossible. He didn't survive the war. No one in my grandmother's family did."

I motioned to Angelika not to translate that. I felt strangely sorry for the old woman, knowing that she had found it necessary to invent a story like that, to justify her life spent in this home.

"She wants to know if you would like to go inside and see it. She hasn't changed anything since she bought it, she says."

"She won't mind?" I asked, incredulous.

"Not at all. Go ahead."

I made my way gingerly down the path to the side door of the main building. Once inside, however, I immediately regretted my decision. The house was extremely dirty and reeked of human waste. I couldn't imagine my scrupulously tidy grandmother in a house like that. I emerged a moment later, trying to cling to some of the nicer details. There was one large room in the front and one in the back. The ceilings were high and beamed; old, cumbersome chandeliers dangled from between the shallow rafters, dusty crystals catching the faint rays of sunlight that weakly illuminated the darkened interior. I imagine they all slept there, in one bedroom, the parents and their ten children. No wonder my grandmother had been sent to live in Nyíregyháza as an adolescent. There had been no room for her.

That was why she wasn't gassed, my grandmother had once told me. Because she had been deported separately from her family and hadn't been holding a younger sibling when she faced Dr. Mengele at selection. Anyone holding a child was automatically gassed. Her whole family had been murdered on the same day. She was the only one who made it past selection and was deemed qualified for labor. But she had never told me anything else, except that she had been liberated from Bergen-Belsen. The time in between her arrival at Auschwitz and her liberation from Bergen-Belsen was a question mark in my mind. How would I ever delve into the secret of her courage and endurance if I didn't know what sustained her through that blank period?

The mayor asked if I wanted to meet the Jewish family that lived in town. I said I was game. We crossed the square to a house of similar stature. The mayor told the Gypsy woman working in the yard that we were looking for Orsi Neni. Zoltán told me that the mayor and Orsi were quite close and had an excellent relationship. He seemed to be trying to say that race wasn't an issue here, especially not now. "She is one of the most beloved people in town," the mayor said.

Orsi Neni emerged from her home, a tiny old woman with very round eyes set in a deeply wrinkled face. Her voice was a crackly whisper. I asked her if she spoke any Yiddish. She shook her head no, explaining that her father had spoken it but she had never learned it. She didn't remember my grandmother, she said, but probably because she had been very young during the war.

"How is it that you were able to come back?" I asked.

"They hid in Levelek," Zoltán told me, referring to a larger town about fifteen minutes north. "The whole town helped, and they refused to give them to the Nazis."

"My grandmother said she was born in Levelek. Is there a hospital there or something?"

Angelika translated for the mayor, but he shook his head. "There's no hospital there that I know of." He couldn't say for sure why she would have been born there instead of in Kántorjánosi, where she grew up.

"Levelek is our next stop," Zoltán said. "I know the registrar there."

Before we left, I asked whether Orsi Neni still lit candles on Friday night and baked challah.

"Of course!" was her answer.

"Do her children do so as well?" I asked.

"No, just her," Angelika said.

How strange it was to find a Jewish woman here who had grown up in the same circumstances as my grandmother but who by some reverse twist of fate had never left home. Orsi Neni still baked the challah and lit the candles, but she was the last Jew in the town, and her children had become completely submerged in secular Hungarian life. I recalled my thoughts from earlier that morning—how easily this could have been me: uneducated, missing teeth, never seeing the world! Would my grandmother have been just like this woman?

As we left, the Gypsy woman, her brows knitted together in her dark and wrinkled forehead, gripped my hand tightly.

"What does she want?" I whispered to Angelika.

"She said she just wanted to hold your hand."

I flipped over my palm to see if she wanted to read it. The Gypsy dropped my hand suddenly, as if it had grown hot.

"She says she doesn't do that stuff anymore," Angelika said.

The mayor was talking to Zoltán about the town. "There is no anti-Semitism here," he said. "Jews, Gypsies, and Hungarians have always lived well together here." It was as if he was presenting the town as a model for tolerance. "We never had this problem of racism," he said proudly.

We drove to Levelek, whose mayor appeared slightly more sophisticated. He was younger and well dressed and had bright blue eyes. He said that his family had come to Hungary during the Polish revolution. "That's why he's good-looking," Zoltán joked. His secretary, who doubled as the registrar, was a sweet and smiling middle-aged woman with ash-blond hair. She embraced Zoltán when we arrived.

The secretary apologized for not having any bottled water to serve us. "The stores are all sold out because of this heat wave," she said.

"Oh, so you mean it's not always this hot?" I asked.

"Would you care for raspberry soda instead?" Zoltán and Angelika both nodded their heads. The soda tasted like seltzer mixed with sugary syrup. It was served on a silver tray with crystal goblets. As if we were visiting royalty.

Ledgers were open on the mayor's table, and he invited me to peruse them. There was the marriage certificate of Laura Schwartz from Levelek to Jacob Fischer from Nyíregyháza, my grandmother's parents. Their names, places of origin, and occupations were all listed clearly. Jacob was a Talmud scholar, which confirmed my belief that his parents had been wealthy—only the wealthy could afford not to work. I saw the record of my grandmother's birth, on January 8, 1927, a few years after their marriage. They had come to report it five days later, on the thirteenth—the very same day my grandfather had been born.

"Perhaps they lived here in Levelek for the first few years, if that's where Laura was from originally. Then it makes sense that their first child would be born here, before they left to open a store in Kántorjánosi."

"The mayor says he can take us to the Jewish cemetery," Zoltán said. "Perhaps you'll find more information on your family there."

We drove to the cemetery in the mayor's car. He was decidedly more upbeat than the Kántorjánosi mayor and seemed very excited to talk to Zoltán and Angelika. It felt vaguely surreal to know that I, a twenty-something woman who easily blended into a crowd in New York City, was the cause of so much excitement and fuss in a small village thousands of miles from home.

A shirtless man met us at the entrance to the cemetery. The sweat glinted like dewdrops on his hairless chest. Angelika translated for me, explaining that the man and his wife had decided to take care of the cemetery about ten years ago, as their home abutted the property. We followed him down a dirt path to a brick wall with a small gate in the middle and waited as he unlocked it.

My hopes deflated as soon as I was on the other side of the wall. All I saw was an empty field, the grass mostly yellow straw. Then I noticed stubs of tombstone poking out from the brush.

"Most of the stones were stolen by Gypsies before he started taking care of it," Angelika said, listening closely as the caretaker explained sheepishly. "They are considered very valuable for the quality of the rock."

"So they're all gone?" I asked.

"Almost."

I had noticed two on the other end of the cemetery and one in the far eastern corner. I approached the single one first, but noticed as I got closer that all of its writing had eroded. I trudged back.

"I can't read the writing anyway," I said. "It's all faded. It doesn't matter; they're probably not here."

"Don't you want to take a look at those other two before we leave?" Zoltán asked.

"All right," I said and took off my shoes to wade through the weeds.

Somewhere close to the stones I must have brushed against stinging nettle. I had never encountered the plant before, and didn't know what it looked like, but the painful feeling spread quickly around my ankles and up my calves—it felt like I was being bitten by a colony of ants.

"Ow!"

Angelika laughed. "She stepped on some *csalán*!" she said to Zoltán.

"Don't worry, Deborah," he said. "It will go away in ten minutes."

When I straightened up, I noticed I was standing in front of the stones. Perhaps it was my stinging legs that prevented me from grasping what I was looking at right away. The writing on the two stones was perfectly legible.

"Woman of Valour, Faiga Leah," read one. "Saintly woman, Faiga Pessel," read the other. The only two legible stones in the cemetery belonged to my great-grandmother and my great-great-grandmother.

"Oh my God!"

The others looked over, pausing their conversation briefly. Angelika looked up from her phone.

"It's them!" I shouted.

They hiked over. "That's Laura's grave," I said, pointing. "Of all the stones in the cemetery, these are the only ones here still in decent shape! There has to be an explanation, Angelika. Can you ask him if anyone ever came by and paid money to have these graves maintained?"

The caretaker insisted no one had ever visited this cemetery or interfered in its upkeep. "It's just a coincidence," he said. "These were the only ones left when I started taking care of the place."

It couldn't be a coincidence, I thought. Then I noticed the message on the bottom of the tombstones: "Descended from the holy Leibel from Oshvari." I had heard stories as a child of the ancestor who was a *lamed-vav'nik,* one of the thirty-six pillars of the world who supported its continued existence with anonymous good deeds. His saintliness had been discovered only after his death, when his charitable efforts suddenly ceased and his beneficiaries came forward. People had started visiting his grave, but if they ventured too close, bad things would happen, until eventually they had to put a fence around it, my grandmother had told me. It was the closest thing to magic I had ever heard of in my world. I wondered now if, given what I understood to be a superstitious stereotype attributed to Gypsies, it was possible to suppose that they might have stayed away from those stones out of fear of that very same legend, passed down among their own.

On the way out of the cemetery, we stopped to pick sour cherries from slender trees with dark green leaves that grew wild along the path. The cherries were incredibly juicy and plump. I watched as Angelika sucked a whole bunch of them effortlessly off their pits, stopping to grind them into the ground again with her shoe. For each cherry she consumed, a whole lot of them might grow in its place.

How incredible, I thought, to have food growing wild on the street. I tasted a cherry, and it was perfectly ripe, emerging from its thin, still-delicate skin in one tart, juicy burst on my tongue. I closed my eyes and remembered the taste of my grandmother's cold cherry soup, the one she served on hot summer days like this one. I wondered if she missed picking the fruit from the tree or lamented the quality of store-bought or canned sour cherries.

On the way back we stopped for lunch in a village called Napkor. Zoltán instructed his driver to pull up in front of an inn with stone walls and a sloping log roof. Potted geraniums dangled from the overhang and onto the wraparound veranda.

"Zoltán knows all the best places to eat in the area," Angelika informed me. "You're lucky."

"I never eat in the cities, Deborah," he said to me in German. "I always stop somewhere along the way, at the places most people would overlook."

We made our way inside, and were greeted by the host, who clearly knew Zoltán well. The restaurant was quite large, but empty at this hour. I glanced at the heads of boar that were mounted on the walls; their black bristles quivered in the breeze coming from the air vents and their pink snouts were ringed with condensation. They served as a stark contrast to the tables set in pristine white cloths, topped with crystal goblets and delicate flatware. The restaurant had an aura of unstudied and effortless elegance, despite the setting.

"We've got to decide which animal we're having," Zoltán informed me once we were seated and had been presented with enormous, leather-bound menus. I skimmed quickly; there were over a hundred options. "They've got to have enough notice if we want to eat within the hour."

Angelika looked at me with a mischievous sparkle in her eye. "Here they only slaughter the animal once you say you'll eat it. Otherwise it's a waste."

"You mean they'll actually go out there and grab a chicken and kill it, right now?" I asked, incredulous.

Zoltán chuckled. "Can't get any more fresh than that."

Angelika mocked my flabbergasted expression. "What, is it better somehow, knowing they already killed it yesterday?"

I turned my attention back to the menu in silence, trying to process the idea. This was farm-to-table on a whole new level.

In the end we all opted for duck. While we waited, ostensibly for it to be slaughtered and cleaned, a series of appetizers were delivered to the table. I pounced eagerly on a cold pear soup, served with sweet strips of *palacsinta,* or Hungarian crepes, as noodles. The flavors were impossible to place, a hint of something like nutmeg, a kind of cream that was neither sour nor sweet, but faintly tart, and a dash of zest that might have been from a kumquat. My spoon came up empty all too quickly, but this was soon forgotten, as our duck arrived in clearly identifiable parts, a crispy-skinned leg each for me and Angelika, a breast for Zoltán, and an assemblage of parts and organs for our driver. The duck was served on beds of caramel-colored mashed potatoes with generous sprinkles of sweet paprika and accompanied by shredded cabbage stained a deep purple by the prunes it had been cooked with. We dug in, and silence reigned at that table until the plates were cleared.

Afterward I marveled at how it was possible to eat such meals, meals that easily outranked the numerous ones I had been served at New York City's top restaurants, in such a far-flung setting and at such ridiculously cheap prices. Was it really as simple as recipes honed for generations, water drawn from deep springs and wells, fertile, unspoiled land that nourished crops and animals? I supposed, in such circumstances, even a Michelin starred chef would be rendered superfluous.

It was late afternoon when we arrived back in Nyíregyháza to visit the synagogue before it closed. The Jews had been rounded up for deportation right in front of it, and it was there that I had most wanted to stand, in the spot where my grandmother's own exile had so horribly begun. The square was now paved over, with decaying apartment buildings serving as wary witnesses around its perimeter. Their shabby terraces with peeling blue paint strips seemed like so many eyes half-closed in fatigue. This was not the Nyíregyháza my grandmother had seen on that day, but it seemed somehow to retain the memory of that moment in its tired bones nonetheless.

The street in front of the synagogue, a stately building with small high windows and a secure gate, was quiet except for the occasional passing car. Now that I was looking directly at the spot where it had happened, I couldn't imagine a roundup taking place there. These were events dramatized in movies, or vividly evoked in books I'd read, but they couldn't possibly happen in such a quiet and ordinary place. Reality would have to split apart for a moment to allow something like that. Life as I understood it, the banal pursuit of food, salary, and entertainment, would have to completely collapse; it would have to be replaced with something alien and otherworldly.

The synagogue was painted pink with white trim. It looked nothing like the shuls I had grown up around, and more like the reform temples I had started to visit recently. Inside, the synagogue had a low, unenclosed women's gallery, and in such a small building, those women would have been clearly visible to the men below. The synagogues I had grown up with had women's sections that were fully separated from the main room by height and enclosure.

This had been a very modern Orthodox community, nothing like the one I remembered my grandmother being a part of.

I asked the rabbi, "Were there any Hasidic Jews living here before the war?"

Angelika translated. The rabbi shook his head slowly.

"None that I know of. From what I heard, there was a small group of them over in Satu Mare, now in Romania, and perhaps another small community in the southern region, but there were no Hasids in this area back then. In the eighties they came to Budapest, the Lubavitchers, and tried to convert everyone. They even tried to convert me. Like I wasn't a good-enough Jew for them."

The rabbi and his associate gave us a ride back to the college, as our chauffeur had left for the day. I heard the two of them talking in exuberant Hungarian in the front seat, and I could just about make out that the conversation was about me. I asked Angelika to listen in.

"He is saying," she said with a laugh, "that he doesn't understand how someone can talk so much and listen so well at the same time, that your brain works so fast. But he says you are very sweet."

"Ach, you are translating for her?" the rabbi said. "No, don't be offended. We just don't often get such intense visitors—we are accustomed to a slower pace here."

"It's okay," I said, smiling. "It's not the first time I've heard that."

Zoltán walked me to my room when we got back.

"I'm so thrilled that we were able to do this," he said. "This is what I want to show, that Hungarians can help! There is no anti-Semitism here. There never was."

When I left Nyíregyháza some days later, I looked out the window at the passing world, thinking that this planet was like a snow globe that received regular shakes. The war had been a particularly vigorous one, and because of that, my grandmother had drifted over to the other side of the world amid the chaos, forever changing the legacy of our family.

During that trip to Hungary, I had cracked for the first time in my grandfather's hometown, Újfehértó, twenty-five minutes from the town where my grandmother was born. The bureaucrat who was being paid to print birth certificates and death certificates and other such documents for people in precisely my position had made us come back three days in a row, and each time she had a different excuse. Here we were on the third day, with our official stamps procured, all fees paid, and the front door to the town hall locked for an hour already with Angelika and I still in it, and still there was this tut-tutting, the opening and shutting of doors with ancient ledgers peering temptingly behind them, the meandering phone conversations in Hungarian that I couldn't understand, and still those certificates weren't printed.

My translator indicated that I might have to wait and receive the rest in the mail. We'd had no trouble procuring the birth and marriage records of my grandmother, great-grandmother, and great-great-grandmother in Levelek. Indeed, the registrar had produced them with a joyous smile. Here in Újfehértó, I felt the tears come and quickly left the room. My eyes began to swim as the cleaner painstakingly removed the padlock from the double doors so that I could exit the building, and outside the scene blurred into brown and gray as I collapsed onto a bench.

Zoltán came and sat next to me, inquiring what was wrong. "I don't understand," I heaved, wishing I could stop sobbing. "Why does she have to be that way?"

The translator explained briefly, "Some people are just like that. Bureaucrats. It's unfortunate but it happens all the time. Not everyone can be a lovely person."

I'm so thrilled that we were able to do this, Zoltán had said to me yesterday evening after dropping me off at the college. *Hungarians can help. There is no anti-Semitism here.* Poor Zoltán. I was sure there wasn't a shred of anti-Semitism in his heart, nor was there any in the lovely group of people he had assembled to assist me in my research, but I know that he would have felt terrible to realize that on the rest of my trip, I would learn something very different from what he wanted me to.

Perhaps my bitterness set in for good once I arrived back in Buda-pest, when I met, for the first time, a Jew who was afraid. Or maybe it was earlier—maybe it happened when I saw what my life could have been like had tensions not culminated in that awful "final solution." Would I have had to live being subject to humiliation by a local Christian population with the power to intimidate me? Surely I wouldn't have access to the rights I have today; I wouldn't have been able to pursue social equality, let alone my education.

In Budapest I met my friend Ella, who took me to the Jewish quarter. Here I saw a living Jewish community, a kosher butcher, a Belzer chasid from Israel who had moved back here with his chil-dren and was able to converse with me in Yiddish, women in *sheitels* escorting young boys with messy side curls, Hebrew writ-ing next to Hungarian, and synagogues and ritual baths and all the familiar paraphernalia. Cholent, a staple dish in Jewish com-munities worldwide, was listed on most restaurant menus.

After we toured the Orthodox synagogue together, Ella and I decided to drop by the Judaica shop next door. A young man was working there, sitting behind a desk piled with books. He had curly brown hair and a nice familiar face, very Jewish-looking. So I asked. I did not see Ella's face behind me go white. Peter—that was his name—drew inward and away from me, his shoulders scrunching up in defense.

"That's a very private issue," he said.

Oh. Where I came from, it wasn't private at all. A Jew, travel-ing, meets another Jew, and says, "Shalom."

"I'm sorry," Ella apologized in a whisper. "She's from America."

"Ah." Peter relaxed a bit.

"What—you can't ask someone if they're Jewish in Hungary?"

Ella nodded. "It's a very offensive question here, almost never asked for a positive reason. You have to be very careful in this anti-Semitic environment."

"It's that bad?" I thought back to the handful of days I had spent in the east of Hungary, where I had seen quite a few cities and villages and towns, and met so many people, and only the dreadful bureaucrat stood out to me as someone who might have been, just maybe, a tad anti-Semitic. But she could also have been a generally rude and unhelpful person, no? Or an overworked and underpaid civil servant? Or a frustrated matron resentful of an entitled American who swooped into her town with chauffeur, translator, and esteemed university president in tow?

"I heard about the Jobbik party, and Gyöngyösi's idea for a list of Jews as national security risks, but that was laughed out of parliament, right?" I said.

Ella's forehead was creased. "He's got eight percent now, but with next year's elections, he'll get twenty percent at least."

"What happened? Is everyone suddenly going crazy? Is anti-Semitism becoming acceptable again?"

"The problem is, in Hungary, it never left," Ella said darkly.

There was still flooding then, so Ella couldn't show me the sculpted shoes that lined the banks of the Danube. Instead, she led me to the larger Dohány Utcai synagogue, with its gracious courtyard, now a memorial, where the Jews of Budapest had been made to await deportation. In the last days of the war, she informed me—when the Nazis had retreated in anticipation of the Russian advance—the Hungarians had taken it upon themselves to drag the remaining Jews down to the river and shoot them into it. To save ammunition they had tied groups of five or six together and shot just one; the rest of the group would fall into the river and be drowned instead.

They had been made to take off their shoes first; big and small, old and new, they had lined the banks afterward. The sculptors had re-created the scene by placing replicas along both sides of the Danube. For weeks, Ella told me, the Danube had been red with blood. "They weren't under any orders," she said. "They just wanted to get rid of the Jews before the world came to its senses again, and the opportunity was lost."

My observations of Jewish life in Budapest absorbed me completely. For the first time, I was not only able to imagine prewar Judaism but also able to see it. The community proceeded as if no time had passed. Did I want to see those ancient tenement buildings around echoing courtyards from which spectral Nazis drove their sobbing victims? Could I visualize the archetypal Jew, his head bent in humility, looking at the floor, all of his movements restrained in such a way as to draw the least amount of attention to himself? What did I know of this life, where one's identity must be kept secret, where one must always look over a shoulder in search of a menacing pursuer? I watched a man step out of a kosher pizza shop and take off his yarmulke, stuffing it into his pocket before he walked down the street. No, I never knew of such privations. I had yearned to take off my Hasidic costume so that I could blend in and be normal, but I never experienced a desire to do so out of fear. It was fear that had kept us so separate in Europe, and that continued to do so in a place like Budapest, but how long would that threat work in America? Even I had eventually realized that those stories of hate and persecution, designed to teach me to keep my distance from gentiles, no longer applied in the New World, in the melting pot of Brooklyn.

I headed for Sweden after that, because it was the only place I had ever heard my grandmother speak of fondly. She had spent most of her time there with her friend Edith, who had been with her in the camps. Edith had accompanied my grandmother's exit from Bergen-Belsen by walking alongside the stretcher on which she was placed by the British Red Cross; she had obtained transport on the same ship to Sweden, where my grandmother was sent to recuperate from typhus in health resorts that had been temporarily refashioned into refugee camps. But I had only ever known Edith as the woman who lived in Chicago, the one who occasionally flew in to New York to see my grandmother, but whom I could never meet. She was not allowed in our home, for she was secular.

In Sweden, as I slowly filled in the gaps in my grandmother's history, I realized that back then, it must not have mattered that Edith was on the verge of renouncing her faith while my grandmother was about to dive in headfirst. It seemed clear to me that faith must have been irrelevant in a world turned upside down by war; rather, it was something to grapple with when the ground steadied itself underneath one's feet.

I had a photograph of my grandmother standing next to Edith

in front of a grand house, with tall pine trees filling the background. I showed this photograph to the woman working at the archive in Malmö.

Operation White Buses, it had been called, the Swedish relief effort that rescued hundreds of Holocaust victims directly from the camps. "But that wouldn't have been her," I said. "She was rescued by the Red Cross. Was there another way she could have arrived in Sweden?"

"They painted red crosses on those white buses," she explained. "That's how they were able to get past the military."

The clerk took another look at the copy of the Swedish alien's passport I had brought with me. Perhaps here, she said, pointing to the stamp from the Statten Uttlands Kommission, or the Swedish Aliens Commission. The way the archives program in Sweden was organized, each city was home to a different archive. Nothing was digitized. The records of the Aliens Commission were located in the Riksarkivet in Stockholm.

I took a train to Stockholm that afternoon, where I was informed that the archive I was looking for was closeted away in a special room that only one expert had access to, and he needed to be called in. I waited impatiently for an hour until he arrived. A lanky, middle-aged man, gray-haired, bearded, with skin the ghastly white color of chalk, he took my ticket wordlessly and disappeared for twenty minutes.

He came back with a slim white box, which he opened on the table in front of me.

"Sorry, this was all I could find," he said haltingly.

In the box was a thick folder containing sheaves of documents about my grandmother, all in Swedish. I was speechless with joy.

At best, I had expected a one-page record of her temporary presence in the country.

I gave the man a spontaneous hug, which almost made him jump out of his skin.

"You don't know how much this means to me," I said. He backed away, his eyes widened in alarm.

"You're welcome," he said once he was at a safe distance.

Another employee helped me with the initial translation. There were pages of testimony about her experiences during the war, which had been collected by international police. It was delivered woodenly, but, although that could have been the translator's work, it seemed somehow to be my grandmother's voice. I could almost hear her saying those words out loud. The testimony had been taken in German, the documents said. Had she indeed spoken a rudimentary German, or was that Yiddish they were referring to? I had never heard her speak a word of German.

She had been one of two hundred Hungarian women, chosen for their ability to perform skilled labor, culled from Auschwitz and taken to various munitions factories throughout Germany, where they were forced to fashion weapons for the Nazi army. They had to have known that they were aiding the war effort, I assumed. Later, I would learn from online research that a memorial had been erected for those two hundred women in the small town in Germany where they had worked, at the site of the former Phillips-Valvo factory where the munitions had been produced. The memorial was erected out of sensitivity to those women who had been forced into the particular cruelty of manufacturing the agents of their own destruction. Much like feeding chicken to a chicken, I thought. I tried to imagine my grandmother producing guns, bombs, or grenades. My grandmother, who could whip a meringue so fine that it hovered over the bowl. Had her fingers shaped cold metal? Had they been blackened with powder? Try as I might, I couldn't envision it.

There was also a list of places and dates in her file; they were penciled on yellowing paper and difficult to decipher, but they turned out to be a detailed itinerary of her time in Sweden. I asked the clerk to show me where the places were on a map. His finger swiped haphazardly from region to region, north, south, east, west, back and forth, as he scrolled down the list in chronological order.

"How could she have moved around this much?" I asked.

He shrugged. "They went where there was room for them."

I knew I didn't have time to make it to all the places on the list. Some of them were a day's ride away. But I rented a car and headed to the lake region in Central Sweden, where spas and resorts traditionally used by Sweden's upper class for a restorative cure had been converted into temporary refugee camps after the war. These were the places she would have recovered in. Afterward, she worked as a farmhand and then as a seamstress, first in a small-town factory, then in a big city.

Sweden's lake region consisted of deserted roads of pebble and dirt and an endless horizon of tall, spindly pines with raw trunks the color of cocoa powder. Loka Brunn, a famous old spa town now restored to its former glory, was deathly quiet. There was a small museum there, designed to explain the town's role during World Wars I and II, but although it was open, there were no visitors or employees in any of the hushed rooms I peered into. This was the region that supplied Loka, the sparkling mineral water available in every café and market in Sweden, but where the production process took place I could not fathom.

I took a dip in the clear, still lake at the edge of town, even though it was barely sixty degrees out, and the sun hovered somewhere behind the towering pines. Two small gray birds skimmed the water for fish. I watched their legs blur like those of roadrunners on the surface of the water and wished I knew what kind of birds they were. Perhaps they had been here sixty-odd years ago, and she had smiled at the sound of their high-pitched trills. I was glad to be here now, alone in the quiet, looking at a scene my grandmother had gazed at all those years ago. It was nice to know that she had been somewhere beautiful, that it hadn't all been ugliness. It was some consolation, I supposed, that she had ended up here, instead of going back to Hungary and getting stuck behind the iron curtain.

Back in Stockholm, I ordered porridge in Café Giffi in Södermalm and noticed all the familiar pastries of my childhood behind the glass display case. My grandmother had made those, but who had taught her how? They were certainly not traditional Hungarian confections, and couldn't have been passed down from her mother, as she'd claimed. The round lacy cookies I remembered were called Tosca flan here. They were sandwiched together with pastry cream, not dipped in chocolate as she had done.

"Are you Jewish?" the white-haired Chinese man who owned the café asked as he brought me my porridge. I had this panicked thought that someone had informed him I might be coming, which I immediately dismissed as ridiculous.

"Yes," I answered in a cautious tone.

"Are you American?" he asked, with even more enthusiasm this time.

"Yes," I said again.

"You look just like Woody Allen!"

I look like a cantankerous old man—great.

"You should meet Leon," he urged. "My best customer. Comes in every day. Also Jewish."

"Sure," I said, thinking that Jews must be a rare thing around here if he thinks we need to stick together.

Leon was eighty-six, exactly the same age as my grandmother. He had come to Sweden as a refugee from Berlin when he was eight years old, before the war. He was very hard of hearing and incredibly lecherous. He'd never been married, he said, but he now regretted it. He didn't like feminists.

"Do you remember the survivors," I asked, trying to steer the conversation away from his obsolete political views. "When they came here after the war?"

"They kept to themselves, mostly because they scared everyone else. They had these swollen bellies, you know."

"Because of the shock of sudden nutrition?"

"I suppose. They ate a lot. They were hungry all the time. They were all trying to compulsively put on weight."

The photograph of my grandmother that I had found in her file had shocked me. I could barely recognize her, with her swollen face, her hollow, unseeing expression.

"Did they seem sad?" I asked.

"Sad? No!" he said with great certainty. "If anything, they seemed very strong."

I left the café after that, wanting that sentence to define my conversation with him. Of course she had seemed strong. It wasn't the depressives who survived the horrors of war; it was the stoic and valiant who made it through. Of course she wouldn't have spent much time lamenting her losses. She threw herself into skilled work, made plans for the future. She wanted to replace the family she had lost by marrying and having many children. I suppose it made sense that she would choose for a husband someone familiar, someone who spoke her native languages and came from her region, when she had lost everything else familiar in her life.

I had pieced together from her file that the Hungarian government wouldn't give her an identity document after the war. She had appealed over and over to the embassy in Stockholm. It was only after Swedish diplomatic interference that she finally received a piece of paper stating she had been born in Hungary but was not a citizen. This had proved enough to apply for an alien's passport, which had then allowed her application for U.S. citizenship to finally be approved, after three tries.

It provoked me deeply, seeing evidence of her travails in this arena. It was unimaginable that someone who had just survived hell should have to be consumed for three years with the maddening process of begging for a home in any country that would take her. She had even considered emigrating to Cuba under the condition that she would only perform agricultural labor. It was written into an agreement she signed with the Cuban government. She had stated, over and over, her intention to emigrate to Palestine! She, who had ultimately married into a fervently anti-Zionist community.

"Everyone was a Zionist then," Leon had told me.

What I couldn't understand was, what happened to that strength that she had so bravely displayed then, completely on her own, in a mad world still reeling from chaos? I never knew her to speak her mind or advocate for her needs. Was this what ultimately marked one as a survivor—the drive to subsume one's identity under the heavier mantle of martyrdom for the sake of the dead?

Ed had asked me to look back in one of our sessions. I didn't know what he meant at first, but he said to close my eyes and it would come. I did so with some skepticism.

"What do you see?" he asked after a few moments.

"I see a mourning dove," I said, surprised that the image had popped into my mind. "It's sitting in a window grate." That's odd, I thought. How did it squeeze through the grate?

"What's inside the window?"

"Nothing. There's just a lace curtain and it's pulled shut across the window." Those beautiful floor-length drapes had hung across the entire wall like curtains on a stage.

"Try to see if you can push the curtain aside and look behind it."

Out of nowhere a breeze came and blew through the open window, lifting the curtain slightly. As it briefly fluttered aside, I did not see what I expected to, which was myself as a child, contemplating the view as I often did at that window. Instead I caught a momentary glimpse of fire and torment; a Goyaesque collage of burning bodies, flailing babies, limbs contorted in pain, mouths open in wide grimaces. I recoiled, and the curtain closed again.

"That's not my past I'm seeing," I said. "I don't even know what I'm looking at. It's like they're living through me."

A few years ago in New Orleans, a tall, brown-skinned man, half Cherokee, half something else, had approached me on the street. "You've got dead people all around you," he'd said to me, his face stern and serious.

"What?" I'd said, thinking he was joking.

"Dead people. Everywhere. They're following you. Probably your ancestors. That's what they're telling me."

"No, you're making a mistake," I told him, laughing nervously. "They can't be my ancestors. My family disowned me. I'm cut off from my community. I doubt my ancestors haven't caught on."

"You're the one who's mistaken," he said, glaring, the tone of his voice impatient. "They know it all. But they're still there, and they want you to know. Don't neglect them."

I had looked around then, at the quiet street, darkening in the early evening. Which ancestors? What were they like? How could I get to know them?

In Hungary, I'd asked myself who I could hope to be if I didn't first know the person my grandmother had hoped to become. Now I wondered if I could have inherited her pain somehow, the burden she carried but refused to speak about, those gruesome deaths she related so woodenly to the police officers who took her testimony—as if it were normal, as if everyone lost every living relative in such a way. Was this why her story seemed embedded into my own sense of self, why I felt compelled to know her dreams through mine?

I had searched all my life for a magic of my own, an answer to my grandmother's inextinguishable essence. I had sought the location of my iron, unbending will, the source of my irreducible strength. In myself, I found only fallibility and fear, but what I now realized I had inherited from my grandmother was the knowledge that home is an internal space you could carry inside you, that it could never be violated, even if your whole world was turned upside down.

My grandmother had unwittingly taught me that to be a whole person, you did not need the certainty of blood relations or confirmed origins; you needed only your convictions. She showed me, through her own story of heroic survival, that I did not need family to survive. Even today, she still models a true independence for me, the kind that renders you free even in the smallest prison, where your mind is a series of doors that open out. Even when ugliness abounded and it felt like the hate of the world was directed at her, she demonstrated that the integrity of the self could never be compromised.

IV

השכלה

enlightenment

Before I was compelled to go off in search of my grandmother's origins, I tried to find my own place in the world, however temporary, starting with the country that I had grown up in but that was still so unfamiliar to me. I took my first step toward that by enrolling at Sarah Lawrence in 2007, at the age of twenty. I had managed to obtain entrance to this storied school on the basis of three essays, with neither a high school diploma nor a transcript, and nary a recommendation to my name. The religious school I had attended as a child did not meet government standards for accreditation. Yet there I was, changing into jeans in the car, combing my hair out after removing the burdensome wig I still wore, stepping briefly into the other world to mingle among these alien folk before retreating back into the community where I felt so confined. I was still married then, but I was dreaming of a day when I would be free.

Sarah Lawrence was integral to my escape. It was there that I looked out into secular society and found it quite different from the descriptions of doom and gloom I had heard all my life. It was a world I wanted to be a part of, and eventually, I was able to act on that desire.

And yet, never was there a time in my life during which I was so keenly and desperately aware of my own lack of selfhood than in those early years of being outside, having given up all the remaining shreds of my identity in exchange for the promise of something new and better. I became a sponge, reflecting the expressions and desires of those around me, parroting accents, mannerisms, and social behaviors in an effort to patch together a temporary identity that would see me through the next phase of my life.

I took up smoking briefly because all the cool people at Sarah Lawrence seemed to be doing it. I would stand outside the library with my friend Heather, watching her inhale the smoke effortlessly, and feel enormously aware of how the cigarette was tilted between my fingers, wondering if I looked natural holding it, wondering if I was somehow part of the club. Was I normal? Was I really a Sarah Lawrence student, just like everybody else? I eyed Heather's long auburn hair and tanned, freckled skin with awe. Would I ever look that American?

Heather was getting her master's degree in poetry. She was from a small town in the Bible Belt. We couldn't have been more different from each other, at least on the surface. She wore cowboy boots and carried a black Prada purse. Her car was a brand-new silver convertible. Incredibly, what she and I ended up having in common was the feeling of being different, and having that experience highlighted at Sarah Lawrence. Neither of us quite fit the mold at a college that advertised itself as a haven for misfits. We agreed that most everyone attending was "different" in the same way. At Sarah Lawrence, a college that prided itself on being the most fiercely liberal college in the slew of fiercely liberal colleges lining the Northeast, everyone was scathingly secular and liberated. Religion was taboo; we had no Hillel house or chapel on campus—students insisted that no proselytizing should be allowed. That was tolerance for you. Heather got a fair amount of shit for wearing a sparkly diamond cross around her neck. She wasn't a Jesus freak like people assumed, but like me, she was carrying around vestiges of her religious past for sentimental reasons, and it kept coming out in her work. Her poetry had a lot of God in it, and everyone took that literally, even though one of the most respected professors on campus had called her "the voice of our generation." The other students smiled politely at her but talked jealously behind her back.

She was a full-blooded Methodist who had once attended church services every Sunday. I often asked her about what it was like to grow up her kind of Christian in the Southwest. She'd tell me that Methodists were different from other Protestants, explaining that she was on the liberal end of the Methodist spectrum, which had some evangelical communities on the extreme end of it. She said she had been awkward and misunderstood in high school. This was hard for me to fathom, because she looked like she would have no problem fitting in, but I guess she felt so different on the inside that she couldn't see that. She dated guys who bought her entrance into the popular crowd, and when she was seventeen, she fell in with Joel, whose family belonged to the Church of Christ. In her hometown, that was the most extreme you could get at the time. Joel's family welcomed her into their church. They were not aware that their son, a devout Christian, was also having sex.

In time, Joel's family thought that Heather was acting strangely, so they invited her to a "Bible study." It turned out to be a group of people who had gathered there specifically to exorcise her. They created a circle around her and chanted. They told her she would feel sick and vomit the evil out, and she did. They had a little bucket for her in the middle of the ring and she retched into it.

Afterward, she was bleeding so much that she went to the hospital. She thought it was the devil, but it turned out to be a miscarriage.

Still, she didn't give up church. She went to a Christian university and swiped her college ID card into chapel every day, as was required. It was only in her last year that she realized she didn't believe in it anymore, at least not in the old way. She didn't want to end up like her friends, married at twenty-two with a husband working in the army and a brick house in the suburbs. She had to figure out a new way to reconcile her desire for faith with the reality of what she wanted from life. So she ran away to New York, which everyone in the South told her was the city of non-believers. They predicted that if she could stay faithful there, she was a true Christian. A part of her held on to that, and she said that was why she liked wearing the cross around campus. Because she wanted to believe that if she had been a true, by-the-book Christian, that's not what would have led her astray—not her desire to blend in, but rather her intellect, her powers of perception.

She went back south for spring break in March and told her family all about me. They insisted I fly out for the remainder of the school vacation. I was thrilled at the invitation, mostly because I hadn't been anywhere yet, although it had been almost a year since I'd left at that point. I'd always dreamed of a well-traveled life, an antithetical concept in a community that valued the stable family unit above all else. Now I was free to go where I liked.

I had to transfer at Dallas–Fort Worth airport, as there were no direct flights to Heather's hometown. At my gate I encountered a handful of men with sun-leathered skin and more heft than I was used to seeing in New York. Some of them were returning from long stints on oil rigs, which seemed to put their overt cheer into perspective.

I sat down between an oilman and an oil-supply man. On my left, the oilman, in a camouflage jacket, turned to me as I sat down and asked if I was Hispanic.

"What?" I did not expect that.

"Your hair is so dark," he said. "I just figured . . . maybe Native American? You look so exotic."

I had never been called "exotic." In New York, I looked just like every other Jewish girl. But camouflage jacket said he'd never been to New York, "and I ain't got much interest in it either," he drawled. I heard the guy on my right chuckle in agreement.

"Do *you* think I look Hispanic?" I asked him.

He smiled, shifted uncomfortably in pants that looked too tight. "Eh, you got a little something different there," he said, pointing in the general direction of my face.

I considered that my official welcome.

"The South is like its own country," oilman said to me as we made our way off the plane a half hour later. He'd discovered it was my first visit. "Hell, we might even secede one day if we get fed up enough."

Heather greeted me in front of the airport with a giant bear hug, almost lifting me off the ground. We drove off in her mom's navy blue pickup truck, passing manicured desert gardens and clean, simple architecture. We pulled onto a two-lane highway, and all I could see for miles were shiny new pickups zooming through a vast expanse of beige. The dusty horizon seemed very far away, but the sky above us was bigger and bluer than any I'd seen, so bright my head throbbed just looking at it. As we zipped past the other pickups, I caught glimpses of tanned faces, broad hat brims, cigarettes held casually in sun-browned fingers.

Heather kept up a running commentary, pointing out everything she loved about her hometown. Although she had come to Sarah Lawrence to escape, she was clearly happy to be back home, albeit temporarily. She knew the name of every cactus plant and desert tree and said that though it was barely March, this area was already in its late-spring season. I remember loving Heather very much at that moment, because underneath her Southern trappings, she was a true poet and saw beauty in everything. I'd never known people like her before, and it struck me then that one of the freedoms I had fought so hard for was this ability to make friends with just about anyone.

Heather turned into a gray stone driveway and around to the rear entrance of a large red-brick house. A kidney-shape swimming pool shimmered silvery-blue to the left; a cactus garden was thriving modestly to the right. I saw a barbecue pit with a small pile of used charcoal at the bottom. There was an ashtray full of cigarette butts between two green deck chairs, and a border collie curled in a corner, soaking up the sun.

Heather's mother, Leann, was in the kitchen, frying bacon for breakfast. She agitated the skillet effortlessly, shaking the bacon back and forth while smoking a cigarette held in her other hand. The smell of Marlboros was etched into the walls, but I liked it. It brought to mind how, when I was a kid, I used to like the smell of other people's laundry because it reminded me of them. Heather had this same natural perfume, a scent I recognized now that I was in her home: an aroma of cigarettes mixed with bacon and Jesus and swimming pools.

We pulled stools up to the granite countertop, and Heather put the bacon and some scrambled eggs on plates for us while introducing me to Leann. A TV attached to the bottom of a cabinet was tuned to the *700 Club*, and a preacher sermonized with a serious face. As I conversed politely with Leann, I could hear the words "Our Lord Jesus Christ" every few seconds, and I pretended not to think that was odd.

A small green parrot flew into the room and landed on my glass of orange juice. I watched him inch around the rim of the glass and dip eagerly into little bacon bits that Leann had prepared for him. She cooed softly at him while he ate, inhaling another cigarette while stroking his feathers. Smoke curled around her fingers and floated upward. She had the finely crinkled skin that I'd noticed on some older women before, the kind that gets dark and mottled from years of sun damage, but it didn't detract from her beautiful bone structure and big, bright eyes.

There was a dinner planned for me later. Leann wanted to introduce me to all of her friends in town. They were dying to find out more about me; most of them had never heard of Hasidic Jews. As for me, I had never met an authentic Republican before until Leann, who was terrified that Obama would take away the money she earned off oil and gas royalties and leave her nothing to live on. She had recently joined the Tea Party and was planning to speak at their next convention. She scoffed at pro-choice politics. "They might as well be forcing abortions on these young women, telling them they're too poor, or too young, or don't have enough help. As if having children was a privilege, instead of a God-given right."

A buzzing beehive of people, mostly women, showed up to the dinner that Leann hosted for me in the local art museum. A stately, elegant building complete with columns and a spiral staircase, the museum showcased a large collection of photographs, mostly of desert landscapes.

A petite matron wearing very high-heeled gold shoes, with her hair teased into a pompadour to compensate for her lack of height, confided in me that Sarah Palin was hosting another event nearby. "I would rather be here," she said, looking up at me through thick false eyelashes. "We're all so bored of hearing her talk anyway." I felt flattered; I assumed if Sarah Palin had a devoted audience anywhere, it was certainly here.

A woman named Melissa introduced herself to me, her voice a slow, melodic drawl. I looked at her face, which seemed unnatural, with permanently arched eyebrows, hard cheekbones, and a mouth that created no lines when it smiled. Her hair was a deep red color that only came out of an expensive bottle; it fell in fat, loose waves around her shoulders, which were draped in a pricey-looking silk scarf.

After she had moved on to make small talk with the person on my right, Heather came over to me and whispered in my ear, "Twenty plastic surgeries at least," and nodded toward Melissa. I shook my head in disbelief. "Nose, boobs . . ." Heather rattled off the cosmetically altered features on ten fingers. I felt sorry for the woman, who had clearly felt that everything about her had to be fixed. She was beautiful now, but in a way that left you convinced she had been even more gorgeous before she invited a surgeon to take a knife to her.

After making the rounds of introductions, Heather facilitating excitedly at my side, I was steered to the buffet, at the center of which rested a gigantic platter of jumbo shrimp. In the middle of the tray was a deep dish filled with bright red cocktail sauce, bloodier in color and thicker in texture than ketchup, but reminding me of said condiment nonetheless. I'd never had shrimp before. Bacon was my big sin; after that I figured I had pretty much checked the whole nonkosher thing off my list. But shrimp was an equally enormous transgression, and I was curious.

I heard myself admitting it out loud: "I've never tasted shrimp before."

The ladies gasped theatrically. A woman wearing her hair in a chignon speared a shrimp with a fork and handed it to me.

"Go ahead," she urged, "dip it in some cocktail sauce. You'll see; it's delicious." Her eyes were wide in anticipation, and she leaned in to get a good look at my first bite. The other ladies edged ever so slightly toward me, and there was a dramatic pause in the conversation as they watched for my reaction. I slowly brought the speared shrimp toward my mouth, feeling uneasy as the cold, wet sea-bug loomed before me, and lurched forward for a quick bite, just a small one off the tip. There was a spontaneous cheering and clapping as I chewed slowly, trying to get past the spiny and rubbery texture to some sort of pleasantness underneath. The faces around me were so hopeful that I couldn't help but smile sheepishly and nod. "It's good," I said, but it came out more like a question than a statement. Satisfied, the crowd dispersed. A few attacked the baked brie and strawberries nearby, while others headed for the champagne. It started to feel like a party.

At some point, when I was drunk enough not to remember people's names anymore, one of the women came over to me and whispered in my ear. "Darlin', do you know," she crooned, "I mean, do you *know*, that Jesus has opened a door for you? Isn't it amazing that a young woman like you, coming from where you're from, ends up all the way over here? Honey, all you have to do is walk on through. You just walk on through that door to Jesus."

All I could see were her enormous fake eyelashes, caked with mascara. Her face was very close to mine, and I felt at a loss for words, so I did my usual routine of smile and nod.

Heather drove us home in her father's pickup truck, and I passed out happily in a king-sized bed. I didn't dream, and this seemed the most striking thing about being away from home for the first time. It was as if the massive canvas of the desert had wiped my subconscious into a blank slate.

Before leaving for the airport, we went to visit Leann's friend Patsy, who distributed a line of women's clothing from her home. Heather needed a spring wardrobe to take back with her to New York.

Patsy's husband, Mark, was a lawyer working in tandem with several thriving local industries and clearly supported his family quite comfortably, but there was a marked difference in the couple's lifestyle compared with that of Heather's family. Their house was much smaller and less ornate, with cheaper terra-cotta floors and tacky Southwestern decor. Heather's mother had decorated their large and opulent house with the best of designer furnishings and fabrics, and I guess I had expected similar decor to be the standard for the rest of the local homes. But Patsy's lawn was dry and had brown patches on it, and the trees sagged tragically, seeming near death. It must take a lot of water to keep a garden healthy in this dry, scalding region, and I assumed most people couldn't afford the extra expense.

Still, Patsy had the manner I was coming to expect from a Southern woman—incredibly bubbly and sociable, with an indefatigably cheerful attitude toward life. She also reminded me of the yenta stereotype; she was curious to the point of being nosy, and her eyes roved shamelessly over your face, as if trying to guess your thoughts. She insisted that I try on clothes even though I said I had no money to spend, and then asked me which was my favorite item.

"The green shorts?" I said.

She turned to her computer and typed something quickly. "Done," she announced. "Green shorts, size six, shipped to Heather's address in New York. She can give them to you when they arrive."

I was at a loss for words. I thanked her shyly and wandered out to explore the house while Heather finished selecting her wardrobe. In the kitchen I met Mark, who had come out of his office in search of a snack. He was a quiet, mellow man, in sharp contrast to his blond, bubble gum–popping wife, and a welcome relief from the constant chattiness I had been overwhelmed by since my arrival. However, like so many of his neighbors, he asked me the now-familiar question: "Have you accepted Jesus into your heart?"

They don't prepare you, in politically liberal environments, for the possibility of meeting a devout Christian who's not ignorant, sexist, racist, and the usual host of other insults I was accustomed to hearing lobbed. They don't tell you how to make sense of a man with a kind face and an earnest manner who's clearly concerned for your emotional and spiritual well-being and can't bear the thought that you could be missing out on the peace he's feeling, the peace he claims is right in front of you.

I was learning that Christians who smell a potential inductee have a universal method of seduction. They look at you like they're reading a crystal ball and say, "You're clearly chosen by God." Man, you sure are special, they say. Why, it would be the greatest shame ever if someone as special as you had to miss out on salvation.

I listened patiently to Mark, until he started to sound eerily similar to the people I had heard preaching the prosperity gospel. He believed he was taken care of financially simply because he believed in Jesus. Look around, he said, this is a wealthy community, and we all believe. Coincidence? he seemed to be asking. I was more than a little horrified. Heather had driven me through the other side of town; poor Hispanic neighborhoods abounded in this region. Did Mark mean to say that they just didn't believe in Jesus as heartily as those who lived in rich white neighborhoods?

I didn't vocalize my thoughts, but I was disturbed. Just then, Heather came out of the other room with a satisfied smile on her face.

"Found everything you needed?" I asked.

She nodded happily.

As we prepared to leave, Patsy pulled me aside with an urgent whisper. "Listen," she said, "I hate to bother you, but—well, you're from New York City, and you're Jewish, so I just figured—I need you to find someone for me."

I was incredulous.

"My best friend's son gone and done converted to Judaism— and she being the pastor of their church and everything. He hasn't spoken to his family since, and they're so worried."

"Patsy, New York is a really big place. And Jews don't all know each other!"

"Would you just try? Please?"

"Sure," I heard myself say, without confidence.

It would have been very funny except that I did find him, easily. He had picked one of the most generic Jewish names in the book: Jacob Weissman. Of all the Jacob Weissmans I found on Facebook, *this* Jacob Weissman's profile picture was a dead giveaway— none of the others had the homebred good looks of a small-town superstar. It may be possible to erase a name like Colt Cayson, but it's more difficult to blot out the linebacker shoulders that come with it, the Gallic cheekbones and strong jaw. For an instant, looking at his picture, I felt sorry for him. That would never be a Jewish nose, I thought. Then I clicked the blue button and requested his friendship.

My message was innocent. We had a mutual acquaintance. I was fascinated by his story, and as I was newly transformed myself, I thought our paths should intersect. He wrote back immediately, eagerly, and we arranged to meet.

Colt's parents are prominent clergy members in the Baptist

community. They live in the deepest part of the Deep South, and they have never been to New York City. I think this is why I wanted to meet Colt, because he had lived a life that I had once romanticized as exotic and foreign. But somewhere along the way, he had broken from his life, as painfully and completely as I had mine, and chosen the world I came from instead. Honestly, I didn't know what to expect.

Any preconceptions I might have had, however, disappeared the moment I looked up from my perch on a stoop in front of a vegetarian café in East Harlem, feeling a shadow loom over me. Jacob was so tall and broad that he literally blocked out the sun. He had a deep, crooked dimple in his left cheek, but otherwise I had never seen so many square angles in one person. It was like you could fold him in half and everything would line up perfectly.

I was twenty-three years old, but in many ways still thirteen. I saw a Prince Charming with an inconvenient yarmulke. A knight in Jewish, if not shining, armor.

So naturally I craved the old Colt, the man I would have gotten to meet had I been around five years earlier. While Jacob offered me a brief biography, he was more excited to talk about who he was now. He was clearly exhilarated by his own Jewishness and even more excited about my own, because my Jewishness felt more real to him than his. There was nothing more real than the Satmar brand of Judaism, he thought, because they were the most intense version of Jewishness around in the present-day era.

"That's not true! The Satmars are a fundamentalist group that broke off from the rest of the Jewish world, isolating themselves," I argued. "In the process, they became extremist, and their original views were distorted. Yet people still continue to romanticize the Hasidic community as a nostalgic preservation of times long gone! In some ways, I think the Satmars encourage this. It certainly portrays them sympathetically."

If Jacob had had the option, he might have become a Satmar, he speculated. I realized that I often made my own mistaken assumptions about different brands of Christianity, so I tried to be understanding, but we both knew that the Satmars did not accept converts. They didn't even accept repentant Jews. So in a way, Jacob had only settled for ultra-Orthodoxy, because it was the highest of echelons in which he could earn acceptance. I tried to warn him that even there he might never be considered one of the gang, but his eyes were still starry and he waved off my concerns. He believed he was a full part of the community.

When I was growing up, I often heard people talk about converts in disparaging ways. Converts were considered dangerous, because although they may have been pious at the time, their past still tethered them to the world outside, one they might still be able to join. Those born inside had no such option, and were thus considered less of a flight risk. In addition, the fervent ardor and enthusiasm of the typical convert was mistrusted. Much like a woman who has an affair with a married man and later distrusts him because he cheated with her, a convert was distrusted by Hasids, who are leery of those who stray from their origins, even if those origins are judged deserving of abandonment.

"Aren't you past marriageable age?" I asked Jacob. In the Hasidic community, marriages were arranged at a very young age, and I was confident that the ultra-Orthodox followed the same standard, if a bit more flexibly.

"I am a little older than would be desirable," he admitted.

"But you converted when you were still young, twenty-two right? Couldn't you have married then?"

Jacob's shoulders drooped ever so slightly. "It's harder, you know, when you're a convert."

I did know. I was only feigning naïveté. I knew Jacob couldn't ignore the fact that he was being blatantly discriminated against in the world of *shidduchim*, or arranged marriages. He may have convinced himself that he was being fully accepted as the real deal by his peers, but he couldn't deny that his status as a convert made him a very unattractive prospect for marriage.

Ultra-Orthodox Jewish fathers do not want to consign their pure and precious daughters to marriages with converts. People would whisper about the family, wonder what was wrong with the daughter that she had to settle for someone who hadn't been born or raised Jewish. There was always the danger of the convert changing his mind and dragging his wife with him, or even worse, becoming too extreme and enslaving his wife in an unnecessarily stifling lifestyle.

"But don't they set you up with other converts, or maybe *ba'al teshuvas*?" I asked. A *ba'al teshuva*, better known as a BT, is someone who was born a nonpracticing Jew but became religious later in life. It's not as bad as being a convert, certainly, but subject to a similar level of mistrust.

"They do," he said. "I've dated a lot of them, but . . ." and here he trailed off. Something in his manner told me that he had swallowed the party line and harbored a mistrust of others like him.

"That's a form of self-hate," I cried.

"It isn't that," Jacob insisted. "It's just that I know my commitment to Judaism is rock solid, whereas other converts and BTs just don't give me the same impression!"

So Jacob yearned for his own pure Jewish princess much in the same way that I yearned for the WASP knight played by Robert Redford in *The Way We Were* (obviously, I am so Barbra Streisand in that movie). Cultural differences may or may not prevent me from shacking up with a Hubble, but Jacob's dreams were even more impractical. I couldn't see how he could ever land the girl of his desires. The circumstances would have to be extraordinary.

"Are you dating anyone right now?" I asked.

"Yes, actually. She's a BT from Los Angeles."

"What's she like?"

His description made her sound like every blond California girl I've ever met. Tan, tall, athletic—and Jewish. He didn't sound especially inspired by her, but not bored either.

We spent the evening walking around the Upper East Side. The more he discussed his Judaism, the more I felt the niggling sense of loss that I had not been able to meet him in his former incarnation, and was instead stuck with his overzealous new character who disdained all the things I had recently discovered I loved.

He called the next day to invite me to his friend's birthday, which was being held at a bar in the Lower East Side that boasted a mechanical bull. These were his non-Jewish friends, and I suppose that was why he felt comfortable bringing me. At the party, he drank some Maker's Mark and got on the bull. I watched him handle it deftly, and it occurred to me that he really was made for that life, riding bulls and taming wild things, and that maybe the wild thing in this case was himself, and he thought he needed taming.

I was there with him because I still had faith in the person he had once been, and apparently he felt the same. "I came into your life so that you could come back to your Jewish roots," he assured me as we walked to the subway. He wanted me to be the Hasidic woman of his fantasies, not the stubborn and independent person I was now. Our desires to be with each other's ghost selves lined up perfectly and miserably.

On our next outing, we went to Brother Jimmy's BBQ on Third Avenue. I invited Heather, thinking her Southern roots would help Colt/Jacob feel more at home, maybe bring out the Southern boy in him. Indeed, as Heather's drawl came out, so did Jacob's, longer and thicker and much more redneck. I was entranced all over again, just listening to him.

Heather had always been a bit of a Jewish fetishist, one of those people who hail from the land of Christian conformity to whom Jews are mysterious and mythical creatures. She found Jacob's new self charming, but she thought he had taken her own natural curiosity too far by converting, and alienating his family in the process.

When she went home, I was left with the task of seeing a drunken Jacob safely back to his apartment near Yeshiva University in Washington Heights. I had to steer him three blocks to where my car was parked, surprised at my own capability in handling a man easily three times my size.

During the ride uptown, I tried to engage him in a seemingly innocuous conversation. Having never been as drunk as he was, I didn't quite understand what it was like to answer questions without being aware of doing so, but my gut told me that if ever I wanted to extract a truthful response from Jacob, now would be the time.

"So, when was the last time you had sex?" I asked. I expected an impressive answer, an amount of time as long as the years he had spent as an official Jew. The ultra-Orthodox are firmly against all premarital touching, and he had already told me that he was fully committed to that way of life, despite the seemingly impossible restrictions (such as no masturbating). I had started to feel a little awe at his commitment at that point, and a willingness to respect him and his choices as a result of that integrity. I was going to forget about the old Colt and embrace the new Jacob, for the sake of our friendship, which was certainly eccentric and therefore worth preserving.

And then Jacob answered my question, and it all went to hell. "I had sex on Saturday with that BT girl I'm dating. She asked me to come over, and I couldn't help myself."

The next day he called to apologize for being so drunk. He remembered that much.

"Do you remember what you said to me?" I asked.

"No." A pause. "What?"

"You told me you had sex on Saturday with your girlfriend."

He was shocked. He couldn't believe he had released that information. There was a long pause, some hemming and hawing, and then a surge of justification and righteousness.

"You don't understand," he finally said haughtily. "The point is, I try. And I'll keep trying. No, I'm not perfect. But I know it's the right way to live and I'm going to work on myself." He was rightly angry at me for tricking him into his admission of guilt.

I tried to understand how it could still be okay, but I was struck by the futility of adopting a set of rules for oneself that were impossible to live by. It seemed self-punishing, self-defeating. Could that experience in itself make him feel good?

I met Jacob one more time after that. It was a Friday in July, and the summer heat had settled into a low, oppressive haze of malignant odors and breezes. We were standing at the intersection of two streets in Washington Heights, and it was a Friday, so young Jewish men were rushing by us on their way to preparations for the Sabbath.

Jacob, who somewhere along the way had managed to attain an excellent education and was still, underneath his beautiful form and passionate religious ideas, one of those very smart, learned men I had come to admire and curate in college, was going to lend me a book by the philosopher Peter van Inwagen. We had tacitly agreed to stop talking about religion and focus on the shared intellectual ground between us. He had always wanted to be a great American novelist, and he admired my success and my ambitions as a writer. And of course he wanted to send me this novel he had written about racism in the Deep South.

He gave me the van Inwagen book, and we talked about philosophy because it was a safe topic we had in common. But when I started to share with him the startling and ecstatic discoveries I had made when I first began reading feminist philosophy at Sarah Lawrence, he gave me a blank, contemptuous face.

"I read all that," he said, waving his hand dismissively. "I think it's bullshit."

"Feminism is bullshit?"

"Yes, I think women are better off in traditional roles."

"You mean to tell me you got two degrees, you read everything there is to be read about this topic, and you still think it has nothing valid to contribute to the philosophical conversation?"

"Exactly."

The revelation disturbed me for days, so much so that I called an old college professor to tell him the story. "How is it possible to be exposed to all that knowledge and still cling to misogynist ideas?" I had always believed that education was the cure for ignorance. But my professor gently reminded me about Quine's theory of the web of belief, explaining that Quine was the first philosopher to challenge the idea that belief systems were build like pyramids. A pyramid, Nathan said, would topple if sufficiently disrupted, but a web could adjust its margins without sustaining damage to its core. It was Quine who postulated that people could be exposed to ideas that challenged their web and simply adjust the web's margins to go on believing in the same way. In the end, no matter how well informed we are, we choose what to believe.

Despite the dead end we seemed to have hit during our heated discussion, Jacob's manuscript arrived a few days later, wrapped in a brown cardboard file. It was very long, close to eight hundred double-sided pages. I sat down to read it out of curiosity. I counted seven violent rape scenes, most of them perpetrated by rich white men against black teenage girls. I wondered if that had been the old Colt, a man who thought that an appropriate literary tool for the critique of systemic racism was the clichéd victimization of the underdog and the vilification of the elite. Perhaps he hadn't really started out any different from who he was now. A new name, yes, but not a new persona. By reading his manuscript, I had gotten to meet him, and I couldn't help thinking that his conversion had proved a marginal improvement. It had brought him to New York. It had made him a little bit more cosmopolitan and a little less arrogant. Maybe that's what he had been going for all along, the discipline, because he sensed his need for it. Did he see himself as one of those rapists, with uncontrollable lust governing his every move, his white maleness inherent proof that he needed to chain a sexuality that he could only view as dangerous?

We stayed Facebook friends, without talking again, until my memoir, *Unorthodox*, was released to a great storm of controversy and shock and anger, at which point he may have unfriended me, although I didn't realize this until a few months later, when I checked out of curiosity.

A year after Heather moved back home after getting her degree, I received a text message from her that said she was dating an army pilot in her hometown. I told her I wished her the best of luck and happiness.

Six weeks later there was another text. It read: "I'm pregnant." "Is it the pilot?" I asked. It was.

"I went for an abortion yesterday and couldn't do it," she wrote. "I'm outcast from the family now."

"Can't you just get married?" I asked.

"It won't change how they feel," she explained. Leann had told her that theirs wasn't the kind of family where daughters got knocked up and showed up in a maternity gown at the wedding. "I don't know what to do," she confessed.

A month went by, and I hadn't heard from Heather, so I checked in with her again.

"Is everything okay?" I asked.

"I had an abortion," she told me. "There was just too much pressure from my mom. Immediately afterwards I regretted it. I'm so angry," she said with a sigh—"but mostly at myself."

Leann was the first person I had ever met who actually listened to Rush Limbaugh and thought women shouldn't have access to free birth control and healthcare because they shouldn't be having sex in the first place. She believed abortion was simply not an option, because God had a reason for everything. I guess that when it came to her own daughter, those values went out the window.

Certainly I'm not foolish enough to believe that hypocrisy is a phenomenon found only in the deeply religious. But I was birthed and raised in a world where what a person claimed to be was rarely in sync with his true nature. In a society that places appearances over every other priority, that kind of behavior is necessary, and makes sense. Some people simply use their faith as a lexicon of behavioral reasoning; without that they would be forced to face their own moral and ethical failings honestly according to a secular code of right and wrong.

It's religion that holds us up to an inhumanly high standard while acknowledging that we are incapable of measuring up, and tacks on the clause that protects us when we inevitably fail to do so. Would there be a need for the incredible acrobatics of justification that religious people engage in every day, like some would a gym routine, if we simply accepted our limitations and dealt within their parameters?

Opening a door for Jesus no longer seemed like a generous thing to do, not when that door was closed when it was convenient. How could they try to reform the Jew over to ways they preached but didn't practice?

I once had a conversation with an atheist who said that the argument for the existence of God was like the argument for a false reality. Sure it was possible we were all living in a computer-simulated video game, he posited, but until any evidence as to that effect was presented, it was more sensible to concur that such a reality was highly unlikely and therefore not a viable part of the argument. I remembered feeling my own de-realization as a child, when everyone around me behaved like an automaton and I began to fear that I was the only person with real, absorbing desires. How frightening that possibility had felt, in that there were moments when I found it conceivable. I supposed then that the atheist had never found himself in that particular frame of mind, and did not know how closely the illusion had loomed before me once, threatening to cross the threshold of reality and invade the tangible world I inhabited.

Perhaps what you might feel is most missing in your life post-religion is the experience and ritual of worship. True, you don't want to bow down in a show of adulation to a nonexistent or misrepresented God, but I think the human psyche yearns, in its own way, to appreciate and admire. We like to praise what is beautiful or great. It can feel like the same instinct that makes you want to hug a tree. When you're feeling grateful for all the wonderful aspects of existence, it's only natural to want to thank someone for them!

Leaving a fundamentalist environment, I was loath to replace it with another; although plenty do, as ex-religionists can be the most vulnerable targets for other spiritualists on a mission to proselytize. I can't count how many times someone has attempted to convert me to their version of religion, which is invariably the "right" version. But for me, it's always seemed unlikely that religion "lite" could impress me after being exposed to the real deal.

Without spirituality in your life, often the only other option seems to be a kind of harsh realism, and your religion can become an amalgam of Christopher Hitchens and science monthlies and maybe some MSNBC thrown in for good measure. But I've always believed in real magic—not the kind with wands and sparkly explosions, but the kind of magic that makes each day a surprise, each moment a new discovery about myself and the world.

In my early forays as an ex-religionist, my friends were often people who didn't seem to need anything more, at least not in the way I did. I miss the thrill that comes with believing in the impossible. I remember how that wild and ridiculous hope opened doors for me in the past, and I wonder how I'll ever manage to achieve anything great again without that spurring me on.

The other day I was reading a wonderful, magical book that illustrates this feeling for me. It's called *The Elegance of the Hedgehog*, by Muriel Barbery, and one of the main characters, a thirteen-year-old girl named Paloma, writes eloquently and passionately in her journal about why she thinks trees are so great. They are literally rooted to the earth, she exclaims, whereas we human beings scramble around on its surface without any real hope of taking root in the same way. Our inferiority in comparison to trees is clear, she postulates; they adapt gracefully to changing seasons and the passing of time while we wail and rail against these forces; they weather trauma with incredible endurance while we sob and sigh over the smallest of challenges; and, of course, they hang around way longer than we manage to. Enough to make anyone feel small, she says, and yet we love trees. They make the world beautiful! They remain unmarred by the human corruption that may poison everything else. A tree's beauty cannot be contained, marketed, possessed. It just is.

It's true that her voice has all the exaggerated pathos of a thirteen-year-old girl. I, too, remember writing passionately in my diary about this thing or the other, always convinced that I had the answers while the adults around me remained clueless. Perhaps that is why I connected so much to this character, Paloma, despite her occasional adolescent tirades. We all have our innocent thirteen-year-old selves lying dormant within us. Remember those days when anything could make you feel strongly? Passivity is a terrible thing to grow up into.

Heather used to stop and hug trees all the time, back when we were at Sarah Lawrence together. She'd say it made her feel better, and I didn't get it at the time, but now I wonder. The other day I put my arms around a tree and closed my eyes and breathed deeply. I imagined what it must be like to be a tree, to feel the security of roots burrowing a solid hold into the ground. It felt particularly comforting to imagine that, because I often suffer from the feeling of rootlessness, a kind of panic that stems from my free-floating position in life, which causes me plenty of anxiety. As I wrapped my arms even more tightly around the base of the oak, I thought, the stronger the root system, the more you can grow. Isn't that how it works?

In my first writing workshop at Sarah Lawrence, I found myself submitting material that would later make it into my memoir: personal recollections from my childhood, peppered with transliterated Yiddish. My fellow writers approached my material tentatively, with both fascination and reserve. Feeling ignorant about the subject matter, they were hesitant to offer feedback, but there were always questions, which I would strive to answer in time for the next class.

When one week I submitted something totally different to be read and critiqued by the class, one of the students opened her comments to me by exclaiming, with great exuberance, how glad she was that I had finally "un-Jewed it."

"I was so happy I could understand this piece," she said. "Your other work was so confusing."

The other students laughed uncomfortably. It was as if she had slapped me in the face. Would I be validated only when I wrote about that which did not mark me as different?

What if the only people who would ever understand me *were* Jewish?

When Isaac turned four, I tried to enroll him in kindergarten at Park East Day School, a Jewish private school on the Upper East Side. After submitting my application, I had to appear before a board to qualify for reduced tuition. The board consisted of three middle-aged Jewish men, the moneyed Jews of upper Manhattan, who asked me why I hadn't enrolled Isaac in the community I came from.

That was the funny thing about Jews that I discovered after I left. The cliquey group mentality that I had sought to escape existed in all the other communities I could find. Everybody was an "us." I was always an outsider.

"Why don't you just put him in a Satmar school?" one board member asked, his voice blatantly accusing.

"Because I want him to have a high school diploma someday. I want him to have a shot at a real education."

"But why us? Why should we take responsibility for you?"

I took a deep breath. I steadied my voice. When I spoke it was quietly and respectfully.

"*Chas V'sholom*," I said, a Yiddish expression, the equivalent of "God forbid." "It's definitely *not* your responsibility. I have faith that everything happens for a reason. If for some reason my son goes to public school, I know that will be because he was meant to. That won't be your responsibility."

I knew these were fighting words. One of the men raised his finger as if to lecture me, but his colleague reached over to touch his arm, restraining him. He turned to me and assured me that Isaac would be accepted.

But my son did not do well in that conformist environment. Much like the community I had grown up in, this Upper East Side congregation was composed of people with similar incomes, backgrounds, and ideals. I had taken Isaac from one uniform environment and plunked him down into another, except here he was doomed to be an outsider by virtue of his different parentage. It was exactly the same issue that had marked my own childhood, branding me an outcast. How could I sentence him to the same experience when the whole purpose of everything I'd done was to save him from it?

Was it the case, I worried, that we could never hope to find a community, Jewish or not, that would match up with the vocabulary we had acquired, the words we used to define the meaning of our own existence?

I could not, no matter how hard I struggled to, carve out a life for us in the full-to-bursting city that was Manhattan. I could barely carve out a space to breathe. I found myself disappearing into churches just to steal a few moments of silence; unlike most synagogues, they were left open to the public every day. I would sit in one of the rear pews, trying not to make any noise. What would I say if a pastor came out and saw me there? Staring straight ahead at the figure of Jesus on the cross, I'd wrestle with old feelings of guilt at being in a church (as a child, I would have to cross the street and walk on the other side, so evil were those imposing buildings) and the new, rational voice in my head that said, this is just a place, and whatever it might mean to others, it doesn't necessarily have to mean to you.

Sometimes, in Catholic churches, there were candles that could be lit for a donation, and although I wasn't sure what they were for, I sometimes lit them, just to see the flame flicker. I'd nurture some strange hope that by igniting something outside myself, I could ignite something internally as well.

I endured by waiting for things to get better. I had never tricked myself into thinking that these early years would be easy, and so I suffered gladly under the notion that it was all temporary, that eventually I would figure out how to live the life I wanted, the one I had given everything up for.

I was in my early twenties and raising a child, therefore not a typical denizen of New York. I had no resources. I went on a few bad dates with people who injured my self-esteem simply because I hadn't yet acquired the language with which to communicate nor the padding with which to protect myself. My friends donated their old clothes to me, so I was able to wear the designer fashions that allowed me to blend in on the Upper East Side. They took me out to nice restaurants, and I was given a front-row seat at the show that is New York City. And the more I learned about people's lives, the more convinced I became that this was not the life I wanted as a replacement. But I could still read books. And Isaac and I spent many Sundays at the Met or the Museum of Natural History, and it was those moments that reminded me why I had done it all. I held on to the hope that I would eventually be able to create a life for us.

To meet the gap between my meager income and the exorbitant rent, I donated my eggs. I pinched the fold of skin on my hip twice a day for a cold injection of hormones until my ovaries swelled to the size of grapefruits and six dozen eggs were harvested from me on some anonymous operating table in New Jersey. It took six months for my period to come back, messy and painful like a miscarriage. This couldn't possibly be worth it, I thought then. Why was I continuing to struggle for the right to live in a city that brought me no sense of satisfaction or home? But where could I go? New York was the only place I had ever known.

It was Jean Baudrillard's *America* that first gave me the idea of driving across the country, just after I stopped attending college. I read the book in the winter of 2010, after finding the new revised edition on a table in my favorite bookstore, and immediately became fascinated with the prospect of discovering the American landscape that was so foreign to me. I was yet unaware of the great tradition started by de Tocqueville, that of the European tour of the New World, but in many ways I already identified as a refugee in the country of my birth, and I felt a compelling need to experience it up close in an effort to define myself within or without its limits.

As a child, my idea of America had been reduced to the skyline of Manhattan, to the mass of the Atlantic that separated my community from its troubled past on the other side. America was the place to which we had come, a stop on the diaspora route, nothing more. Now here I was, exiled from a community of self-imposed exiles, neither a part of my past nor of my present. If I was an American, how was I to be one?

When I had read the great American writers, I'd found myself struggling to identify with the motives of their characters. I could not decipher the language of their culture or place their actions in any context. In Hemingway and Fitzgerald, I found the most sympathy in the stories that took place in Europe. I felt at home in *A Moveable Feast*, in *This Side of Paradise*, both for the descriptions of old European culture that felt so familiar and for the depiction of the alien on foreign soil. I came back to the old European writers for comfort, and ventured into Flannery O'Connor and John Steinbeck only when I felt brave enough to do so.

So I took Kerouac's *On the Road* with me on the flight out to San Francisco in June of 2011, while Isaac spent the requisite portion of his summer vacation with his father. I hoped to gain insight into the American tradition of the road trip, the sort of aimless back-and-forth momentum that kept Sal and Dean swinging like a pendulum over the map of the United States. What was the source of this restlessness that kept them from settling in one spot and calling it a permanent home? Was it some grand appetite for the giant parcel of land that was their birthright, a desire to claim it all as one's own?

Baudrillard had started in California, Geoff Dyer explains in his introduction to *America*, and so I thought I would start there, too, the farthest point, and work my way back. I chose San Francisco, not Los Angeles, for what I was looking for wasn't necessarily the source of America's cultural mainstream, but its social inclusiveness. The Bay Area, I had been told, was a liberal bastion, the equivalent of New York without the Jews. It seemed a strong starting-off point, a place where I would not be too much out of my element—a place where the self-proclaimed strange could blend in.

I arrived just in time for Gay Pride, when the city comes riotously alive with parades and performances and parties that spill onto the streets. Nearly naked men streaked by, leaving clouds of colored glitter in their wake; women whose fat spilled in luscious rolls over skimpy costumes danced provocatively on stages; buttoned-up lesbians in short haircuts revved the engines on their bikes aggressively, as skinny, lip-glossed femmes clung to their waists. I was at once titillated, overwhelmed, and ecstatic. It seemed all the people around me were engaged in the business of being their most extreme and unrestrained selves, blissfully oblivious to anything else. The rest of the country might as well have disappeared; you could almost believe that America had been transformed into a place free of judgment and censure.

I stood in a crowd in front of Dolores Park to watch the Dyke March. I looked on curiously as a young woman waving a rainbow flag climbed intrepidly onto a streetlamp, aided by others in the crowd who supported her while she yelled encouragement. A generous portion of her back was visible between the hem of her shrunken men's suit vest and the waistband of her low riders. To me, she seemed a symbol for the tidal wave of American unrest in that moment, an icon of enthusiasm that would inevitably slide down that lamppost, aided by the grease of her own sweat, back into the crowd.

I was with two lesbians I'd met earlier that week: a lithe, golden-haired Scandinavian woman who had snagged a Jewish brunette for a wife. They seemed like a poster couple for the perfect gay relationship. I felt, for the first time, a sense of regret that my mother, who identified as gay, had not been able to actualize her own form of happiness for herself. I sent her some pictures of the event from my phone, telling her I wished she could be there to see it for herself. To which she replied, "I've got the parade here in New York, it's plenty." And I thought, for her it probably is.

The next morning I went to Humphry Slocombe in the Mission District to try its famous Secret Breakfast ice cream, realizing too late that the bourbon it contained was raw. I couldn't walk a straight line for the next three hours, and so I stumbled happily around Haight-Ashbury listening to dreadlocked guitar players strum three chords. Everything was foreign, which felt both delightful and frightening at the same time.

After a few days spent discovering the city's breathtaking

S-curves, its variety of one-dollar tacos, designer coffee, and tai chi enthusiasts, I picked up my car from an acquaintance who had driven it out from New York for me and ventured north. I crossed the Golden Gate on a brilliantly sunny day, but the bridge was suspended in its own personal cloud of fog. It reminded me of the biblical cloud pillar that had been said to follow the Jewish people in their forty-year exodus through the desert; I drove through it feeling thrilled by the blindness it imposed, as if I were relying on some higher, truer compass to see me through to the other side. As soon as the fog lifted, I found myself in Marin County, and the expanse of verdant fields rolled down on my right side to Sausalito and the shimmering Richardson Bay below. I veered west to Muir Woods, snaking along the one-lane road that curved sharply around the jagged edges of Mount Tamalpais. I sidestepped the glimmering peninsula of Stinson Beach in favor of the rarely appreciated Bolinas, a town so surrounded by natural reserves that it was practically off the map of civilization. Bolinas had a general store and a saloon, complete with swinging door. Inside was a pool table, a jukebox, and a very grumpy bartender who clearly didn't like serving the occasional tourist. I stopped there only for a quick Coke before shoving the half door open again with my hip, strolling past the lagoon to the stretch of beach that overlooked Bolinas Bay, where a local man, originally from Texas, sat in his usual spot nursing his third beer of the day. I stayed long enough for him to share his earnestly expressed, hardly flattering opinions about Jews, although he could only attest to having met two in his lifetime. I congratulated him on finding a third. "Better yet," I said, "she came to you!"

I turned south on Highway 1 and drove back through San Francisco to the hazy beaches of Pacifica and the hairpin turns of

Devil's Slide, which offered breathtaking views of frothy waves crashing against the rocky shore below. This then gave way to Montara and the blink of a town named Moss Beach, where two new friends of mine, whom I had been introduced to at a group dinner in San Francisco, lived in a light-filled house overlooking the ocean.

Their names were Justine and Max. Max was a performer who traveled frequently, and Justine was a writer who spent most of her time in that remote house, working on her magnum opus. She invited me to stay with her while her husband was on tour. We discovered that we had the same birthday, although thirty years apart. I was, at first, mostly confused by her overt efforts at friendship, and I responded clumsily when she told me she saw herself in me. "What part?"

It does get better, she wanted me to know.

"How did you do it?"

"It's this right here," she said pointing at her house, at the ocean below it, at the fog that wrapped itself around the town like a woolly scarf. "I carved out the space I eventually realized I needed. I created the stability and peace that I longed for."

And it did seem that simple. She had left an urban life behind to live in the middle of nowhere, with her flowers and animals and fog tentacles, and retreated into the active space that was her mind. Like me, she felt assaulted after spending too much time in a city. Her thoughts needed more room to grow. We were all different, but it took us too long to realize that the mainstream formula for happiness might not fit and that we would have to find our own.

We walked alongside the ocean, just the two of us, with no one else around. The beach here was ringed in rocky ground upon which grew diverse and colorful species of moss; stretches of yellow and purple and green extended from the narrow highway out to the drop, after which a slight strip of sand gave way to indifferent slate waters. Here and there a harrier hawk swung low to the ground; a scrub jay squealed frenetically in the brush. As I walked, I contemplated the value of a life lived in the wild, experiencing for the first time the peace inherent in isolation, and felt the first images of my future germinate quietly within my soul. If I was to find a real home someday, I thought, then it would be like this, surrounded by trees and water and birds, my identity allowed to grow into itself, privately and powerfully, without being shaped and molded by any community of humans.

I can build a home, too, I thought. If I can't do it here, because it's too far, then I'll find the right place close by. It's out there somewhere, I felt with conviction—just waiting for me to find it.

It was time to make my way back to my origins, and I left San Francisco with my last coffee and doughnut from Four Barrel on Valencia Street. It was too early to encounter any traffic on the Bay Bridge, so I quickly reached the steadily flattening landscape of Sacramento and the other inner-California towns, passed the initial dryness of the Sierras to the first and most blissful stop on my route: Lake Tahoe, the largest alpine lake in America, a voluminous basin of crystal clear water rimmed by ice-capped mountains and dignified firs. I pulled up to the rocky shore and parked my car on the side of the road, venturing out to the water's edge barefoot and thrilling with anticipation. Although snow was visible on the surrounding mountains, the lake waters were warm and gentle, and best of all, I could see straight through to the pebble-lined bottom. There was no murky sediment to be stirred, no weeds growing between the stones. The lake was pristine. Locals paddle-boarded nearby; I saw a parasailing team land on the opposite shore. Everything was a brilliant blue, a sharp contrast to the land-scape I was about to enter and spend the next few days in. I knew this, and it made me want to hold on to the moment even more tightly. I knew I wouldn't see anything this beautiful again for a long time. I looked down at my toes, the nails of which were painted bright red and glimmered from under the surface, and wondered if I had ever imagined entering a body of water this freely as a child. I had once worn a baggy swimdress just so that I could splash in a pool with a cement-block wall that obstructed the sun. I had never before felt the pleasure of lake water on my skin, and it was enough to let the current swish around my ankles. I withdrew and headed back, leaving wet footprints all the way back to the car.

I drove out from under the shady pines of Tahoe, over the Nevada border to the sad, blinking-light town of Reno, venturing farther and farther into the part of state that stretches on for hundreds of miles without even a gas station to save you from trouble. There would be only a handful of lived-in places until I reached my first overnight stop, Salt Lake City. I took those miles like they were mine to take; it was easy to let my speedometer creep up to 95 without feeling like a daredevil—the scenery hardly changed, and the air felt less resistant than normal. Two hundred miles into the desert, just before the town of Winnemucca, I noticed, too late to slow down, a small tornado funneling a coil of tumbleweeds just ahead of me on the highway. I increased my speed and tore through it, my chest tight with fear, but felt only one deep, enormous tremor as I passed. Dust devils, they were called. Better to go through them quickly, I assumed.

In my approach to Battle Mountain, the town that Jeannette Walls opens her memoir with, I noticed rows of army tanks exiting from what looked like massive garages dug out of the mountainside. The ground here glittered with metallic rock, bronze, silver, and jade, and the air felt thick, heavy with silence, as if some things were deliberately left unsaid in this part of the country. Army uniforms abounded in the town, which had a casino/diner and an old hotel but was deathly quiet on this hot summer afternoon. I stopped for a milkshake and tried to make conversation with a few people, but they would have none of it, so I simply took in the scene and tried to place Jeannette and her family there in my mind's eye. Certainly no Jews had ever been spotted here, I thought, and wondered if anybody here knew enough to tell the difference. I did not feel especially noticeable among the quiet folk who kept their heads down and their voices low, as if it was too hot to waste energy on thinking or talking.

Soon I was back on the road, racing to catch the sunset at the Utah-Nevada border, where the Bonneville Salt Flats lay just west of Salt Lake City. I got there just in time. I crossed over and parked in an empty lot that seemed to serve as a station for freight trains; one of which stretched down the tracks as far as the eye could see this late in the day. Looking back at the receding brown mountains, I saw the sky above and between them pulsing bright pink, the cloud streaks of orange and purple. I had caught the sunset at its apex. Off to the east, a lone Joshua tree stretched up from the flat landscape against a quickly darkening horizon. The rest was all salt mud, looking almost like an enormous ice floe in the distance, reflecting the vivid neon sunset so blindingly that the effect was Narnia-like. The roaring sound of wind rushing over the flats filled my ears; the dazzling silver surface mesmerized me. I felt like I was in another galaxy. It was like no other vision I had seen or imagined, and for the first time on my trip, I felt floored by the place I stood in, unable to communicate or relate to it, feeling my foreignness emphasized to the nth degree.

I took off my shoes and let my toes squish into the cold, stiff salt mud. It did not give, like I was afraid it would. It was not a quicksand, simply a soft solid. I ran and ran and ran around the empty flats, shouting soundlessly into the harsh wind. After about fifteen minutes, I felt as if I had imprinted myself on it in some way, albeit temporarily, and I got back in my car, toes encrusted with salt crystals. I drove past the darkening flats along a quiet highway, into the compact, symmetrical skyline of Utah's capital.

After a quick night at the Hyatt, I was ready to abandon the bland, featureless city, with its poker-faced churches, its indifferent sculptures and fountains. I slowed down as I passed the Mormon headquarters, only because I noticed a group of women congregated outside, dressed in long pleated skirts and high-necked shirts, their hair modestly slicked back, who could have easily been mistaken for the peers of my youth. It was strange to see such a long-ago memory from my past projected onto this celestial wet dream of a city. If I talked to those girls, would they be like the girls of my childhood, thinking and acting in chorus?

I drove through Utah's hill country, where clusters of modest mountains huddled under the scant coverage of stunted conifers. After three hours I seemed to cross an invisible line drawn in the sand as I descended yet again into the purple-veined skin of the desert, looking back at the fertile landscape that had so bluntly come to an end behind me.

I drove for five hours straight, in what felt like nothingness, on a one-lane road, and felt grateful for the red pickup truck in front of me. Its Utah license plate made me feel more comfortable about traversing such a long stretch of uninhabited and inhospitable desert. Surely someone lived here. Eventually there would be a gas station.

There were none until I reached the Green River, at the intersection of Interstate 70, and I exhaled a breath I hadn't been aware I was holding. How long would I have had to wait for a kind stranger to pass if I had run out of gas? Would I have survived on the measly supplies I'd packed in the morning?

The water of the Green River was an anemic brown trickle, but it was enough to support some life, as evidenced by the tiny settlements on its banks. After I filled up my tank, I swung left on I-70 and headed for Moab, home of Arches National Park.

It was ninety-eight degrees in Moab on a July afternoon. I climbed as far as I could past the red rock sculptures but didn't make it far enough to see the famous arch formations. I became anxious to get to Colorado, where I would be spending the night.

The road back to the interstate was a narrow dirt path that trailed the Colorado River, which was hardly six feet wide. Its waters churned and frothed like milk being steamed for a cappuccino. Bright green shrubs bordered the river's edge, but the landscape reverted to dry red earth only two feet from the bank. I passed gated entrances to ranches, but there was nary a cowboy in sight.

I drove through what could be considered a town, which boasted seven houses, all in various states of egregious disrepair. A roof had almost completely caved in on one; another had windows made of cardboard and plastic wrap. On one of the rickety front porches, I spotted a toothless, bearded man in mud-caked overalls, cleaning his shotgun. He glared at me as I passed; I shivered and sped up.

Turning the dial of my car radio this way and that, looking for a station, I could only find one discernible program—a man ranting about Obama being a Muslim terrorist. It struck me then that I had never been farther from my New York roots, and suddenly, looking around once again at the endless flatness, the enormous sky, I longed for the familiar feeling of being hemmed in, of being cradled by tall buildings and low-hanging skies.

This is America, then, I considered. Not the teeming, vibrant metropolis I had left behind on the East Coast and rediscovered on the West, but the vast stretch of emptiness in between, the dusty, arid stretches of desert that nurtured nothing but a feeling of being so isolated as to be cut off from the world and its events. The peripheries of America had been transformed into hectic landscapes; immigrant communities and transplanted hopefuls had built great cities, but here, in America's gnawing belly, it was clear that you were either swallowed up or spit out. I drove the rest of the way through Utah's parched southeast region feeling a tension grip my spine.

I relaxed slightly once I ascended into the winding, mountainous roads of Colorado's ski country. I passed the perched chalets of Vail, noting the elegant, manicured gardens and contemporary vacation homes with a sense of guarded relief—this at least was familiar in the sense that luxury will always be familiar to a New Yorker who grew up just across the river from the vast wealth of Manhattan. By the time I hit Denver traffic, it was two hours past nightfall. I stopped at a roadside bar called the Grizzly Rose, where a neon sign outside announced that it was Ladies Night. That meant free drinks.

Inside the cavernous space, beers were being sloshed onto the bar en masse. Chili dogs were sold for a dollar apiece straight from the kitchen window. Cowboys lingered over pool tables in dark corners, and smack in the middle of the room was a polished wooden dance floor, packed with women in tube tops and Daisy Dukes doing something I could only interpret as the hora, while country music played on the loudspeaker. As the women dipped and clapped, their glittering crosses jangled distractingly over their tanned chests. I wondered how Christian culture had evolved to allow one to worship Jesus and dress like a stripper at the same time.

Here my foreignness came back to smack me in the face. I did not own a pair of shorts that skimpy, nor did I know how to bat my eyelashes and keep my mouth shut when a cowboy offered to buy me a drink. How could there be so many American places in which I had no possibility of finding the familiar?

The next day I would drive to my last stop: Chicago. I felt hopeful that, in Chicago, I would find what I loved most about the West and the East, gathered there in the middle of the country in a summit of two cultures. So the next morning I zoomed past Iowa and Nebraska without stopping; it seemed there was nothing there but corn, rows and rows of it. My GPS said it was a sixteen-hour drive from Denver to Chicago, but I did it in twelve, stopping only once for gas, chips, and beef jerky. What a thrill it was to find myself again on a booming highway, a silvery skyline thrusting powerfully ahead of me! It could easily have been Manhattan; the traffic was similarly aggressive, and the New Yorker in me swerved confidently through it. I gawped at the impressive architecture as I followed the directions to my friend's address, which turned out to be a brownstone very similar to the one I grew up in, tucked into a small side street a block away from elevated tracks, like the ones I heard rattling through my childhood dreams every night. It could have been the same neighborhood. Instantly I was soothed by a false sense of the familiar.

My friend and I went out on the town as soon as I arrived, because I insisted I could sleep later. Here was a city I wanted to get to know. Here was the possibility of finding my groove. We listened to battling saxophones at a jazz club, ate deep-dish and stuffed-crust pizza at 3 a.m., and made plans to get the city's best brunch in the morning. The life here is the same as it is in Manhattan, I thought.

Before I left, I visited the famous sculpture *Cloud Gate*, known as "the Bean," and made my way through the Art Institute. As I turned a corner from a room filled with Manets and Boudins, I found myself suddenly face-to-face with a famous Nazi propaganda poster, *The Eternal Jew*. The familiar image, that of a wizened, humpbacked Jew holding coins in one palm and a whip in the other, set on a bright yellow background, seemed discordantly out of place in a museum of art. Nothing could have prepared me for its assault on my consciousness. Underneath the poster was a description of the temporary exhibition of Nazi and Soviet propaganda posters from World War II.

I stepped inside the room, which was quiet, lined with brown carpeting that muffled my footsteps. Dimmed as if in a theater, spotlights shone softly on the yellowed posters stretched and displayed in glass cases on the walls. Many of them contained Jewish symbolism juxtaposed with images of horror and evil; always there was the ugly face, with its hooked nose, its piercing eyes peering from under thick, dark brows, and its menacing scowl.

I moved from poster to poster, feeling as I progressed through the exhibit that each one resonated with something inside me, that in every image was something recognizable, something horrible yet true.

It is this that terrifies me about the stereotypes I learned growing up, and the ones I'm still incorporating as I make my way through the world as a new sort of wandering Jew—that there is always a speck of truth packed into the core of each accusation, and that I will never be able to fully rid myself of that self-affront. I did not want to leave my world only to be forever chased and haunted by the identity it bestowed on me. I had been raised in America without knowing what it was to be an American—it was that problem that I had hit the road hoping to resolve.

Here in the Art Institute, I felt that the rest of America was busily involved in discussing the influence of Jews in art and culture, but that the physical Jewish presence was concentrated only in negligible pinpricks throughout the country, a speck here and there, except for the powerful communities that coalesced into a blob on the East Coast, ignoring the presence of the rest of the world. Here in Chicago, I felt I wasn't even real, but just an apparition. I felt keenly that I had no identity other than the abstract of the Jew; I could pretend to blend in, but it would be a false construct that would deflate upon first test like a pricked balloon. I could write the word "Jew" on my forehead, and at best I could hope for a simple lack of recognition in the other's eyes; at worst I could expect to be treated like a crazy person.

I left Chicago that night, anxious to return to New York, vowing never to venture out into the unwelcoming territory of greater America again. The sun set over the flat, impoverished plains of Indiana; Ohio and Pennsylvania passed by me unnoticed in the night, because I drove intently without stopping, until I crossed the Verrazano-Narrows Bridge at dawn.

To get to Manhattan, I drove through Brooklyn, and even in those early hours, the city was sweltering and stagnant in the summer heat. Although the streets disgorged their familiar spectral memories, nothing about New York City struck me as particularly welcoming on that day. I came home to nothing more than a feeling of homelessness, a paucity of roots that had been underlined and emphasized the whole way across the country, finally forming a coherent bowl of emptiness in my soul. My grandmother had always said that it was bad luck to present an empty dish; she had filled any borrowed container with gifts of fruit or cake. "No one wants to open the door to an empty container," she had said. How true, for I had opened mine to just such a ghastly vision.

V

רוחניות

spirituality

I may not have recognized myself in America, but on my very
first trip to Europe I experienced the immediate, reverberating
sensation of making contact with something old and almost, but
not quite, forgotten. And so I kept coming back, thinking that if
I felt that again, that maybe this time around I'd understand what
it was.

Three years after leaving I found myself in Paris in a café by the
Arc de Triomphe. It was spring, and the maple trees surrounding
the Place Charles de Gaulle were in full blossom. Down the avenue Carnot, two rows of plane trees were still only puffed, their
thin, gnarled limbs spreading tremulously from a satiny-barked
trunk. As I finished my *café sans lait,* I felt a lump in my throat,
remembering how my grandmother thrilled to the blossoming
trees each spring, calling out their names as we passed them, explaining to me what made each species unique and special. Cedar

was prized for its aromatic wood, acacia for its delicate yet strong leaves. An occasional linden tree would remind her of Europe. How she would have loved Paris, I thought. How sad that she never got a chance to visit.

When I was a child, I watched my grandmother light the traditional Jewish *yahrzeit* candle every morning on the same table, where it would burn for twenty-four hours until the next one was lit. It was a grieving custom, but in this case the expression of it was subversive. It was not permissible to mourn relatives who had passed so long ago—Jewish law limited the mourning period to a maximum of one year. After that it was considered imperative that the grieving move on; after all, one had to accept God's will. But my grandmother never stopped lighting those candles, and although she claimed that they were for this one or that one, I knew that the one flame represented the souls of her entire family, from her two-year-old baby sister to her seventeen-year-old brother, all of whom had been gassed in Auschwitz.

I carried that mourning with me. I spent nights lying awake picturing the faces of all those dead children, tormented by the idea of their aborted existence. Was I really here simply to replenish the family, as my grandfather had said? Was it up to me to birth their souls into the world so that they could live again?

Or was it enough, I considered now, looking down into the dregs of my coffee cup, to retrace their path, so that they could be seen—so that their memories could live on forever in my spirit?

I looked up at the blossoming trees, their leaves glowing a pale, luminous green in the sunlight, and asked myself, Would my grandmother have wanted to visit Paris? No matter how eloquently and nostalgically she talked about Europe, not once did I hear her express a desire to revisit. Was it all burned landscape for her, a wasteland of murdered souls and spilled blood? Or did she feel rejected by Europe, in the sense that it had spit her out and sent her to America, refusing to recognize her birth as legitimate?

Either way, here I was, struggling with a portion of what she must have struggled with, feeling at once rejecting, rejected, and at home.

That dizzying emotional cocktail had first stirred within me the previous September, when I found myself magically whisked away to the City of Light on a spontaneous trip that would last only four days. Sabine, a friend whom I had met through a group of Yiddishists in New York who strove to preserve a dying language, was preparing a performance of old Yiddish melodies and needed help with their reconstruction; she was a renowned French opera singer with a performance scheduled at the Olympia.

I was thrilled to walk the narrow, winding streets of Paris. Everything about the city lived up to my expectations, if not exceeded them. I stopped sleeping altogether, not wanting to waste a moment of my time there. Sabine eagerly showed me what she considered Paris's most interesting and secret corners. When the first night of Rosh Hashanah arrived, she took me to a Masorti synagogue (Masorti being the European equivalent of Conservative Judaism). The rabbi was an Alsatian Jew, and he, along with his wife and children, had a shock of platinum blond hair and pale blue eyes. They looked like a family of Scandinavian supermodels, not Jews. Some of the other members were Moroccan, and the congregation alternated between Ashkenazi prayer styles and warbly Moroccan melodies.

Sabine did not speak English, and I did not speak French, but we communicated in Yiddish. It was my native language and the birth language of the people who raised her, one she had been studying for three years and was speaking moderately well. When the rabbi delivered his sermon in French, she leaned over every so often to deliver a summary of his points in whispered Yiddish. The other congregants eyed us curiously. I could tell that Yiddish wasn't spoken much around them. It had once been the language of these people, but it had gone the way of the ghetto, been obliterated from the European map.

Only a dozen people attended the service on Rosh Hashanah, arguably the most important Jewish holiday of the year. Even the most lax of Jews show up at the temple to pay their respects on this holy day. I surmised that Paris simply didn't have many Jews left, and I had flown here expecting that, anticipating a city wiped clean of Jewish remnants—something I had been assured was true of all Europe since World War II.

After the service ended, Sabine and I rushed to the metro to make it in time for a celebratory holiday dinner hosted at her aunt's garden apartment in the neighborhood of Belleville. We entered the house from the side, through a pair of sliding doors that opened onto a secluded, leafy yard. Inside, we found a brightly lit, noisy room, teeming with people. Twenty friends and relatives were there in total, from all over the world. At least ten languages were being spoken at once. Food was already being eaten and distributed, and while I noticed the familiar gefilte fish and pomegranate seeds, there were a lot of foods that looked exotic and unfamiliar. One man wore a colorful woven headdress; others had knit white caps draped over the sides of their heads. Sabine sat across from me and introduced me to everyone in French, but I couldn't find anyone to communicate with. The couple next to me was Israeli and spoke only Hebrew; the man on my right was Hungarian and spoke neither English nor Yiddish. Finally, a young woman across from me identified herself as German, and I attempted to Germanize my Yiddish just enough to be understood.

As a child, I was taught that there was only one way to be Jewish; everyone else was just faking it. Even when I widened my circle to include the American Ashkenazi Jewish population at large, I was still faced with the same homogeneous approach to Judaic practice. It had never occurred to me that just over the Atlantic Ocean lay a whole new world of interpretations and traditions.

The next morning, I resolved to visit the old Jewish quarter in Paris, located in what was now the flamboyantly gay district of the Marais. It was a typically gray Parisian day, and I biked nervously over the Seine, trying to avoid being knocked off the road by street traffic. I had never biked in a city before. Here I was, though, biking in Paris! I was wearing my retro sunglasses and a flowing cashmere wrap to keep me warm, and my hair whipped past me as I cycled leisurely along bike lanes, nodding in thanks as cars and buses paused to let me by. I felt like a girl in an advertisement for a feisty French perfume.

By the time I made my way into the heart of the Marais, wide boulevards had given way to the narrowest streets I had yet encountered in Paris, streets too narrow for anything bigger than a Smart car, so narrow that when I looked up, the roofs seemed to cave in toward one another so that only a sliver of sky remained visible above them. On the rue des Rosiers, a short cobblestoned alley said to have been the original main street of the Jewish quarter, the air was redolent with the smell of fresh falafel. Everywhere I turned, tourists stood holding foil-wrapped pitas, trying not to drip tahini everywhere. After a quick look around, however, it seemed that falafel was the only thing remotely Jewish that the rue des Rosiers had to offer. I bristled at that; I hadn't grown up eating falafel, so it didn't necessarily feel Jewish to me—more Middle Eastern than anything. Just because there was a Star of David on the store's awning didn't make it Jewish.

I walked my bike over to the center of the street, where it formed a T shape with a longer alley that led out into the rest of the Marais. I passed chic clothing boutiques and quaint bakeries that claimed to sell "Yiddish specialties" like knishes and rugelach. No one inside these bakeries could speak Yiddish or boast of any knowledge about where their goods were prepared or whether the recipes had been passed down or simply reinvented by French pastry chefs. Certainly the challah looked nothing like the fluffy braided loaves I had grown up with; they were simply brioche under a different name.

But at the center of the rue des Rosiers stood a small, unassuming machine, looking almost like one at which you'd buy metro tickets. Its touch screen leaped to life when I put my finger on it. I could choose from a dozen videos, in French with English subtitles, which turned out to be testimonials collected from people who had actually lived on the rue des Rosiers, describing what life was like back when that street was the heart of the Parisian ghetto. I listened to them all, and had to put my sunglasses on to hide the tears slipping defiantly out of the corners of my eyes. Luckily, no one in Paris thinks it's strange to wear sunglasses on a cloudy day.

One of the videos really moved me. An older man, identified as a professor now living in the United States, recalled the shame he once felt when revealing his original address. "It was like saying you had failed to make something of yourself. The rue des Rosiers was a place of stagnation, where only by the pulling up of your own bootstraps could you hope for something better."

He's talking about a ghetto, I thought. I certainly knew of the lost ghettos of Europe and their conditions. Even the Lower East Side had once been a stagnant, stinking ghetto for Jews, the Irish—any poor, oppressed immigrant, really. And then it struck me: Williamsburg was a ghetto. I might have been raised in one of the last ghettos in existence. Although the original ghettos were mandated by society and the government, and Williamsburg had been a self-imposed isolation, the result was the same: a bubble, an invisible wall that effectively divided the lives of those on the inside from those on the outside.

The man in the video seemed both nostalgic and dismissive. He clearly had nothing wonderful to say about the rue des Rosiers as a place to grow up, and yet his voice was tinged with regret over knowing that the place of his birth was gone for good, never to return. It made me wonder what exactly I was mourning, having shown up here expecting something and feeling angry that anything remotely Jewish was gone. Did I want to bring the ghetto back? Of course not, but it would have been spectacular to have discovered a world in which, for once, I could find the familiar, could feel instantly at home. It was roots I was looking for, thinking that of all places, the ghettos of Europe would most likely feel like they were a part of me and my past.

I chided myself after I watched the video. It was a good thing that the stifling ghettos were gone. But I guess it would have been comforting to see some sort of modern, thriving Jewish life in its place, instead of this cold absence, this lack of proper commemoration.

I walked onward, toward the end of the street, where I had spotted a sign that read "Judaica." But the shop was closed, and the posters framed in the window were crude and unflattering portraits of Hasidic Jews sweating and lifting dumbbells, part of a collection titled "Oyrobics."

I certainly did not get the French sense of humor, I muttered to the British man next to me who was ineptly handling his falafel. Then, suddenly, as I was about to bike out of there in a huff, I heard the most incredible sound. It was a shofar, loud and steady, coming from the upper stories of one of the buildings nearby. I raced toward the sound, shaking with excitement at the prospect of a real live Rosh Hashanah service in what had once been the Jewish ghetto. Could there still be a Jewish community in the Marais after all?

But alas, I couldn't find an entrance to a synagogue anywhere on the street. Bystanders watched me zoom from doorstep to doorstep with bemused curiosity, their hands holding their falafels frozen in front of their mouths as they waited to see what would happen next.

And then I saw a young man, dark-skinned with thick, curly hair covered by a small *kippa*, a knapsack weighing down his thin shoulders.

"You're Jewish!" I exclaimed triumphantly. "Do you know where that sound is coming from?"

He seemed taken aback by my urgency. In broken English he said, "That's what I'm trying to find out. Wait here and I will ask the falafel salesman."

He emerged from the storefront a few moments later, saying that he did not know where that particular shofar was being blown but that there were apparently two synagogues nearby. *Two syna-gogues?* On a street I had assumed to be devoid of Jewish life?

I found myself following the dark-skinned man down a dimly lit alley and wondering about the likelihood of any situation that involved following a strange man down an alley ending in a happy conclusion. But a second later, there we were, in an archway that led to two doors, one to a Turkish synagogue, the other to an Algerian one. He went right, I went left, and suddenly I was behind a thick velvet curtain, in another world.

I should mention that I had decided to wear red jeans that morning, which, it occurred to me as I was entering, might not have been the smartest fashion choice given the circumstances. However, once inside the small sanctuary, I was relieved to find that all the people attending this service could easily be mistaken for a troupe of supermodels on break between *Vogue* shoots. The women were tan, thin, and lustrously maned; their wrists were bedecked in bangles, their necks draped in silk scarves. The men were equally lovely and well-groomed. *Boy, they sure make good-looking Jews in Paris*, I thought.

But after I had digested all that, I noticed something else. There was a real service going on, with a rabbi on a *bimah* in the center of the synagogue surrounded by men in prayer shawls, sing-ing songs I did not recognize, lyrics I could not place. All of these people clearly knew one another; I was the only stranger. They had been coming to this synagogue for years, nurturing their own tra-ditions, passing down their unique melodies and prayers. All the while I had been growing up in a Satmar sect in Williamsburg, these Algerian Jews had been doing their thing, as legitimate and authentic as their Hasidic peers.

How had I never realized that there might be Jewish communities all over the world whose practices and perspectives had nothing in common with my own, yet were just as connected to our shared heritage as any other?

As I left the synagogue, an old, wrinkled woman wrapped in a metallic-threaded shawl was lighting candles off to the side. She looked at me with bottomless black eyes.

In that moment, gazing at the flames she hovered over so protectively, I knew I had found a piece of my new identity. I was a global Jew, someone who could be open to everything it meant to be Jewish, who could discover the complete length of its broad and colorful spectrum. I would never again think in terms of limiting myself to one dot on that map when I could be the epitome of the wandering Jew, absorbing the diversity of the Jewish experience anyplace I happened to be.

I tried to express this later, as Sabine and I sat down to a lovely lunch in the newly trendy Gambetta neighborhood. The restaurant was on the ground floor of a boutique hotel called Mama Shelter; its ceiling was low and made of slate, with poems and designs sketched on it in colored chalk. For a moment it felt like we were in SoHo. There was nothing old-school glam about the environment here on the outskirts of the fashionable, chic core of Paris. I no longer felt like such a tourist.

Sabine interrupted me to introduce her friend Amélie, another Jewish denizen of the city. Amélie was beautiful in a throwback way, slightly plump with high cheekbones and a full head of curly red hair. She did not seem Jewish, but when I shared that observation, she pulled out a Jewish star from under her black turtleneck. In heavily accented English, she said with a laugh, "Now you know I really am!"

I turned to Sabine. "You've worn your Jewish star everywhere—I've never seen you hide it." I turned back to Amélie. "Do you feel self-conscious wearing it?"

"You can't wear a Jewish star in the open in Paris," she insisted in a hushed voice. "Paris is—how you say—very racist. You can't be Jewish here."

After everything Sabine had shown me, I was convinced that the Jewish community was undergoing some form of renaissance; Sabine's brazen announcement of her ethnicity to the world had felt like an indication of the nascent boldness of the contemporary European Jewish community. I looked at her questioningly as Amélie took a seat at the table.

Sabine acknowledged my look with a cringe. "It's not quite so bad . . ." she said, trailing off as she made a face at Amélie, as if her friend was just being a bit hysterical.

"No, really it is," Amélie insisted. "You don't know because you coming from New York," she said in her heavy accent, "and Sabine tells me in New York it's all Jews, nothing but Jews. This is why I want very badly to go to New York. Here in Paris, Sabine, she only spends time with Jews. She doesn't live in the real Paris. I live in the real Paris, and you cannot be Jewish there."

"Is that true?" I asked Sabine, shocked.

Sabine hemmed and hawed. "It's partly true," she acknowledged. "Although"—she looked pointedly at Amélie—"I do have some non-Jewish friends, but I admit I choose to spend most of my time with Jewish people. I have very strong feelings about my heritage and my identity. I want people around me who support that, who allow me to strengthen that identity."

I asked Amélie, "How is it that you are more assimilated than she is?"

"Because my parents are more scared," she said. "They did not want to put me in a Jewish school, or send me to a Jewish camp, like Sabine's family. When they came back to Paris after the war, they changed their name, pretended their family had never been Jewish. It was very bad then to be different. Where I live, there are no Jews. I never belonged to a Jewish community. My boyfriend is a Catholic, and his mother knows and she *hates* me."

"It's like the Dark Ages," I said. "Who still reacts that way?"

Sabine sighed. "That's how the *goyim* are in Paris. Very different from America."

"But Sabine, when you went out with me to that fancy restaurant the other day, why did you wear your star if you knew the environment would be more discriminating? Why not tuck it away?"

"I refuse to be intimidated. I want people to look at my star, know who I am, and then observe me and see that I'm just like them. I'm always polite and friendly. What fault can they truly find with me besides that star?"

I hadn't considered that every time Sabine ventured outside her community, she was being brave, standing up for an entire people. I couldn't have even fathomed that in New York.

When I said good-bye that day, I hugged Amélie and Sabine very tightly, thinking that in some ways these girls were more Jewish than I was, despite where I'd grown up. They were making sacrifices for their identity daily, just like our ancestors did. They couldn't take their Jewishness, or other people's acceptance of it, for granted.

The next day, before I left, I had lunch with Amélie one more time. The waiter overheard us speaking in Yiddish and shared with us his own memories of a Yiddish-speaking grandfather.

"What is your name?" I asked the waiter.

"Denis," he said.

"We'll give you a nice Jewish name," I kidded with a smile. "How about David?"

He nodded happily and Amélie giggled.

I noticed that Amélie was wearing her star outside her sweater that day, and I remarked on it.

"You've only just met me, after my whole journey into Judaism. I didn't always wear a Jewish star," Amélie said.

"What do you mean?"

"My grandparents had different names, after the war. They were hidden children during the Holocaust, so my parents didn't even really know we were Jewish. I found out when I was seventeen, and I literally had a nervous breakdown. I lost my mind; I started getting panic attacks. I developed agoraphobia. I even had to be institutionalized for a month."

I was gaping at this point.

"Now I'm okay, but then . . ." she trailed off. "My psychiatrist asked me what was wrong, why I was suddenly feeling so terrible, out of the blue, and all I could say was 'I'm Jewish!' He didn't understand, but I now had to worry when I walked out on the street, if people would still love me, or if I had to work harder to earn their love, to somehow compensate for this new flaw in my personality."

"I definitely know what that feels like," I said.

"But then I went to Israel! For the month that I stayed there, my symptoms completely disappeared! I felt like I was home. I thought I was cured. Then I came back to Paris, and my anxiety resumed immediately. Now I'm on a whole cocktail of medications, and I still have to employ all these methods of distraction when I'm outside, like I can't walk on the street unless I'm listening to music. Otherwise I just wonder if people are judging me, if they're looking at me and thinking I look Jewish. This is why I want to come to America, to New York. In New York there are so many Jews like you! I want to live there, or in Israel. Somewhere that's Jewish."

"It's like we are going in opposite directions," I said. "Yet we have so much in common." She was trying to be as Jewish as possible to resolve her internal crisis, and I was running as fast as I could from a leash that someone was trying put around my neck, with a little tag hanging from it saying "Call this number if lost." At least that's what it felt like. Everyone seemed to think they knew better than I did about my Jewishness, whether I was or wasn't, or what sort I should now become. "We're different, but our anxiety and feelings of displacement are the same," I told her.

I wondered how I could tell Amélie that America doesn't feel like home to me when she thought I was lucky to be from New York. I put my feet on European ground for the first time and immediately experienced the sensation of roots growing deep into the hallowed soil. It is here in Europe, where to be Jewish-identified is now an anomaly, that I feel most clearly defined. I may not have visited Israel, but I have seen my Zion. The land of my ancestors, the map of the diaspora, this is my Israel. It is the wandering that is home, at least for now.

My son knows he's one of very few Jewish students in his new school in the rolling hills of New England, but I always encourage him to share his culture and heritage with his peers as much as possible. I think of my experience in Paris and am thankful that he doesn't have to be wary of that sort of blowback, that he can at the very least trust that most people won't try to exclude or deny him anything because of his blood. But I also want him to know that a form of rejection is a part of his history. How to explain that to him without scaring him? I would never discuss the Holocaust with him at this age, or any of the other great persecution epics like the Spanish Inquisition, but I want to tell him the ethnic story of the Jewish Diaspora, about how his ancestors lived under very different conditions than we do now. I decided to show him *Fiddler on the Roof*, to explain to him what Jewish life had once been like, without exception—that it had taken a big war and a lot of change for us to live the way we were living now. As I watched him try to process that, I realized just how different the two of us were—I had never been able to see myself outside that identity, and he was struggling to place himself inside it. Had we really made the break then? Had I freed him from an imposed legacy and allowed him to define himself?

On his Thanksgiving break in 2012, I took him to southern Spain. He had been learning Spanish in school, and it was an opportunity for him to practice his language skills. I showed him the grand mosques and cathedrals that dotted the Andalusian land-

scape; we were transfixed by the flamenco dancers who still carried on a tradition that represented a merging of Gypsy, Moorish,
and Jewish musical influences. This was the seat of Jewish thought
in Europe, I said to him. It was the first port through which Jews
entered the continent, and it was because of the Inquisition and its
consequences that they were scattered in all the countries to the
north. Maimonides had studied and written here, I said, remember Maimonides? A sculpture was erected in his tribute in a square
in Córdoba, the ancient Roman city where he had lived. I still
have a photo of Isaac dancing excitedly around it.

We stepped into the tiny room that constituted one of the only
three restored synagogues in the whole of Spain. It was smaller
than my first apartment. Etchings and carvings in the stone wall
had been recovered, but otherwise there was nothing on display
except for a brass menorah in a case on the platform.

"Why isn't there any stuff?" Isaac asked me. I didn't know what
to say. We had been to so many lovingly restored cathedrals, all of
which had been large and grandiose and had boasted many beautiful objects and artworks. He had a point.

"I'm not sure," I said. "Maybe because everything was destroyed
and they couldn't find it."

The synagogue didn't take more than three minutes to walk
around, that's how small it was. A box asked for a donation of fifty
cents on the way out. I remembered the pricey admission fee to La
Giralda in Seville and felt irritated at the comparison. At the
Sfarad House across the street, a similarly low fee was charged—
and like the synagogue, the Jewish museum was incredibly small,
with limited offerings.

I asked the man working behind the desk if he was Jewish, or
if anyone who worked there was.

"Unfortunately no, ma'am," he said apologetically in a strong accent, "but all of us care very much about the history of the Jewish presence in Spain and are working very hard to the interest of preservation."

"So *are* there any Jews left in Córdoba?"

"Very few. We used to have eleven, but then the rabbi's son went to England to study, so now we have ten."

I couldn't fathom how ten people managed to hold on to the idea of a community in the historic wasteland that was southern Spain. I had not come across any other reports of Jews in the region.

"But they are all older, and their children move away, so it is expected that there will not be any Jews anymore, in the next generation in Córdoba."

"What about *la convivencia?*" It was a term I had heard tossed around in every museum and tourist site. Spain was trying to rewrite the history of Andalusia by pointing to a nonexistent "golden age" of tolerance and claiming it was a model for peaceful coexistence in the modern world. *La convivencia* was the label for this idea, and I knew the museum employee would recognize it.

"Unfortunately it's just an idea. It's not really quite possible for Spain to recapture the time when many different cultures thrived amongst one another. That era was before Spain became a real independent state."

Isaac was very excited to explore the museum and he raced ahead, calling to me when he saw something he wanted to show me. I was very pensive as I walked through the small house. Any one of the garments on display, of those that were real and not created based on a design that was surmised to be authentic, could have belonged to a man who was tortured and burnt at the stake.

Yet that feeling faded as I realized that almost everything in the museum was an "inspired restoration," as opposed to a real found object.

I looked down at the one-sheet guide the man had given me. It talked about the history of Jews in Córdoba. We were now in what was still called the Jewish quarter, but according to the document, any homes that had once been occupied by Jews were destroyed by riots in the fourteenth and fifteenth centuries.

On the way out, I pointed that out to the man. "So, if the so-called Jewish quarter was completely razed after the Jews had already been expelled, why still call it the Jewish quarter? Not even the ground I'm walking on is Jewish! It's been inhabited by Christians for centuries." He must have felt put on the spot. I'm sure no one had asked him that many questions.

"It's called the Jewish quarter in memory of the people who lived here before."

"But look around," I said. "This is now your cool neighborhood! This is your SoHo, your Village, like we have in Manhattan. Do you have any idea how insulting it is to have your trendiest, most expensive neighborhood invoke the memory of the people who were oppressed and tortured here? Spain has made no effort to reach out to the Jewish community or welcome them back. The right thing to do would be to give this neighborhood to them. No wonder there are only ten Jews left."

I wouldn't live here in a million years, I thought. It would make me sick. I walked out of the museum feeling flattened.

"You're upset because they don't have any more Jews here, right Mommy?" Isaac asked.

"Yeah, I guess so. But I also thought there'd be more to see.

This was the biggest Jewish community in Spain. We've been touring mosques and churches everywhere—those weren't destroyed. Why couldn't they have left just a little bit behind for us?"

I was ready to leave, but on the way out of the quarter, now mobbed with model types sipping cappuccinos, I passed a small jewelry boutique. There were handmade Jewish stars on display in the window. The jeweler was an old man who didn't speak English, but I pointed to the one I liked and he gave me the price. I laid the money on the table, and he opened the case and gently lifted the necklace from it. He looked at me, and motioned putting it on, a questioning look on his face.

"Yes, I want to wear it," I said.

And I walked out of that shop with that star on my neck, not hidden under my sweater. I held my head high and walked down the street holding Isaac's hand, making sure to meet everyone's gaze. I was Jewish. My roots were right here.

When we landed back in New York, I felt for the first time in my life like a full container, one my grandmother would have said was worth opening a door for.

I still feel the need to establish my Jewishness immediately. "Can't you tell just by looking at my nose?" I ask jokingly. "Hand me a bagel and shmear." However, it is precisely in the parts of the world where Jews are underrepresented that I feel most Jewish. The irony of this does not elude me, of course. And yet, to discover my authentic Jewish identity, it feels almost as if I need to have a space cleared for me in which to do that, a space clear of preconceived notions, empty of past or communal influences. Besides, there's nothing like being surrounded by *goyim* to make you feel the need for a nose job.

One of the first things I did when I moved to New England was befriend one such *goy*. Richard T. Scott had just moved into his new studio when I met him in the spring of 2012. Tall and slender, with red hair, freckled skin, and a high forehead, he looked distinctive and out of place in such a casual environment. He wore linen pants, aviator sunglasses, and wide-brimmed straw hats. He was a contemporary figurative artist, he said; and then his appearance made sense. The work that hung on the walls of his atelier seemed to combine the elegance of classical style with the disturbingly haunting subjects of the modern world. It was an odd yet moving juxtaposition.

Richard was ambitious, but until recently he had felt mismatched with the mainstream values of the art world. It was anomie, I told him—the experience of individual values mismatched with society's as established by Émile Durkheim in the late nineteenth century. It was this precise experience that had led me to break from my own community, or so I believed, and what was driving me to the pursuit of my true self.

Richard had always been particularly inspired by classical painters such as Rembrandt and Hammershøi. But at the New York Academy of Art he was taught to admire modernists. After a period of frustration, he wrote a letter to the controversial Norwegian painter Odd Nerdrum, asking to study with him. To Richard's surprise, Odd accepted him.

Eventually, Richard realized that there was a whole community of people who felt exactly the way he did, in the sense that their aesthetic ideals did not match up with what was accepted in society. It was called the Kitsch movement, and Odd was the father of it. Created in protest against postmodern art philosophy, Kitsch embodied an aesthetically humanist position in what it saw as an antihumanist technological society. Artists who were acutely sensitive to this experience were drawn to the Kitsch movement, finding a home among people who similarly identified as pariahs and outcasts in the modern art world. They tended to prefer the use of classical techniques to paint contemporary subjects as a way of expressing their unapologetic love of beauty and how they valued its role in artistic expression. As I looked at the various works produced by Richard and his peers, I recognized the experience of marginalization and alienation as strong themes.

I spent many afternoons poring over the art books in Richard's studio. I became fascinated with Odd's work, more so when I heard the stories about him that Richard shared. Many of Odd's portraits were of himself as the alien. In real life, he was one, having been essentially exiled from his home country. He was dogged by accusations of tax fraud, although it was plain to the Kitsch community that this was a ploy. Anything to destroy Odd, Richard told me. Norwegians are conformists, he said, and Odd isn't afraid to be political, and they just can't stand that.

Later Richard would tell me that a mistake in the government accounting had been discovered, that the amount of money really involved had become too negligible to legally pursue in court to the full extent that Norway had planned. "So they'll give up now," I said. "Odd will be able to go back to Norway."

"I don't think they'll ever really give up," he said. "I think Norway will always be looking for a way to get him, and Odd is always going to have to deal with that. But at least now he can return to his house on the Norwegian coast. He can go home."

When I tried to meet Odd in his house outside Paris, I had to go through Richard, who had to go through Odd's son, Börk. Odd never stayed in one location for long; always moving among his various homes. "Is he paranoid? Or justly afraid?" I asked Richard.

"Who knows?"

Odd had found a way to deal with his feelings of alienation early on, by surrounding himself at all times with people who shared his experience. He became a teacher. Potential students from all over the world could apply to study with Odd, living in his home for months or years at a time in exchange for assistance with Odd's work. In this way, his homes throughout Europe were havens for refugee artists, young men and women escaping from worlds in which they felt misunderstood and coming to a place where they felt accepted. Richard had been one of those students. He had finished up a degree at the New York Academy of Art, where he had felt like the poor boy on scholarship who would never amount to much. He had worked for artists in New York City whom he didn't respect. He had nothing back home in Georgia, where he had always been considered strange. New York had very little room for an artist who did not follow the mainstream. It was a professor who had advised Richard to write to Odd.

In the end, Richard became Odd's best and most renowned student. The work he produced under Odd's tutelage went on to gain international attention and catapulted him into a world where collectors and art critics fawned over him, and galleries competed to display his work. It was a sharp contrast to the tepid reception Richard had experienced in his early days, when his ideas were dismissed because he lacked the credibility of education and parentage. I identified strongly with this reinvention, as I saw it. Both of us had experienced sudden and complete transformations in our lives.

In Norway and in Paris, Richard and Odd had slowly developed an intense master-student relationship, and Odd had then entrusted Richard with his estate in France for three years, during which time Richard had painted furiously. By the time I met him, he was avidly preparing for several exhibitions, all scheduled to take place within a three-month period.

Being prolific wasn't enough for Richard, however. "I want to paint something great," he said to me. "Not something that will sell, but something that will end up in a museum." He often painted portraits for money, as he lived off his commissions. This required him to paint pretty things, as opposed to the more provocative work he felt drawn to do. "For once, I just want to paint something for myself, even if others feel it's too disturbing."

Then Richard asked me to pose for him.

"I want to paint a version of Rembrandt's *The Jewish Bride*," he said to me. He told me I was probably the first real Jew he had ever encountered. He felt he could now have the kind of access to the character that would enable him to paint not just the visage but also the soul. "I've always had a fascination with that painting. I've been looking for an inspired way to present that idea, something new, but still embodying the spirit of the original work."

I had never seen or heard of *The Jewish Bride*. It surprised me that Rembrandt would have painted Jews, and I mentioned this. Richard pulled up an image of the painting on his phone. The two people in it did not look especially Jewish to me.

"I think he wanted to show the humanness in oppressed people. See how they look careworn but they're dressed in fine fabrics? And the colors—they're very luscious. It's an attempt to paint them as the bourgeoisie. So at first glance, the image is of prosperous newlyweds, but on second look, most viewers would notice the finer details, and they'd realize they'd been duped. There was a kind of outrage about it. That was what Rembrandt was aiming for."

I looked at the image of a woman, not too young, with a sweet, submissive smile, looking up at a middle-aged, balding man who has his hand on her breasts, as if to denote fertility. It felt like an image of me, back when I was a submissive Jewish wife. I didn't want to be painted like that.

"That's not the kind of Jewish woman I am," I said to Richard. "That was back in the day when all Jews lived in ghettos. When they only married each other, and married young. That was me when I was seventeen. But that's not me now."

Richard nodded. "Maybe that's the answer to my problem—maybe that's the way to make it new. A Jewish bride, but one like you—strong, independent, free."

I was skeptical. I was also reluctant to pose. I had never thought of myself as a muse or a model. I was the writer, the observer. It was the world's job to pose for me, in a sense.

But after a while, the idea started to appeal to me. My excruciating self-consciousness was becoming a real problem. In many ways, I had chosen the life of an observer because it made it easier to deal with that painfully self-aware feeling all the time. If I ever wanted to make my way back into the world without having a panic attack, I needed to learn how to get comfortable in my skin.

About a month later, I told Richard I would pose for him. He just had to come up with the idea first.

In the end, we came up with the idea together. I knew that if I could summon the bravery to do it, the painting would strip me of my last defenses and build a sense of self-acceptance in its place. For that reason, I steeled my gut one Sunday morning and dropped my pants.

It was the first time that I had been looked at by anyone, let alone looked at in daylight.

"I've seen lots of vaginas before," Richard said, as if to soothe me.

"Yes, I know, but you've never seen one menstruating."

"That's true."

"Couldn't you have gotten one of your many models to pose like that? They're so used to being naked."

"They never would have agreed to be seen that way. They want to be painted at their best, portrayed as idealized versions of themselves. Their modeling is vain; it's an ego thing for them. None of them would have ever agreed to this." Richard furiously mixed colors on a palette as he glanced between my legs.

There didn't seem to be any difference to me between modeling naked and modeling naked while menstruating. I suppose nakedness, in all its forms, had always been made to seem offensive and shameful to me. I remember being told the story of Kimchit, the biblical woman who never allowed the beams of her own house to see her nakedness, that's how modest she was. She was rewarded with seven sons in the high priesthood. This story would give me goose bumps in the shower. Was I offending God with my body? Was I horrifying the very ceiling beams above me? To this day, I get in the bath and feel a shiver, like I'm being watched.

Where I come from, rabbis believed that menstruation rendered women into unclean beings, who therefore had to be regulated in order to protect the male community from contamination. I had been made to feel dirty and ashamed for the same bodily cycles that were responsible for my most important contribution: life.

I was taking it back.

When Richard showed me the composition sketch, he asked me if I could come up with something that was symbolic of a Hasidic ritual that he could insert into the landscape, something that would speak to my story. But there was nothing ritualistic about my past that felt like a part of my identity now. All the traditions I had once engaged in felt sexist and oppressive to me.

No candles, no prayer shawl, I insisted. Instead, I asked for a blue heron to be in the painting. I had first developed a fascination with white egrets in Louisiana, sitting by the banks of the Mississippi to watch them scavenge their daily repast. I had never been to the South before, and the birds I had grown up around were city pigeons. My grandmother had displayed an unusual love for birds; she left food on the porch for them every morning. So occasionally I was able to see a cardinal, and rarely, a blue jay—if I ran fast enough in response to my grandmother's urgent call to "come see!"

The egrets were like exotic birds to me. They made me feel as if I had traveled a long way. Perhaps they were the pigeons of the Mississippi, but they might as well have been swans. They were so white and so elegant. Their stick-limbed legs remained perfectly still as the gray water slopped around them, bits of the river's surface shining white when it caught the sunlight. Every so often, they'd dip, so fast you could miss it if you blinked, and up they'd come with a gleaming silver fish in their beaks. One gulp, and that was gone, too, and it was back to watching and waiting.

I thought the egrets represented patience. They were very committed to the task of procuring food, but they were also willing to put in the necessary time and effort to do so. I reflected that I had not met many people who could match their life skills. Humans wanted instant gratification; egrets seemed to understand that the reward would be there at the end, if the work was done right. I liked that. I, too, wanted to wade into the Mississippi and wait for treasure to swim by.

Then, shortly after I moved up to the little dead-end street in New England, a bird I had never glimpsed before moved into the small pond at the entrance to our road, fed through a stream coming from the lake. All summer long, this blue heron stood at the edge, barely protruding from dense shrubbery, waiting patiently for his meals. As I walked or drove past every day, there he was, so still you might mistake him for part of the foliage, so beautiful it made me wonder what he was doing in this ordinary corner of the world when I had thought that there would never be anything beautiful to see again. It was only after I looked it up online that I realized blue herons and egrets were one species.

In my local coffee shop I met a man who carried *The Tibetan Book of Living and Dying* and a handmade pot of ink to fill his quill with. He told me that the blue heron was a totem animal, speaking to self-sufficiency and multi-capability.

"I thought it was about being patient," I said.

"That fits, too! It's what it says to you that matters. Do you identify with the heron?"

One late summer day I had witnessed the heron ascending into flight. It had lifted itself awkwardly and fitfully into the air, seeming to struggle against something. When it finally leveled out, it climbed ever so slowly into the sky, its wings working with visible effort. But after achieving the necessary momentum, the bird relaxed into a graceful and deliberate stroke, flying the way I had expected it to fly. It looked free.

"I identify with the fact that getting up there is tough, and should look it," I said.

I walked out of the coffee shop feeling heavy with the desire to get off the ground, just like a heron. It felt as if I had been beating my wings in vain for years.

The heron returned again this spring, to my little floating dock, where it paced all afternoon, catching perch and sunfish. It was a solitary creature, concerned with providing for itself, never once allowing for play. After gazing at it for a few hours, I suddenly realized I had been wrong. The heron was afraid. It was anxious. The egret stood in the Mississippi and fished all day because it was afraid it would run out of food, that the river would someday stop being a bounty of meals. It gorged on fish as if each one were its last. I felt sorry for the heron on my dock, maintaining such a vigilant watch all day. He could not simply have faith that his needs would be provided for.

When Richard showed me the final sketch of the painting, in which the heron's leg was grasped in my outstretched hand, I saw it. Had it been a coincidence or a subconscious rendering of the split I felt in my own identity? The image was so clear that I couldn't unsee it if I tried. The heron was the *kaparah*, the bird sacrificed by Hasidic Jews once a year before Yom Kippur. The ritual was designed to confer one's sins on the bird; with the subsequent murder of the animal, the sins were erased, compensated for by the sacrifice.

Every year I had visited the *kaparah* vendor and grasped a chicken by its legs as I swung it over my head while reciting the prayer of guilt and repentance. When I had been pregnant with Isaac, I had swung three chickens over my head at once, one for my sins, and one female and one male chicken for the sins of my fetus. Sin was something taken for granted; the human being growing in my uterus was sinful just for existing.

Looking at the painting, I saw myself grasping the heron as if to lift myself up along with it. The image carried a dual interpretation of atonement for guilt and a struggle to break free. It was the most truthful depiction of myself that I had ever encountered. I would always be struggling between my past and my future, between my roots and my potential for self-fulfillment. But looking at myself, frozen in that struggle, didn't seem like a terrible thing. It was beautiful. *I* was beautiful.

After the painting debuted at a gallery in New York City in early spring 2013, I helped Richard take it off its stretcher and roll it up in bubble wrap. We packed it into a cardboard cylinder, and with Richard this time, I again headed to Paris, where Odd was having one last vernissage in his house in Maisons-Laffitte. Odd would want to see the painting, offer his advice on how to improve it. Then it would be hung in Richard's gallery in Paris.

Paris felt even more exciting this time around. I enjoyed the sunlight at an outdoor café on avenue Carnot, gazed at the Arc de Triomphe, looked forward to a weekend full of adventure. Then I descended into the cool tunnels of the RER station, where I boarded the commuter train that would take me to Maisons-Laffitte. Richard was already there, no doubt helping with the last-minute setup for the exhibition. I was wearing jeans and a blazer, and I felt pleasantly attractive, as if I'd have no problem fitting in with the crowd. I emerged into the downtown area of this famous horse-racing suburb, the place where Hemingway went to gamble in his memoir, *A Moveable Feast*. Here there were no sidewalks, only unpaved ground; horses hooves marked the depressions in the grass. Magpies pranced fearlessly in the green, and dandelions grew at the borders of gated estates.

Odd's estate was on a beautiful street, from which one could see across the Seine to the hills on the other side. Only his self-portrait, overlaid on a ceramic tile, marked the address—there was no name on the bell. The gates swung open slowly for me, and I walked down a path bordered by lush trees, into a small clearing from which I could finally see the house, in typical grand chateau style, with shrubs and trees growing with wild abandon all around.

Inside, the house had been emptied of furniture. In each beautiful, high-ceilinged room, Odd's work had been hung; a tour of the entire house yielded a veritable lifetime of achievements. Although Odd was in Berlin for the duration of the exhibition, some of his children, specifically two sons and two daughters, milled about providing guests with information or a glass of champagne. They were all in their teens, with glowing skin, Scandinavian bone structure, and ethereal blue eyes.

I walked from room to room, my high-heeled footsteps echoing on the stone floor. The work was mesmerizing; up close, its power to transform put all those books I'd read to shame.

Soon, the guests were asked to gather in the main room, where a renowned composer, Martin Romberg, had prepared a concert for the evening. A cellist and a pianist started to play, and as they reached the high notes, I could hear the return calls of chirping birds in the dusk. I was inexpressibly moved.

It was only later, after I had finished looking at all the artwork, that I suddenly realized that the house was full of Aryans. Norwegians, Swedes, Austrians, Germans—of course the people most likely to be interested in Odd's work would be those ethnically related to him, but still! Was I the only Jew here? My heart started to race. Had anyone noticed my nose, I wondered?

The next day, in Richard's gallery, a Norwegian family came by to visit. The daughter was a painter studying with Odd. The grandmother was a successful artist in her own right. She reached out to caress my face.

"You are a Jew?" she asked, in an almost adoring manner.

I chuckled uncomfortably. "How can you tell?"

"You have such a beautiful Jewish face," she said. "When I was a child, I had a Jewish friend, but we had to smuggle her over the border during the war and I never saw her again."

She asked me if I would come visit her someday, and I said sure.

It struck me as strange that this fetishizing of my Jewishness felt no different when it was positive than when it came in the form of ignorance and anti-Semitism. Everyone wanted to define me by my Jewishness, while I struggled to define myself outside of it. Each time I thought I had arrived at a consensus, someone would come along with a comment like that, and I would lose my carefully constructed balance. It was a precarious identity at best, I was beginning to realize.

On Sunday, we headed to Odd's house again, this time to welcome him back from Berlin. The inner circle had gathered in the kitchen to prepare dinner. Kristoff, the Austrian who showed Odd's work in his Oslo gallery, and Helene, his wife; David, a Kitsch painter from Venice; and Richard, Odd's most prominent student. Börk, Odd's eldest son, milled about in an expensive-looking suit. I was not much use in the crowded kitchen, so I made my way into the grand sitting room, where my favorite of Odd's pieces was hung: *Volunteer in Void*, a figure suspended in a mythical galaxy. As I perched on the edge of a trunk, contemplating the large work, Aftur, Odd's only brunette daughter, entered the room.

She approached me and in halting English asked, "It is true that you are Jew?"

I froze. I felt at once accused and singled out, but also as if a small and delicate bird had accidentally landed on my finger and I must not scare it away. "How did you know?"

"Um, because of your nose?" Aftur said innocently, asking if she got it right.

"Who told you that Jews have noses like mine?"

"My father. My siblings always called me the Jew, because I have brown hair."

Aftur looked like Leisl from *The Sound of Music*, with straight-edge cheekbones, a delicate jaw, and piercing blue eyes. Her teeth shone like pearls in two neat rows when she smiled, a dimple just barely emerging from one hollow cheek.

"You don't look Jewish to me at all," I said, laughing. "So take comfort in my expert opinion."

"My father is one-eighth Jewish," Börk informed me, joining the conversation suddenly. Trembling with excitement as he spoke, he told me that when he was in school, his peers often called him a "fucking Jew." He said this to me as if to equate his experience with mine, as if it was the common ground we shared.

Minden, the youngest daughter, all platinum blond tresses and translucent complexion, piped in as well, asking, "Is it true you grew up Orthodox?"

"Yes," I answered once again.

"I saw a movie about that," she said eagerly.

"Oh really? Which one?"

"*Witness.*" And she smiled like a cat waiting to be petted.

I explained the difference between Jews and the Amish, in slow, deliberate English so that she would understand.

The situation devolved into a barrage of questions about Hasidic Jews from all of Odd's children. In the middle of it all, Odd and his wife, Turid, arrived; I heard them clattering into the front hall. Soon, Turid was standing at the edge of the circle, listening, asking questions. Odd barreled in and out of the room at intervals, his dramatic, Harry Potter–like robes gathering the dust on the floor.

"I hear you are quite the rebel," he said as we were introduced. But as soon as we shook hands, he disappeared again.

A bit later, Odd exclaimed from the doorway, "You are the wandering Jew!" He lifted his fist as if to demonstrate some icon, like the Statue of Liberty.

"What shall we give you to drink, Deborah?" he asked.

"That depends on how you want me to behave," I said coyly.

"Only enough so that you won't be boring," he pronounced and left the room in search of mulled cider. He returned with glasses for all.

"I am one-eighth Jewish, do you know, Deborah?"

Dinner was served outside in the rapidly cooling twilight. The Venetian had made magnificent spaghetti, someone else had tossed together a superb salad. There was excellent wine. Odd mentioned Epicurus, his favorite philosopher.

"Did you know," I asked him, "that in Hebrew the word *apiko-res* is used to denote a blasphemer or heretic?"

"How interesting that they use his name this way!" he exclaimed. "As if to be for pleasure is to be against God and morality.

"I am an oligarchist," Odd said. "Only because it's the only kind of politics you can say you have that will shut people up; you see, no one knows what it is!" He chuckled then, seeming very pleased with himself.

After dinner, we all retreated into the Fire Room, named for its fireplace. Chairs were arranged in a semicircle, with Odd at one end and his children, friends, and admirers around the other. I watched as every person made their way over to Odd, as though petitioning for his attention, while he granted them the calm glow of his gaze in turn. I did not feel the need to speak to him, only to go back inside myself to find that little girl in the purple dress, and once more say to her, *Did you ever think this is where we'd be? Some-*

day, when you're older, I told my present-day self, *it will be like saying you met Rembrandt.*

"Thank you for your spiritual talk, Deborah," Odd said to me as I left. I wondered about the content of our conversation and its spiritual index.

I looked at Odd in that last moment in his home, and it struck me that no matter how alienated he may have believed himself to be, he had surrounded himself with the most effective buffer: a community and a family.

What was my buffer? Moving to the middle of nowhere was exactly what I needed, but now what would stand between me and the past? Better yet, what would bridge that gap created by anomie, so that I could cross the ravine between myself and the society I longed to grasp?

VI

באַשערט

meant   to   be

I had to cut ties with everyone I had ever known when I left. I said to myself that I would build a new community, a new family, but the rules about relationships seemed different on the outside, and more confusing. Could I ever hope to cement connections with people in a way that would feel as permanent and enduring as the relationships in my former world?

In the beginning, I experienced a need to cancel out the bad sex of my marriage—the only sex I had ever known—with good sex. So I had two one-night stands with men who were simultaneously gorgeous and stupid. It was a conscious decision; I sought physical stimulation only, not mental.

I was still trying to figure out the morals and expectations of romance in the real world, especially regarding sex. Different generations seemed to have different attitudes. The kids I went to college with were obsessed with proving they could hook up carelessly and repeatedly without consequences, as though carefree random sex were some testament to hipness. Older women described free love but not free sex. They could select as many lovers as they liked but did not feel the need to keep emotions out of the picture.

I fell in love for the first time in New Orleans. My mistake was thinking he was like the other two men—ridiculously hot and brainless—and that I'd never get attached.

It was my first trip on my own. I was so excited to visit New Orleans, which seemed, from the books I'd read, to be very exotic for an American city. Almost as good as going abroad, I figured, which was something I could not yet afford to do. New Orleans was everything it was hyped up to be and more. Small, and in many ways squalid and unassuming, it had all the magic and mystery of a town clearly outside the boundaries of convention. I explored happily on my own; I had only three days there, as Isaac was with his dad for the Jewish holiday of Rosh Hashanah 2010, and I wanted to make my time count.

In New Orleans, riding that flimsy little skiff out into the swamps just outside the city, looking for gators, I saw cypress trees with their entire root systems exposed, like gnarled old ladies lifting their dresses. Their roots came up in knobby knees designed to deliver much-needed oxygen. Maybe I'm a cypress tree, I thought. My roots were never deeply entrenched in the ground I grew from, and I was constantly coming up for air, but surely I could hope for some form of stability and strength regardless.

Maybe the person I am is the kind who can put down temporary roots anywhere, who can be at home not just in one place but in the whole world, because she takes home with her in her heart.

I didn't know if that would turn out to be the case, but it was around that time that I began hoping.

My room in the French Quarter just off Bourbon Street had a terrace that was linked to the terrace right next to mine. Whenever I went out there, my neighbors were inevitably perched on the two chairs available, drinking beer and making idle comments about the goings-on below. They were from Kentucky, a sweet couple in their late thirties who were taking a break from the caretaking of an elderly parent. I did not see them leave their room or change out of their pajamas the entire time I was there. When I left, they assured me of their plan to drive to a Saints game, but I don't believe they ever went.

My second night in New Orleans, after having explored the swamps during the day and toured the various music venues in the evening, I wandered back to my hotel room in the French Quarter at around 4 a.m. I had to squeeze through the intoxicated crush of people on the main drag to get in, but once upstairs, I checked the balcony, and sure enough, my new friends from Kentucky were still going strong. The terrace wall was lined with empty, crinkled beer cans.

I was feeling amped up, so I decided to stay up with them for a bit until I felt tired. But two minutes into our conversation, we heard a sudden uptick in street noise. Turning toward Bourbon Street, we saw a crowd—no, a mob—pouring into the little side street facing our terrace. The faces I could make out were twisted into expressions of anger, and the mob was clearly screaming something I couldn't understand; something had happened, or was about to happen.

"What the heck?" Jolynn from Kentucky exclaimed, her jaw dropping.

And then, suddenly, the group stopped right underneath our porch. I looked out over the railing and saw a burly white man in a buzz cut and camouflage punch an already prostrate skinny black man over and over on every part of his body. Blood pooled at an alarmingly fast rate, but the whole thing was happening even faster. I remember looking for the ubiquitous police presence that had made me feel so safe all day, and there they were, sitting back on their horses, not making a single move to restore order.

The crowd was cheering on the aggressor, but then suddenly it got quiet. The victim lay motionless on the sidewalk, beaten to a pulp, most likely dead or near death. The man in camouflage had disappeared. Onlookers, perhaps sensing it had gone too far, dispersed as quickly as they had arrived. An ambulance whizzed around the corner and swallowed the body. Within five minutes, our street was back to its usual nighttime hum.

I was speechless, but Jolynn and her husband seemed to have recovered in the time I was turned away.

"What was that?" I asked.

"That dude was eyeing that guy's girlfriend earlier," Don said. "Probably wouldn't back off. It's his own fault."

I said good night and retreated back into my room. It's okay to beat a man to death for looking at someone's girlfriend the wrong way? And the police just let it happen? No, it was okay for a white man to beat a black man to death for the slightest provocation. That's what that was.

It was the first moment that weekend that New Orleans seemed hard, volatile. I had known very little about the city before I arrived; of course I had heard about Hurricane Katrina, but there didn't seem to be so much storm-related damage around me as there was storm-related anger, bitterness, and violence.

The next day, as I was on my way to One Eyed Jacks, where a bingo burlesque performance was scheduled, I accidentally bumped into a black man who was walking on the narrow sidewalk with his friend and who either deliberately or undeliberately failed to move aside just a bit to accommodate my walking the other way. He was wearing a clean white wifebeater and had very shiny skin marred only by bullet-shaped scars on his right biceps.

He turned around and apologized profusely in an affected manner that made me suspect he had done it on purpose. His sorry sounded like "I'm not sorry," but I got the feeling that he was just angry and it wasn't about me.

"No worries," I said.

He stopped in his tracks. "You a Caucasian lady and you talking to me?" he asked incredulously.

"I'm not Caucasian!" I said, laughing. "I'm Jewish!"

"Wow," he said, shaking his head in wonder. "I couldn't tell. How are they different?"

We got to talking, he asked me where I was from, and I told him.

"No way, you from Brooklyn? I grew up in Brownsville."

"How'd you end up here?" I asked.

"Long story. I just got out of prison." His companion gave up at that point and walked away.

"Are you staying with friends here?" I asked.

He squirmed a bit. "I'm trying to find a job as a line cook."

I thought, Oh, he's homeless. He didn't look it.

"Did you eat today?" I asked.

"Not in three days." The tough guy act was down, the smile sheepish and vulnerable.

I tried to get into Noah's but they wouldn't let me in with him.

The bar across the street didn't mind, and the bartender was nice, sympathetic even.

"The steak for my friend, please," I said, and slipped the bartender a twenty. I waited until he was served before leaving to make the show.

There was a line outside One Eyed Jacks, which was hard to find otherwise because of post-storm scaffolding. I tacked myself on the back of it and started fishing through my purse for the ticket I had bought earlier. As I felt around the bottom, among wadded receipts and lip balms, I sensed a group of people come up behind me and felt a bit self-conscious, being on my own. I decided not to look at them and pretended to be very busy with my bag search.

"Hey," a voice said, deep and almost Queens-accented. I looked up: a man, not very tall, hands tucked into pockets of baggy, unfashionable jeans, broad shoulders underneath the most ridiculous shirt embroidered with colorful flowers, but what a face! Or as we would say in Yiddish, what a *punim*! Think Harry Connick Jr.'s genes mixed with those of Daniel Craig.

"Hey, yourself," I said. I wouldn't be giving him the time of day in Manhattan, I thought.

Behind him I was vaguely registering the presence of his friends, two female, one male. But neither of those women were his girlfriends, I deduced.

"Where you from?"

"Manhattan. Are you from Queens or Long Island or something? You guys visiting?"

"Ha! No, we live here. I was born and raised here."

"You don't talk like you're from here."

"You think locals talk like hicks?"

"Shouldn't you have a Southern accent?"

"Not in the city, honey. Maybe in the backwoods."

His name was Conor. By the time we'd made our way into the bar, I had already decided to let him talk to me because it would be better to have the company of his group than to hang out at the show alone. Plus, I would be able to say I went to New Orleans and hung out with real local people.

I was introduced to Conor's friends, Amanda and her husband, Pat, who commented drunkenly on the size of my breasts, and Tops, who was nicknamed for the size of hers. Conor offered to buy me a drink, but I hadn't yet figured out how to handle my liquor at that point, so I told him I didn't drink.

"That's great—me neither," he said. "I'll get us some Cokes."

"You're lying," I shouted over the crowd noise. Alcohol had been everywhere I looked in this city.

"You're saying you don't drink to get in my pants! No way that you live here, in the city of Bourbon Street, and don't drink!"

"I'm serious," he said. "I'm sober ten years now. I used to drink, but it wasn't good for me." He wore the same expression in all his remarks, the kind that challenged you, made you think his mouth was about to crease into a smirk, but it never quite did. His eyes danced though, like he was enjoying himself.

It's not like I was sold, not nearly, but I won't deny that I had noticed his enormous blue eyes and, with some curiosity, the chunky cross he wore around his neck and kept a shirt button open to reveal. (So he was a goy *and* he had bad taste.)

The show was witty and daring, and I enjoyed it very much. I sipped my Coke, and Conor stood next to me the entire time, his hand on my waist. I had never been paid this much attention. I thought, Okay, he has good game.

Then he leaned over, hand on my shoulder, and whispered in my ear, "You're beautiful." Oh, he has very good game.

I pretended not to hear. "What?" I shouted.

He said it again. I was impressed but still not sold on the whole redneck hillbilly thing he had going on. Well, I'm on vacation, I told myself. I can do this for one night, just to see what it's like.

After the show, instead of going back to my room, I hung around outside with Amanda, Pat, and Tops, trying to figure out what to do next, while Conor was in the bathroom. Amanda and Tops confided in me that Conor hadn't shown interest in anyone since his divorce a few years ago and that they were happy to see him have a good time. They invited me to spend the rest of the night with them.

"Well, what are y'all gonna do?" I asked, my acquired Southern accent kicking in by association.

"What *can* we do?" Amanda said.

"Strip clubs and bars, pretty much," Pat said. "Bars are out of the question for Conor, so . . ."

When Conor came out, he said he'd just finished doing the carpentry work for one of the classier strip joints. He offered to take us, show off his skills. A carpenter! Perfect, I thought. I bet this man has never read a book in his life. This will be excellent fling material.

We went, and us girls sat together at one table while the men retreated to the back of the club, and I had a grand time trying to get the dollar bills to stay put on the women's bodies. It didn't feel nearly as seedy as I'd expected it to. One of the women was Creole, and her skin glowed with a coppery tint in the dim lights. She slithered gracefully on the stage like a serpent. Also, the wainscoting was indeed magnificent.

And then Conor piled us all into his pickup truck, assuring me that after dropping his friends off at his house, he'd definitely drive me straight back to my hotel.

"Come see my garden."

"You can garden?" I asked.

He nodded, with a smile that showed he knew I didn't expect it of him and that he got a little bit of pleasure out of popping my bubble of assumptions about him.

His house, which he'd built and decorated, was beautiful, all drooping tendrils of ivy and stained glass and hand-carved furniture. What girl wouldn't be seduced at that point? In the romantic comedy, this is where the previously one-dimensional dude gets all deep and sensitive, and the girl is suitably chastised for her judgmental attitude. It's a classic. I got suckered in.

I stayed for a ginger beer, which I pronounced disgusting. We all sat out on the front porch for a while chatting, and I was thinking how cool it was to have come to New Orleans for the first time not knowing anyone and then to find myself on some random porch, temporarily inserted into the social dynamics of other people's lives.

Eventually, I interrupted the conversation to quietly ask Conor if he could take me back to the hotel.

"You can stay here," he offered, only somewhat jokingly.

"I have to take my medicine." I wasn't lying, but my thyroid pills definitely weren't a matter of life and death. I was just trying to do the smart thing, which I had always prided myself on, and I knew it didn't look good on paper for me to sleep over at a strange man's house, even if nothing happened, especially when I had a perfectly decent hotel room to return to. Flings were nice in theory, I supposed. Maybe I wasn't quite up for it.

"Wow, that is the best damn excuse I've ever heard," Pat said, only slightly less intoxicated than when we'd first met.

"I bet I could come up with something way better if I was looking for an excuse," I retorted.

"Hey, don't worry about it," Conor said. "I'll drive you back right now." And I could tell he was kind of happy to get away from his friends, and a bit embarrassed for Pat.

I was quiet and self-conscious when we were alone in Conor's truck, and I pretended to be interested in the nighttime scenery outside as we drove along quiet streets to the French Quarter. Once we hit Rampart, the streets were suddenly choked with traffic and people. The area around Bourbon Street was cordoned off for pedestrians, so Conor parked his truck and insisted on walking me the rest of the way back to the hotel.

Just outside the door, he asked for my number and offered to show me around the next day before I left for the airport. I knew my time would be tight but I gave him my number anyway, thinking he would never call, that it was just a thing people did to look decent.

Then, ever so slowly, just like in the movies, in that way you never think will really happen to you, he leaned in, gently gripped my waist, and kissed me. He kissed passionately but with restraint, and we stayed like that for about five minutes, as the crowds continued to stream past us, and neon lights flashed. When he pulled away, I was out of breath, and he seemed a bit disoriented as well.

It was the kind of kiss that makes you see the world differently. The night was newly awash in color. Even Conor's face had suddenly come into sharp relief; it seemed to have attained new characteristics that made it more memorable. I blinked, because it was almost like he was a whole new person.

"I'm gonna call you, girl," he said, waving the paper slip with my number on it as he backed away. I smiled, and he watched me walk into the lobby before he left.

On the elevator ride up, I resolved never to think about it again.

My phone rang as soon as I landed at JFK the following afternoon. Did he really want to pursue something with a woman who lived twelve hundred miles away and had no plans to return to his city? I guess in the beginning I kept up the conversation because I was so curious about his intentions. It wasn't until much later that I realized I had already started falling in love with the memory of him.

I spent quite a few weekends in New Orleans after that. I like to say I fell for a man and a city at the same time, and boy can that have an intoxicating effect! I know that now; I still have a tendency to fall for the foreign, for the man who comes in an exotic package.

Somehow I was persuaded to get on the back of his motorcycle, and I held on to him tightly in sheer terror as we whizzed around the city. Later, it became a thrill I wanted to repeat, over and over, and we'd ride for hours, sometimes skidding in circles in City Park, where the late-afternoon light cast long, syrupy shadows in the grass. I'd focus my vision on one spot and everything else would fade out of focus. The world became reduced to the small yet mobile space we occupied, the two of us on that bike. We came to a stop at Lake Pontchartrain to watch the sun set in wide, spreading arcs above the silvery horizon. The waters turned neon pink, the palm trees became black shadows against the chemical sky, and it seemed a very glamorous backdrop against which to be carrying on a romance.

I did not need much more to be seduced. Sex with Conor was

good. It was the first time I really enjoyed sex for its own sake, and it was enough to prove to me that with the right person, sex could be exactly what it was cracked up to be. For that alone, being with him was a valuable and transformative experience.

At the time, I wasn't able to understand why it was different with him. We weren't doing anything particularly special. We laughed a lot. We were very comfortable with each other (although I suspect that wasn't new to him the way it was for me). I had an uncontrollable physical attraction to Conor that I couldn't explain. There were things about him that I would have written other men off for. I did it all the time. I found tiny, insignificant reasons not to be attracted to people. But everything about Conor seemed perpetually, painfully perfect to me. I would look at his blue eyes and feel my gut wrench in response. I couldn't eat around him because he made me so nervous. I would watch him polish off a whole plate of oysters with enormous gusto while I became the girl who sipped lemon water.

"Why is it good with us?" I asked him once.

He shrugged. "It's chemistry," he said. It seemed so simple to him, not even worth questioning. Some things you just couldn't explain.

But I rolled that answer around in my head. Chemistry. Was I really capable of experiencing that supposedly ordinary reaction that ignited between two people at random and unpredictable permutations, that was constantly happening all over the world, that I had always assumed was unattainable for me precisely because I was somewhere off the grid on which these circuits were sparking? Was it really possible that Conor, a man decidedly and fixedly on a grid, if not at the center of it, was chemically connecting with an aimless, broken piece of wiring like me?

That's what I felt like. Like a dead piece of wire that someone had temporarily spliced with a live one, and for a few brief moments I bucked and shivered with electricity. Then it was gone.

One day in New York, my phone buzzed when Conor sent a photo. In it he had wrapped a curly phone cord around his head and topped it off with a black fedora, so that it looked like he was dressed in Hasidic garb.

"See? I'm one of your people," he texted.

I didn't know whether to laugh or be offended.

Conor tried to learn Yiddish for me. It was exactly the opposite of how I had expected to be treated by an Irish Catholic man from the South, who should have known next to nothing about Hasidic culture. Instead of making me feel like a freak, he made me feel endearingly quirky. My past made me interesting to him but did not define me—in his presence I felt valued only for my ability to intrigue him with my wit or sex appeal. It felt cleansing to me, as if I was being purified by his gaze.

I teased him about hiding his books in his nightstand, so that none of his friends would know that he liked to read. He spent most of his social time watching football with his friends and grilling whatever animal they had managed to kill that day. He made fun of me for valuing intellectual activities more than what he considered good old-fashioned American pastimes.

One Friday night in New Orleans, Conor pulled up in his pickup to take me out to dinner. I was wearing high heels and a nice silk shirt, and he called me the Yiddish word for princess, which he had managed to track down from a Tulane professor. I pointed to his work boots and called him a stable boy, and we resumed our usual banter.

The wait at Irene's was forty-five minutes long that night. Because the presence of him was enough to cancel out even the most vigorous hunger for me, I suggested we skip dinner and go somewhere else instead. We went to the Spotted Cat on Frenchman Street, reputed to have some of the best live music in the city. The saxophone player winked cheekily at the two of us, sitting on our bar stools with our knees touching, our identical bottles of spring water sitting untouched on the bar.

Later, outside, a man sitting on a crate in front of a typewriter stopped us. "I am a poet for hire," he said. He wanted to sell us a poem. "Give me your names," he said, and we did laughingly, not yet committed to the idea of purchasing a poem yet to be written. "Come back in twenty minutes. It will be ready then." Before we moved on, I asked him who his favorite poets were, and he stared at me blankly. I was chagrined by his lack of response. I thought longingly of the poems I had read in my classes at Sarah Lawrence, of the sinewy ecstasies of Crane and Whitman, the terse fragments of Anne Carson, the smooth rolls of Wallace Stevens.

Somehow, we never did make our way back to pick up the poem that had been written for Conor and Deborah. It seemed trivial then, the forgetting, though now I long to return to that night so that I could see what he had written, if there was any foreshadowing in it, if it was a missive I should have heeded.

Even though I had girded myself for every possible danger in life, I had not been prepared for Conor. I had not considered the possibility of falling for his kind of man, and so had not adequately checked myself at earlier opportunities. Why would I fall for the guy with the one-eyed pit bull in his backyard? How could I have been convinced to ride on the back of some dude's motorcycle? I believed myself above him and his crowd simply on the basis of my Upper East Side address; like most New Yorkers, I had bought into the mystique of superiority that came as a consolation prize for life in a harsh and lonely metropolis. I had anticipated falling for the suave lawyer, an emotionally messed-up writer—but never a redneck with a shotgun collection. That certainly wouldn't fly on Park Avenue.

Very early the next morning, when it was still dark outside but just barely, Conor woke up so that he could open his business, a salvage company that had been in his family for generations. The light from the bathroom illuminated the right side of his body as he dressed, and I noticed the tattoo on his shoulder as if for the first time. It was crudely drawn, the ink pale and blurry. I asked him about it, and he clapped his hand over it.

"Don't look," he said. "I got it when I was sixteen. I couldn't regret it more."

I wondered why I found his confessions of a wild past anything but a turnoff. Conor never failed to remind me of the foolish, reckless person he had once been; he had told me about the alcohol, the violence, the bad judgment, all of it. And although I knew I was the kind of woman for whom these things were deal breakers, I was breaking all of my rules with this man, and I couldn't stop myself. I was doomed, and I must have known it.

The night we celebrated his birthday, I realized that it wasn't a fling. It was January, and in the early morning after his birthday we walked to the coffee shop a few blocks from his house, and the weather was beautiful; flowers were still bursting from between cracks in the concrete, and the winter sun was gently warming even at that hour. I looked at his face, and it was that glance that I remember most vividly, because I got a pain at the pit of my stomach as soon as I saw his enormous blue eyes turn translucent in the sun and his whole face crinkle when he smiled. It was the pain of a premonition, because that same spasm would come back to haunt me in later months and years, the pain that I suppose could be called lovesickness, which I had never encountered before and didn't understand. I thought it was telling me to run away.

We've got to stop this, I said to Conor. There is no future in it.

I wasn't ready to get my heart broken by the first guy who happened to buy me a Coke. What I didn't account for was the fact that I might be preemptively breaking it myself.

The last time I saw Conor, he fell or had fallen off the wagon. It was the weekend of his nephew's confirmation, and he had flown to New York to attend. I had agreed to pick him up from the airport, and Conor asked me to join him and his family for the weekend, out in the Hamptons. It was confusing at the time, being introduced to his family, because they all seemed to think I was so important. And yet, we were not together. I sometimes think I filled a need for Conor that weekend, a need to show off someone presentable to gain his family's approval. I could see that they all considered him a wild card. He did run his mouth a lot.

We slept in the same bed and hugged and cuddled, but we did not kiss or do anything else. This was for the better, but at the time it felt wrong and terrifying, like a form of rejection. Then we went out on Saturday night with his party-hardy cousin Katie, and he ordered three identical drinks from the bartender. They were golden brown and had cherries in them. He gave Katie and me our drinks, and I peered at my glass.

"Shirley Temple?" I asked.

"No, silly goose," he said. "That's a Manhattan."

"What's in it?"

"Bourbon. And some other stuff."

"Oh." I was so surprised. He'd never gotten me an actual alcoholic drink before. We'd always had this thing, our matching Cokes or club sodas.

"What's yours?"

"Same thing." I was so stupid, too. I didn't get it. I thought it was his first drink. I had observed the tension between him and his sister; I knew they'd been fighting for years before I first met Conor. I thought he was being tempted to drink because he felt bad. He had been so emotional last night, going on about how I was the only consistent person in his life, which seemed to say more about everyone else than about me.

So I watched him drink. I got drunk first, of course. Inexperienced, I downed my cherry-topped Manhattan in one delicious gulp. I think we each had three Manhattans. I hit my max and cried while we shimmied on the dance floor. Katie let me bawl into her jacket. But then I was over it. It wasn't until we hit the third bar that I realized that Conor was beginning to be affected. I'd never seen him like this, slushy almost, his usual crisp manner and presence blurred into a sort of miserable blob.

I urged Katie to help me take him back to his sister's house. But she wasn't ready to be done with the night, and I ended up leaving her at some other bar while I carted Conor home. He was completely gone. I worried about getting him into the car, but I should have been more worried about getting him off of it. He collapsed onto the hood and refused to move for five minutes despite my begging and shushing. It was 3 a.m. The lights in the house were out. Conor's sister said she'd leave the back door open for us, so I dragged him around, through the little door in the fence. But before we made it to the back door, I heard a loud thunk and crash. Conor had tripped over the barbecue and knocked it over. He lay sprawled on the ground pathetically. Something clicked quietly and quickly in my brain that I would later qualify as disappointment. He wobbled back to his feet and beckoned me close, drunkenly.

"What?" I whispered. I was angry now.

"Please," he slurred. "Don't let . . . them . . . see . . . me like this. They can't see me like this."

So he was aware of that much, at least, aware that he had gone too far because he didn't know how to stop, aware that in this moment he really was an alcoholic, aware that his deciding to drink was bad and put his family in a terrible position.

I sighed. "Okay."

I snuck him upstairs, where he fell into bed, already asleep as I pulled off his shoes, jacket, and belt.

He was very blasé about it the next day, refusing to admit that his drinking was a problem. It had always been drugs, he said, in complete contradiction to what I had heard before. Alcohol had never been his problem. Anyway he had been sober for ten years now, he could have a drink once in a while, and would I just give it up? He confessed that he had started drinking again a while back.

We saw each other for the last time on Monday, after the whirlwind weekend.

"I don't do crazy," I said, after trying to have an honest conversation with him about his well-being. Then I walked away without saying good-bye.

But he was the only man I had ever fallen in love with, at the time, and I realized that in many ways we were the same. I was as vulnerable as an alcoholic. I thought I was above self-destructive behaviors; I had always deplored them in others. But alcohol and religion have something in common: they are ways of coping with a scary and difficult world for people who feel they can't manage otherwise. Sure, alcohol is something you choose, and religion is something I was born into, but for plenty of people, it's vice versa.

Do I do crazy? I hardly know what I do at this point.

I became afraid, as time went on, that Conor had ruined me. I regretted being seduced by him; it felt as if he had somehow damaged the mechanism in my brain that powered my attractions. I couldn't muster the slightest crush. I suppose, in a situation like that, all it takes is for one person to come along who can at least rival the appeal of your last love. That would be Jonathan.

"Don't let your baggage get in the way of really going somewhere in a relationship," Jonathan's text message said portentously. He'd been talking about what kind of clothes I would look good in and how he wanted to buy me a gift, but I was making it difficult— no, depressing, he said. This was because I had insisted I wasn't a doll to be dressed. I was fine with his having twenty pairs of shoes in his closet, or rather, his suitcase, but he needed to know that those sartorial habits were never going to extend to my wardrobe. One pair of shoes in a carry-on would always be enough for me (one very nice pair).

Jonathan was a film and TV director who traveled to his work locations with three large suitcases filled with clothes, shoes, and accessories. When we met, his house in Los Angeles was on the market and he was dying to move to New York. I had been hired to work as a consultant on a TV show set in Brooklyn; he was working there on an outgoing episode, and I was preparing for an upcoming one. On my first day, when I was desperately trying to keep track of all the people I was being introduced to and what their jobs were, I had given him the mental nickname of "scarf guy," because he wore an expensive-looking ribbed cashmere scarf wrapped artfully around his neck, even though we were indoors and it was very warm. (The only way that's not a crime, I thought, is if you're gay.) He had tousled dark hair and a neatly groomed black beard with thin streaks of white running through it. His skin was dark and weathered like a skier's.

He kept looking over at me, his blue eyes gazing intensely at me from underneath a dark and furrowed brow. I couldn't decide if it was a Hollywood thing or if there was something on my shirt. When he insisted on leading me to all my meetings, taking over from the assistant that the studio had sent, I thought it was because he wanted more time to ask work-related questions. When he dragged me to the set and plunked me down on a director's chair with a set of headphones and asked me to listen for nothing in particular, I figured my time was being monopolized for other reasons. He liked me, which I found immediately suspicious and then inexplicable. He was too well dressed, too cool, too L.A.

I gave him the same treatment I gave every guy who showed interest in me: a combination of withering scorn, acerbic wit, and the occasional glance of outright disbelief. Yet it wasn't working, and I didn't understand why.

When Jonathan called a couple of evenings after our first meeting, I took his innocent questions on my notes at face value. Then he called again, and again. And there we were, arguing about fashion and relationship baggage.

I learned that Jonathan had been raised by born-again Christian parents. He told me that he, too, had married young, and it hadn't worked out; he mentioned he had a nine-year-old daughter. Oh, wow, I said; does she live with you or her mom? How often do you see her?

"Oh, once every few months," he said nonchalantly. "On the short breaks between work commitments." I was flabbergasted. Should that have been my red flag?

Or maybe the red flag was the fact that he didn't read. Ever. Oh, he read scripts, and he read books, if you considered listening to them on audiotape in the car "reading." But he never longed for the pleasure of picking up a book and perusing steadily through its pages. Yet I could tell he was interested in me because of my story; he told me he had immediately purchased the audio version of my book and was halfway through it within weeks of our first meeting.

"Can you imagine what people will say," he asked, "when they see us together? My God, it will blow their minds." He seemed excited more by the idea of me than anything else.

"Why does that matter?" I asked, confused.

He would get such a kick out of seeing how people dealt with the contrast between us, he said. I had this vague sense that I was only talking to his shadow, that in truth he was standing outside of our conversations, directing from behind the scenes, while I spoke with his stand-in.

His intensely sexy text messages often had me fumbling for a response. "The first time I'll touch you, it will take your breath away," he assured me. "I can't wait to have you up against a wall, my mouth on your neck." They were always specific descriptions, as if he was describing a scene in one his scripts.

One night, after I had ignored a few of those texts, he called and asked me, as soon as I picked up the phone, "Are you not able to enjoy sex?"

"I can enjoy sex just fine," I answered. I can. Conor gave me that much, the certainty that I was sexually functional, that I had not been rendered defunct by repression and trauma. I had not removed all of my clothes with him, though. I had clung to the last pieces of underwear, as if by shedding them I would be crossing the line into some unforgivable territory. I wondered if I'd ever achieve the ability to really strip myself, physically and emotionally, for another person.

"Then what is it?"

If only it were that simple. I had no idea what it was. Was I shy? I could flirt, but only in metaphor. Was I afraid of the real thing, or was it just that vulgarity turned me off? I must have brought some of that with me from my upbringing.

My ex-husband hardly ever masturbated because it made him feel guilty. There's no way Jonathan emerged from a rigidly observant childhood unscathed, I surmised.

"Jonathan, how often do you masturbate?"

"Never."

"That's crazy. Nobody 'never' masturbates."

"Why would I masturbate? If I want some, I can get some."

I pressed the point, but Jonathan was adamant. He was offended that I would think there was something wrong with that, but I did. I couldn't put my finger on it exactly, but I knew it wasn't normal. Even I masturbated, and I was plenty messed up about sex.

I had just come back from yet another visit to my gynecologist. Although the fuss around my vagina had died down after I left my marriage, and had remained that way throughout most of my relationship with Conor, ever since our breakup, my difficulties had resumed, albeit to a lesser degree. I was beginning to wonder if vaginas were simply organs that demanded perfect happiness in order to function.

No gynecologist had ever been overly thrilled to have me as a patient, but my current one, Megan, was really starting to show her frustration. To her, my nether regions presented an infuriating conundrum. Nothing in her education equipped her for the battle with my irascible and mutinous vagina.

When Megan and I had originally sat down in her office for a first consult, I think I did my best to prepare her for the unique situation she would be dealing with. I gave her the basic rundown without going on for too long, using all the appropriate medical terminology that had been thrown at me over the years, and she dutifully took notes.

It started with vaginismus, at least I think so. I'm almost sure. I got married, I couldn't have sex, I received multiple diagnoses, but that was the one that stuck. I fixed it with dilators and hypnotherapy, at least to the point where I actually had a functional, if not happy, vagina, and got pregnant.

After giving birth, I developed a condition rarely seen outside menopause, a shedding of the vaginal walls related to a sudden drop in estrogen. I was a medical anomaly, but at least they had a cure for it. It went away, and over the next few years, it and many other things came back.

Burning, itching, discomfort, you name it. Put it on a microscope slide and it looked like everything or nothing. I was given all the diagnoses, all the ointments, all the pills.

"Just warning you," I had said. "My vagina is very unhappy."

I started calling my vagina "unhappy" after reading *The Camera My Mother Gave Me*, by Susanna Kaysen. I requested it at the library during the period when I was dilating in preparation for sex with my husband, to give me something to do while I clenched down on those plastic tubes. It was a memoir of one woman's vaginal pain, a no-holds-barred catalog of gynecological malaise so obnoxious I'm surprised it ever got published. Perusing the Internet for reactions to the book lent credence to my newly found conviction: no one wants to know that much about vaginas.

Which is unfortunate, because unhappy vaginas do not like to be ignored.

After the initial examination, Megan predictably tossed three prescription medications in my lap. A steroid, an antibiotic, and a topical painkiller.

"I don't know what exactly is going on in there, but one of these is bound to get rid of it."

I was back in a month, as promised. Megan took one look and threw up her hands in disbelief.

"I told you so." I smiled. I was used to this. I had gone through this with other gynecologists.

Megan wrote another prescription.

"If this one doesn't do it," she said, "I don't know what else I can do. The options are kind of limited. For most people, we just alternate between them."

I came back a month later just to prove my point.

"I don't want to give you another prescription," Megan said.

"These things are harsh on your pH. They have serious side effects."

We had discussed my diet and lifestyle. I was off wheat, dairy, corn, soy, sugar, and preservatives. I was taking all the probiotics. Everything else was feeling great.

"I think you should see a naturopath," Megan advised.

"Are you saying Western medicine can't help me?"

"You saw what I can offer you. It's not helping. I don't want to be irresponsible and keep dosing you with the same stuff. This is all I have. But there's something out of whack in your body that a naturopath might be able to help you with."

How do you tell a naturopath to heal your vagina, I wondered? Does he have an exam table with stirrups? Or does he just recommend herbs and remedies? Our local naturopath was male. I simply could not imagine walking into his office and telling him the story of my unhappy vagina.

If all of it was in my head, as the very first gynecologist I had ever visited had told me, then it was up to my head to establish friendlier communications with my nether regions. For now, out of respect for its crankiness, it would have to be off-limits. Until I could figure out what it really wanted.

"You don't just become a new person," I said to Jonathan on the phone. "You go through a childhood of repression, a few years of sexual trauma, and then you run away—it doesn't mean that you start from the beginning."

"What are you saying?"

"I wanted to prove to myself I was unaffected. That all it took was escape from unhealthy sexual attitudes and an oppressive environment, and bam, there was my repressed sexuality back in its rightful place. But it comes back to haunt you. You have to deal with it."

"I don't understand. If you have a good lover, then the sex is great. It's that simple. What more is there?"

What's more is everything else that's involved in the process of getting off. How you see yourself. How you see the person with you. How safe you feel. How scared you feel. Does sex make you feel better or worse about yourself after? Violated or complete? Dirty or clean? All those things matter.

I didn't know how to say that to Jonathan, because the idea that sex was simple to him frustrated and terrified me. What did I have in common with such a person?

"I didn't get to wipe the slate clean. Those are permanent markings. I'm going to have to figure out a way to draw on top of those markings and incorporate them into a new and beautiful picture. I have to make the ugliness in my past an integral part of what's beautiful in my future. That's not going to be easy. Not as easy as starting from scratch."

"But tell me this in real terms, not in metaphor. What does it really mean?"

"You don't necessarily recover from sexual dysfunction, but you can work around the handicap." It sounded way less pretty when I said it that way. Maybe that's why I liked talking and flirting in metaphors. Everything just sounded better.

"That's not really that profound," Jonathan said.

I paused, swallowed. "It's just true. For a lot of people, not just for me." *And I wish you knew how to help with that.* But Jonathan wasn't deep. He was a movies guy. To him, it was all about what you see. Not what you think. You never get to see what the actors are thinking, I thought. If there's one thing I learned working on a TV set, it's that. I'd watch them on camera, and they'd rattle off their lines so articulately and convincingly that I'd assume they were drawing from personal experience—then they'd show up in the director's tent and barely be able to stammer through half a sentence. Did they choose this job particularly for that reason, for the gift of other people's words with which to tell a story, any story, even if it wasn't their own? Or did they have to create a mental vacuum in order to make space for someone else's words—get in a zone, in a sense? I worried that Jonathan looked at me like he looked at his actors: as someone to put in a spot marked with duct tape, someone to hand lines to. I felt as if I was being ever so gently manipulated into a story he had already written and planned out in his mind.

I never actually said to Jonathan what I meant when I talked about sexual dysfunction. I never told Conor, either. It wasn't that I needed the specifics to be out there; I just needed a little more understanding than most. The only problem was, I met very few men in whom I could have faith that they would extend me that understanding. Did I really deserve that extra mile? What was I willing to offer in exchange?

A month later, Jonathan came to New York to shoot another episode of the TV show we had worked on together. He had sold his house in L.A., but he hadn't yet found a place in New York, so he stayed at the Trump SoHo and commuted to the set in Brooklyn. He worked eighteen-hour days, including weekends. My phone would vibrate under the pillow around midnight, and I'd wake up to see his name on the caller ID. We'd talk for ten minutes, and I'd listen to him fall asleep on the line, and then I'd lie awake and wait to feel tired again.

Often on these phone calls Jonathan would give me fatherly lectures, words of advice or concern. I didn't quite know what to do with them. I thought it was nice that he cared so much for me, always inquiring about how I was really doing, wanting to hear what was on my mind, eager to share his perspective. Yet it wasn't sexy. I couldn't imagine sleeping with him as I listened patiently to his parenting guidance.

"I just want to inspire you," he would say. "I like to be a person that inspires others."

After we said good night, I stayed up, tossing and turning. Although we had seen each other only a few times, his image was burned into my brain. Jonathan is dark, swarthy even. I had never dated dark-haired or dark-skinned men because they reminded me of my father and my father's brother Uncle Sinai, who still liked to heap abuse on women, me being his favorite target.

I remembered acknowledging to myself, back when Jonathan had befriended me on set, that he reminded me of my dad. Not in a specific way, like his facial features matched up, but in the coloring, the lean body type, the big, jolly smile that showed two rows of teeth. There was a vibe about him that I associated with the men in my family.

I did not have daddy issues. That wasn't why I was attracted to, or kept attracting, older men. It couldn't be, I said to those who accused me of suffering from them. I had not so much been hurt by my father as I had wrestled with his mental and physical absence. Not only was my father completely uninvolved in my upbringing, but also I was constantly aware of his inability to be consciously present. If I carried a scar, it was that of an excision. How to fathom the filling of my personal space with a male figure when none had featured in my original story?

This was my problem then, I thought. I lacked the ability to even imagine a man in my life.

"We have to try to meet again," Jonathan said one night.

I thought, if I meet him and it goes well, I'm doomed to fall for a man who doesn't even make his permanent home nearby. A man who works so much he has no time for anything else. Who sees his daughter on breaks between episodes. Why would he want to see me, I wondered, if he knows he has no room for me in his life?

And there was another fear. Since Conor, I hadn't seriously dated a man for more than two years. Of the few men who had tried, most had triggered an anxious response; I would feel dizzy and nauseated and make an excuse to leave quickly. I didn't want a repeat of that experience. What if I met Jonathan and had a panic attack? It would be late at night, the environment would be crowded, there would be alcohol involved—all of those things were triggers for me. It would be devastating for me to have to confront the idea that any future romantic encounter would always evoke a fight-or-flight response in my body. If someone like Jonathan, whom I had been talking to for months, couldn't penetrate my walls, no one could. And I would have to go home and live with the knowledge that even the most well-intentioned man couldn't get me to let my guard down. My fear would be set permanently, like pottery left to dry in the sun.

There was a pit in my stomach as I walked toward him in the dim light of the restaurant, already thinking of ways to shorten our meeting. He was in a corner, wearing his ubiquitous scarf, tied in that same signature way. He stood up to hug me, and we both held on a moment longer than normal. And just like that, my anxiety dissipated like a rain cloud banished by the sun. I felt as if I were seeing a very old friend from a distant past, like a friend from home. He radiated warmth and affection.

I sat down. We joked awkwardly with the waiter. We smiled at each other. He looked straight at me, just like he had when we'd first met, the kind of gaze that most would find disconcerting but that I interpreted as a desire to really see me, as a commitment to get to know me. I let him stare.

At one point, after a bit of small talk, I reached my hands out across the curiously long, narrow table between us. I couldn't reach his end of it, but I let my hands dangle there anyway, as if to illustrate the physical gap between us.

"Let's not do this," I said. I had told him over the phone that I didn't want to do dinner or drinks. I didn't want a date. I wanted a friend, a lover, a real connection. I didn't want to go through the alienating motions of convention.

"What?"

"Let's not put a table between us." I was reminded of the table that had separated me from my future husband ten years earlier, when we had met for the first time.

"Let's not do that whole dinner thing when we get together. We don't have to do that. Why can't we just hang out, go for a walk, just be around each other? We don't need to structure it."

"Come sit here," he said, smiling. His seat was a silver booth built into the wall. I came over to his side. We kissed, and it was familiar, as if we kissed the same way. Our spontaneous impulses, although generated individually, felt like they traveled along the same track. His movements anticipated my own.

"You're perfect," he said, looking intensely into my eyes. "You're so unexpected. I've never met anyone like you."

In my head I heard Conor whispering into my ear, "You're beautiful." It was that simple. All I needed was a man to tell me I was worth loving.

Jonathan took me upstairs to show me his room. He opened the enormous closet, and sure enough, there were his twenty pairs of shoes, his three enormous suitcases.

He pointed out all the little details of the room he was so proud of. The rain shower, the flat-screen, the glittering view of Manhattan, the vista of bridges crossing the river to Brooklyn. Then he put his hands on my neck, pushed me up against a wall, and kissed me hard and fast, tugging the Hermès scarf tied at my neck so that it acted as his personal harness. He threw me down on the bed and tried to kiss me again, and I giggled into his mouth.

"What?" he said, lifting his face off mine to look at me.

"C'mon, this is funny!"

"Why?"

"Because people do this in the movies! People don't do this in real life!"

"Of course people do this. I'm doing it and you like it!"

"Yes, but it's also funny."

He lifted my hands above my head, kissed me again. I kissed back, but I turned him over so I was on top of him. We began to wrestle, pushing each other to see who could maintain control.

"You don't have to dominate me," I said to him.

"But you want it."

"I want equality. We can take turns. You don't have to be the boss."

There was something exhilarating about the energy between us that night. We stayed fully clothed on that bed for a while, playing the same game. One of us would let the other take charge until the other felt the need to take over. After a while, I felt as if someone had opened a pressure valve in my body and released me of tension. I was an uncoiled spring. We lay side by side for a bit, holding hands, not talking.

I reached my hand under his shirt and around his waist. The soft skin of his stomach, scarred from motocross accidents, felt intoxicatingly warm. I lifted my head and looked at him and felt completely and wholly attracted to him. Everything about him seemed beautiful all of a sudden; his jaw testified to his tenderness, his eyes spoke to his compassion. Every feature I focused on seemed evidence of his best traits. Before, his face had been an unreadable mask; now, it was a poem only I could interpret.

"You're just . . . lovely," I said out loud, wishing there was a better phrase I could use to express my epiphany.

He looked away. "I'm really moved . . . the way you just said that . . . people have complimented me before, but when you say it, it sounds real."

"You mean because I'm so stingy with the compliments?" I said, laughing.

"Because you're so brutally honest. I know you don't feel the need to lie just to please people."

"That's true." But I never felt like I could trust others to do the same. This was what I had found most bewildering about my new world, the skillfulness and ease with which people set about deceiving each other. It was as if everyone were in a chess match and cheating was the only way to come out a winner in life. Jonathan had professed not to be a player, but in my mind, if you were born into the game, you played—whether you liked it or not.

"What do you need?" he asked, as we were lying on the bed together, staring up at the ceiling.

"What do you mean?" My head jerked up so I could look him in the eyes. It was an unexpected question. "You mean, right now? Nothing. I'm fine. I'm happy." And I was, in that limited moment, a moment that had only just begun and would end very soon, never to be reclaimed. I didn't need anything more; just lying there next to him was enough.

He nodded thoughtfully. "Okay . . ." he said, as if calibrating something in his head, perhaps trying to figure out what I would require of him and whether he could measure up.

We didn't do anything more that night, which was a credit to Jonathan, who never pushed, even though I might have given in had he tried. But he urged me to go, as I had a two-hour drive to New England ahead of me. As I got up to leave, already feeling the coldness that came from being separated from his body, I felt a sudden, immense sense of dread. Jonathan's face was once again an unreadable mask.

"While I'm gone, someone will come and sweep you off your feet," Jonathan said. He was flying to L.A. in two weeks to shoot an episode for another popular TV series.

Did Jonathan assume I charmed everyone I met as much as I charmed him? Or did he wish he didn't carry the responsibility of being the only one to make it past my prickly exterior?

I told Jonathan I had no expectations, and I didn't, at least not conventional ones. What I didn't tell him about was the disease that lived in my brain, programming it to expect the worst, filling it with images of grief and disaster. After Jonathan walked me to my car and kissed me good-bye, I drove away from him feeling as if the worst result had already happened, pre-living the ache as if I could prevent it by doing so.

I proceeded to torment myself all week, losing my ability to sleep, eat, or focus, going back and forth between my rational mind, which assured me there was no reason to worry, and my gut, which screamed, "You're in deep shit! You'll never recover from this!"

I cried a lot, which upset me. I had been doing so well for months now. How could the entrance of a man into my life cause me to fall so far behind? Would it always be like this, me thinking I was okay and then falling apart again when I tried to let someone in? I was losing it, but at the same time that my emotions were exploding at the seams, I recognized how shameful it was. My response was not in any corresponding proportion to the event.

I became deeply suspicious, suddenly convinced that Jonathan was hiding something. Or that he was lying. Something was off.

And then of course I wondered if that voice in my head came from the little child in me who had only ever been deceived and hurt. Was I doomed to see pain in every risk? I understood that the way I was feeling wasn't normal, wasn't okay.

Perhaps I willed the ending into being. I often felt that I manifested my own worst fears into existence simply so that I would have to confront them and thereby neutralize their power. I did fall for Jonathan, mostly because he had looked into my eyes and said I was perfect, and I tended to deduce from that sort of comment that a man could really see me, and I longed for nothing more than to be seen. So I fell hard and fast, and he promptly had a change of heart. Where before he had been attentive and solicitous, he was now cold and indifferent. I couldn't bear to drag out his rejection, so I called him on it.

"I never wanted a relationship," he said. "I just liked you. You were like no one I had ever met before. But you see my life—it's crazy! I have no time for you; I don't even have time for my own daughter. I don't want to do this with you." Gone was the man who had wheedled and seduced, and in his place was an amnesiac. I was flabbergasted at his ability to turn on his own word.

I said good-bye and felt enormous relief as I walked the slick streets of Manhattan in the early-evening drizzle. No more wrestling with my suspicions, trying to figure out whether to listen to my gut or to my reason. No more fear, no more feeling like I had put my power in someone else's hands. It was back in my control. At the very least, I could draw my walls around me again and retreat into safety.

I'm still okay, I said to myself. *I got out just in time. This won't destroy me.* As I told myself these things, an ever-present voice began to grow powerfully in the back of my mind, like a climbing weed, threatening to take the place of every healthy thing in its presence. *You'll never be able to have faith in people again. Whatever shred of ability you still had to trust someone else is definitely gone for good now. You're officially ruined.*

No, I told that voice. *You don't get to say that.*

I pounded the pavement as if every time my shoe slapped the ground was a confirmation of my own ability to stay upright, to keep moving forward. I had not been knocked down, I told myself. I was still standing.

"Why do you look so happy?" people kept asking. I glowed for weeks afterward. It was the glow of empowerment. I had survived the one thing that I thought still had the power to destroy me. I had been hurt, and it had not been the worst thing.

When I was very young, my family members would often use a particularly cruel manipulation technique to get me to confess whatever they wanted to hear. They'd change the tone of their voice into something sugary sweet, dangling the possibility of love as a reward for my action. Just say this, they implied, and you'll finally be one of us. We will finally love you like you've always wanted. For a long time, it worked. I always reached for the apple, and my fist always came up empty.

I stopped reaching after a while. When Jonathan came into my life I immediately recognized that familiar swinging fruit and I almost laughed at how silly it was. Surely I knew better than to fall for that. It was so clear to me at the very beginning that the apple was attached to a string. And yet, that fruit kept dangling in front of me for weeks, and eventually that old instinct won, and I reached. Once again, I was played for a fool. It brought up memories of each humiliation I had ever endured at the hands of the people who raised me.

What I learned, though, walking away from that, was that I could never really hope to erase the desire for love. I didn't need to. Love is a basic human right, and although that right was denied me, that doesn't mean that I have to accept a future devoid of it.

Some people wonder if I can recognize love when it comes, considering I've never known it. This is true, and something I fear, but although the energy that has come into my life under the guise of love may only have been a poor imitation, I have decided that if the fake kind can feel so good, then I want the real thing. It's enough to keep taking risks and to keep getting hurt.

Members of my community are rooting for me to fail. They want to point to my unhappiness and say that it's proof that no good can come of leaving. And it's true that leaving is only the first step to a solution; it takes a lot more work to actually build a new life after that. And failing is likely for many who try, and was always a distinct possibility for me. I understand that, and I'm even fine with it. Failure is okay. It will be enough for me to achieve self-ownership. I don't necessarily need to have it all to feel like it was worth it, but I want to. Because I don't want all those women to look at me and say, "She left but she never really found a better life. So, it's possible to leave, yes, but the situation is hopeless."

I want to prove the statistics wrong. To do that, I have to find a new algorithm; I have to find the factor that changes the formula. Abuse minus healing equals love. Or is it pain minus love equals happiness? Is it grace plus acceptance equals peace? I'm determined to try them all.

VII

סודות

secrets

As I endeavored to discover my romantic needs, somewhere along the way I started to suspect that they were darker and more complex than I had previously imagined. Perhaps it was that night in the winter of 2012, when I went on a date with a man named Otto. He was German, very tall and broad-shouldered, with a strong nose. We spent the evening wandering around Williamsburg, the cool part on the north side of the Williamsburg Bridge, and we talked and laughed, and it was fun, but the energy between us was strange, almost crackling with aggression. I had never encountered it before and didn't quite know what to make of it.

We ended the night at the foot of the bridge, in a little park that marked the boundary between the two communities, one old, and one new. My past was literally behind me as I sat on the steps leading up to a statue of some general on a horse, facing the twinkling lights of new developments ahead.

I don't know how it was we got the idea to role-play. It just happened. He was German, I was Jewish, we were in Williamsburg—it seemed the right moment for just such an experiment.

"Let's pretend it's 1939. You're a Nazi, and I'm a Jewish girl you found on the street."

And wouldn't you know it, he did just that. He stood up, his large figure blocking the light from the streetlamp, and loomed over me like some cartoonish shadow. He demanded to see my papers with the straightest face I had ever seen. As I withdrew into myself in some strange, otherworldly response, he leaned closer, more threateningly, as if he was serious.

I pulled my knees to my chest and wrapped my arms around them, as if I could roll into a ball. Looking up at his impenetrable face, I felt inexplicably and powerfully targeted. It was real, like going back in time, to some other dimension of possibility. Was this what it had felt like to some other girl who could have been me? Would she have seen someone's fury and power so focused on her and shrink under its gaze, like a turtle withdrawing into its shell?

Afterward we were both embarrassed by what we had done. Otto for getting so carried away—and me for feeling as if it were real. It wasn't real. We were just people, people who responded to each other intensely for no reason we could discern. It was as if there was some secret dynamic at work.

What did I go looking for in Otto's eyes that night? My tormentor, perhaps?

I found another German a few months later, Christopher, a Harvard professor and distinguished author of a book that examined the source of Third Reich ideology. We walked around the

West Village after a literary conference, and we kissed. There was nothing magical there, but there was something in his German accent, in his paternal manner toward me, that felt like it was awakening a sleeping beast inside my chest.

During my time at Sarah Lawrence, I met a young woman who worked as a dominatrix in a Manhattan dungeon and who confided to me that she repeatedly had visits from "rabbis" who wanted her to dress up as a Nazi and beat them.

"They're not all rabbis just because they have beards!" I said.

But that anecdote stuck with me. Were there really men from Williamsburg, raised by Holocaust survivors, who sought to put a face on their inherited persecutors and reexperience the pain their parents and grandparents endured? Was this simply survivor's guilt, or was there something darker, and more erotic, in that impulse? More important, did I suffer from the same affliction?

I had never articulated to myself a desire for pain, but I had noticed my desire for power, both in myself and others. I considered that what had drawn me to Conor was the recognition that he could see all of my deep-seated aggression and not feel dwarfed by it.

Once, I removed his belt and restrained him with it, and he simply looked at me curiously. I didn't know what to do with the power once I had it, considering I was so sexually inexperienced, but I felt a fleeting sense of satisfaction then, being in charge. And Jonathan, too, understood something about that, the desire one might have to experience a power struggle in a relationship, as a way of enacting the inner struggle in oneself. I had sought a battle that would transform me, and while the one I got wasn't exactly what I wanted, I can't say it wasn't what I anticipated. I expect to be transformed. I demand it. No matter how painful, something in me was crying out for the stick, and for the chance to overpower the one who wielded it.

Of course, there may be a simple answer—I was controlled and overpowered as a child, and here was my opportunity to relive the experience with a different ending. And yet, there was also something very seductive about giving up, and I didn't enjoy finding that out about myself.

I'd found myself celebrating the birthday of an Austrian man on one of my nights in Paris. There were six of us: a brassy sculptor from Haiti, his formerly Mormon manager, a Norwegian art collector, Richard, myself, and Kristoff—the Austrian, whose birthday fell on Hitler's birthday. Kristoff had the classic Aryan looks of the most vicious Nazis, the ones who greedily participated in murder by day and hugged their children at night. Those angular jawbones, those cold blue eyes, the wide and hollow smile—it was terrifying, but also hypnotic. I felt as if I could not tear myself away from his company.

What an evening it was—that lively dinner, with bottle after bottle of wine, the boeuf bourguignon in rich amber sauce, Kristoff's steak tartare looking almost perverse on his plate, with the raw egg glaring brazenly in its center. Of course a Nazi would eat his food raw.

He wanted to go to a club. We were all very drunk. I found I could hold my liquor better in Paris than in the United States, but that wasn't saying much.

At some point, Kristoff said something cheeky to me, I can't remember what now, and I instinctually reached out and slapped him.

At the moment my hand made contact with his cheek, I experience a brief tremor, of something I still can't describe, like a pull in one's gut.

He cradled his cheek, grinning in that creepy way of his, like a jack-o'-lantern. "I like it when you hit me," he said. "Hit me again."

I did, to my surprise.

"I would like to hit you as well," he said, but I pulled back. The loudest voice in my head said I was afraid.

"Honey," the ex-Mormon woman whispered in my ear, pulling me aside. "Be careful. That kind of behavior will get you raped."

What could she mean? I pulled on Richard's sleeve. "Richard, did you hear what she said?" I mumbled drunkenly.

"No, what?"

I told him.

"Wow."

"So, in her mind, any woman who acts provocatively gets raped? That's ridiculous."

The woman must have overheard me. She came back to me and said, "No, sweetheart. I was just telling you that because I know you recently left your religion, and I've been there. The boundaries are all blurred, and you're testing the world, I know you are, and I don't want you to get hurt."

We went to another club. This one was elegant, tucked away under a restaurant and accessed through a secret staircase. The Norwegian had thrown his money around; Cuba Libres were offered to all. Kristoff downed his in one gulp. I was leaning against the wall opposite the bar, sipping water now, and everyone around us was talking, except Kristoff. He had gone very quiet.

His gaze seemed to fall just below my face. I saw his hand, as if in slow motion, reach out toward my chest. I darted away so fast it was almost as if he hadn't just palmed my breast.

Richard saw and stepped in between me and Kristoff, scolding him soundly. I thought that, in America, Kristoff would get arrested. In Europe, this sort of behavior must be indulged, or at least accepted.

Maybe the ex-Mormon was onto something. By allowing my aggression to surface for all to see, was I simply asking for danger in return?

Markus was helping me learn German. We had met online; I wanted to brush up on my language skills before I embarked on the trip I had planned to retrace my grandmother's steps through Europe. Our conversations quickly diverged from linguistics, however. He was descended from Mennonites on one side and Nazis on the other. His grandmother had boasted about kissing Hitler's hand, he said.

"It's not so much about what your grandparents did," I said to him on the phone one night, "but about what you would have done if you had lived back then. Can I feel sure that you wouldn't have gotten swept up in that craziness and killed someone like me?"

"Can you be sure that you wouldn't have killed me, if you had been the German and I had been the Jew? Can you ever really be sure of anyone until you see them in those circumstances?"

"I'm not capable of that kind of hatred or violence. I'd rather die than participate in such madness."

"What if you had been raised by avowed anti-Semites? Who, then, is really in full possession of themselves?"

"Did you know that Judaism actually believes in the precept of visiting the sins of the father upon the son? I grew up knowing that our suffering was an atonement for the enlightenment. But in the same way, I was taught that the Germans will always be judged as evil for what their ancestors did. We would have to hate them forever."

"But you're not your upbringing anymore. You're you."

"What if I'm both? What if I can't decide?"

When I finally did come through Germany on my way to Sweden from Hungary, traveling had ceased to feel in any way romantic. I had taken a direct train from Budapest, stopping only one night in Salzburg; and so Austria passed in a blur of drunks and street festivals. The people seemed red-cheeked and lively; they danced in public squares and seemed very efficient at having fun. I moved like a morose shadow through their crowds, feeling an inexplicable weight on my back. Their happiness made me sad.

Of course you can be happy now, I thought as I was trying to squeeze through a bawdy group in lederhosen. All the Jews are gone.

It was a ridiculous thought, but it felt true nonetheless. In my brief tour of Salzburg I had not found one memorial to the Jewish community that had once thrived there. Salzburg was the first city invaded by the Germans to have its Jews deported by Austrians who were only too happy to collaborate. The city is famed for conducting an enormous public book burning in its main square. Yet this site was now a banal tourist attraction with a lovely fountain and horse-drawn carts eager to ferry visitors around town. The old synagogue, now a touristy hotel, did not even boast a small commemorative plaque. In Google searches, I had discovered that Austria's reasoning for failing to erect memorials to the Holocaust was fear of reprisal through anti-Semitic vandalism and attacks. Their answer to anti-Semitism seemed to be to appease it instead of uprooting it.

What remained instead, Google informed me, was something called *Stolpersteine*, or stumbling stones. These were small memorial stones embedded in the streets of Salzburg and other cities, in apparently random places. Yet after a thorough tour of the small city, I had not come across even one. When I stopped to ask two young girls who were DJing in a public square, they looked at me with extreme confusion and said they had never heard of such a thing. I explained myself more clearly in German, insisting that the stones had to exist. Perhaps they might know where I could get a map of them? Now they were annoyed. "They are here, but hard to find. Maybe in that street up there to the right. But we don't know."

There were no stones to be found in that street up to the right, even though I scoured the narrow alley at least five times, eyes glued to the cobblestones. In another square, young men and women in white garb were performing a traditional Austrian folk dance, and a crowd had gathered. I retreated to my cheap hotel on the outskirts of town to grab my suitcase.

I took the next train to Munich, but I couldn't figure out if Munich was the train's last stop or if it continued. Because the stops were not announced in advance, I had to be ready to get off at any moment, as the doors remained open for only a minute or two before the train moved on. As we pulled into each station I checked the monitor on the screen and looked at the platform signs to gauge where I was. At one point, I looked up at the screen to see it read "München Hauptbahnhof" and raced to the door before it closed. The conductor, a thin, older man with a fluffy Bavarian mustache, was just about to lock the door.

"Munich?" I asked.

"Ja, Munich," he said and urged me off through the half-open door.

Only when I had descended did I realize that the platform sign read "Rosenheim," not "Munich." I quickly exclaimed this to the conductor, who shrugged and slammed the train door in my face.

Suddenly I was not in a train station, but in Auschwitz. I had just witnessed an act of unspeakable cruelty. My chest contracted, held, and then burst. I collapsed in a fit of tears on the platform, and in the distance I saw a line of people on the other end of the station, watching silently.

Who was that crazy girl, the only one to get off that high-speed train, standing there on an empty platform on a cold cloudy day, bawling her eyes out?

When I finally arrived in Munich Central Station, having found a local train, it was pouring rain outside, and Markus was late. I made my way to a bar. He was coming all the way from Frankfurt, where he lived, having offered to come show me around while I was in Germany.

"Are you sure that's a good idea?" I had asked him. "We may end up hating each other. It's a long drive for you." I was nervous; I felt that most often these things didn't work out in real life. What if our words dried up as soon as we saw each other in person?

"I'll take that chance," he had said.

At the bar I ordered lentil *Eintopf* in German. The bartender asked where I was from; she said my accent was *zuss*, or sweet. I didn't know if I should take it as a compliment or condescension, but I was at the very least glad to see my origins were not quite clear.

"Why don't you guess?" I asked.

"I don't have the faintest idea," she said. "Usually, I can tell right away, but your accent is a mixture of many places."

I smiled into my soup. "I am this way as well. A mixture."

Two men proposed marriage to me as I ate. It was three o'clock in the afternoon, and they were both very drunk. They stood too close to me, their beers sloshing in their glasses.

One said to me, "*Ich habe kein aphange*"—which literally translates to "I don't have a dependent," but in Germany was a way of saying, "I'm single." "Why don't you come with me to my place?" he offered with a grin.

"Why is this my problem, that you are single?" I asked.

Onlookers told me not to be concerned, that this was Bavarian culture. "We are very friendly," the guy said, while gripping my hand tightly. I extricated my hand and excused myself from the bar, where my two would-be husbands had already argued over who would pay the bill. I wanted to shout, "I'm a Jew!" just to see what would happen, but I felt hyperaware of how alone I was in Munich at that moment.

I went to wait for Markus by the entrance. He was stuck in traffic. Across the stairs, a group of youths dressed in black, with tattoos on their necks, smoked cigarettes with idle, dismissive expressions.

How is it that you tell apart a Nazi and a punk again? What did a skinhead look like anyway? Were they like metalheads? There were plenty of those standing around. I suddenly realized that I didn't know how to tell if someone was a Nazi or not. I wasn't going to delude myself into thinking there weren't any left. And it wasn't as if I could feasibly travel under the radar here, not with my nose. So I had planned to stay far away from any Nazis. This did not seem so simple now, in Munich Central Station. Every face seemed menacing, and I felt more and more skittish as the time passed. A random set of eyes met mine coolly, and I cringed and looked at the floor. A tall man smoked a cigarette a little too close to me, and I felt my heart rate speed up. Was I imagining his leer?

Finally, my phone vibrated. "Come to the Starbucks," he texted. "I'm here."

I didn't want to go back into the crowd. "Can you meet me at the exit?" I asked. "I'm feeling a bit overwhelmed."

He did. I was too afraid to watch for his approach, but inevitably I looked up and there he was, impossibly tall, built like those guys on the cover of romance novels, but with an impish smile instead of a full-lipped pout. He was walking slowly because of a recent knee injury.

I still don't know how to explain the feeling I had then, which I had never experienced before, of looking into a completely new face with the conviction that it was somehow supremely familiar to me. I looked at him and felt instantly as if I knew him and had known him always.

It's like family, I thought. Nothing about him felt strange or unpredictable.

We argued over who would carry my suitcase in the rain.

"You're in no shape to carry it. I'm a feminist. Let me do it myself!"

"*Genau*," he said. "Be a good feminist and hold your tongue."

We bantered like that all the way to his car, on the drive to the hotel he had booked, and in the supermarket we visited to buy groceries. We teased and argued and laughed, stopping only for necessary conversations with the cashier and the hotel receptionist. There was no question then that something had conspired to bring the two of us together. Those phone conversations that had seemed so engaging then were banal in comparison to the electricity that now held us in thrall. We couldn't look away from each other's eyes.

We ate hastily in the room, stuffing slabs of dark brown bread with creamy goat cheese into our mouths. We had been sitting on the edge of the bed, and inevitably we fell into it after the last crumb had been brushed off our laps. I remember not being able to contemplate doing anything else. He was enchantingly corporeal; I felt like I had conjured a golem of sorts, a lightning rod for my projections and complexes.

Here was a real German, 100 percent authentic, descended from Nazis. And he didn't hate me. That story that I had grown up with, the one I had believed for so long, that there was an entire nation of people on the other side of the Atlantic who still burned with hatred for me because I was Jewish . . . well, here was a pin in that balloon. The heat of his skin on mine, the smile in his eyes, his shy movements—these made him human in a way I never could have grasped intellectually. I felt instinctually that there was no real line between us, racial, cultural, or emotional.

He was nervous but trying to hide it. Only I felt, for first time in my life, unafraid. Once, he faltered, and I said without knowing I would say it in advance, "Come on now, be a good Nazi and put it in the Jewish bitch."

He made a sound that was half laugh and half cry of pain.

"I'm sorry, was that inappropriate?" I couldn't help laughing at the ridiculousness of this, of the cliché I knew I was participating in. "I'll stop talking now."

"Good," he says, laughing, putting his hand on my mouth. "Let me do my job, yes?"

We rolled around on that bed for what felt like hours, our energy ebbing and flowing but our bodies never disconnecting.

It was late in the evening when we finally managed to shower and make upstanding human beings of ourselves. He wanted to go out. I would learn soon that Germans are perpetually hungry, whether or not it's mealtime. We wandered out into the cool, rainy night. He draped his sweatshirt around my shoulders.

"It's okay, I'm fine," I said. "You wear it. You'll be cold without it."

"Don't be ridiculous. Do what I say. After all, I'm the *Herrenrasse*." That was German for "master race." He was following up on my joke from earlier. I checked myself internally—was I all right with that, or did I feel a twinge? Was it okay for him to make jokes about it, too?

"I have to admit I do get a kick out of this a bit, but at the same time I feel guilty for doing so."

"Guilty?"

"I'm joking about something that shattered my grandmother's life, that was responsible for the gruesome murder of most of my ancestors. How good can that feel, do you think?"

"*Ja*, of course, I understand. We don't have to joke about it then if you don't want to."

"I don't really know how I feel. The part of me that's still a product of my past kind of wants to chop your head off."

He grimaced. "Great. Good to know."

I had this sensation of a very old wound starting to close, to heal over, in my spirit. Nerves tingled and came alive, muscles twitched and shuddered, and my body throbbed from the sweet pain of it.

"Let's not do any Holocaust stuff just yet," I said. At that point in my trip I was already tired of what had started to feel like an expedition to dig up a trail of anti-Semitism that ran through Europe.

"That's fine with me," he said with a smile.

We drove south into the heart of Bavaria in his little stick-shift hatchback. About an hour from Munich, the Alps loomed into view, more impressive than they had seemed from a distance on the way from Salzburg into Germany. We settled into a small bed-and-breakfast in the sleepy town of Murnau am Staffelsee, perched just at the foot of the mountains. The owners, Gina and Frederic, were a charming couple; she was a painter and he was a cook, and together they had created an artistic retreat, one which also served sumptuous meals at the attached Cantina. The property had numerous nooks and crannies to hide in, with sculptures and plants and cozy seats. A plump gray cat sunned himself in the driveway.

Markus went to pet him, crooning and cuddling the now purring cat with almost childlike enthusiasm. It made me smile.

"Look," Markus called to me where I stood with the luggage. "He's rolling over on his tummy, look how happy he is. Isn't he the cutest?"

I went over to scratch him behind the ears.

"That's Max," Gina told us. "He lives here. Let me show you to your room. I hope we'll see you at dinner later?"

I nodded. "I've read rave reviews about your restaurant," I said. "We're really looking forward to it."

Our room was a charming alcove suite on the second floor, with a porch that faced west, where the sun was already setting behind the sloping, tiled roof. Amber light striped across the bed and on the floor. It was as if we had found a place where time stopped and held its breath, just so we could discover each other in that sacred space between inhale and exhale, before we had a chance to think about how this would work when the moment inevitably came to an end, and breathing resumed.

We took a walk around the picturesque town. Outside the church, I saw an enormous memorial, cast from granite, with fresh roses and daisies laid at its base. It was titled *"Unsern Helden"*—"To Our Heroes." It consisted of the names of local citizens who had died fighting for Nazi Germany.

"Can they do that? Can they turn them into heroes now? How is this even legal?" I said.

"Not everyone wanted to fight in the army," Markus said. "A lot of them were forced."

"Don't you think a more appropriate title for this memorial would be 'Our Victims,' or perhaps 'Our Martyrs'? *Heroes*—don't you see what that implies?"

He shrugged. Out of the corner of my eye I noticed a young teenager with a blond buzz cut glance over at me surreptitiously. Had he understood what I had said? Was he a skinhead? I pointed him out to Markus.

"Don't talk so loud, yeah?"

"But that's the point! I should be nervous about talking about it, here, where it happened? Where supposedly there is the best Holocaust education in the world? Do you see any memorials here for the Jewish heroes who died?"

But there were none, not in that town, and not in any of the other small Bavarian towns we visited in the area. I did not bring it up again, but I decided that the absence of memory was a kind of denial. To avoid the issue was to pretend it had never happened, and in that sense Bavaria was similar to Austria—it had become convenient to forget. It wasn't fair to hold Markus responsible for that, but even though there were no lines drawn between us when we were alone in a room, outside it became easier to see him as on the other side of some great gulf.

At dinnertime we wandered over to the Cantina, a lovely whitewashed grotto carved out of the property's east side. Inside, it was already lively with the sounds of beer glasses clinking, dishes and cutlery being sorted in the back, and the vibrant chatter of diners. Every table was full, as the restaurant was open to the general public as well, but Gina spotted us. She approached us looking regal, wearing a floor-length robe and her hair wrapped in a silk turban.

"Come outside," she said. "I always keep a special table for the guests."

We followed her out the back door into an enclosed yard, full of rustling ferns and trickling fountains. Under a broad umbrella sat a lone table, its slatted wooden top draped in a mantilla. Red roses floated in a bowl at its center. Three men already sat around the table drinking red wine from stemless glasses.

"A table for friends," Gina said, smiling and nodding at the others. "Away from the noise. Here we can actually talk."

The men each introduced themselves; they weren't all local but they seemed to be good friends of Gina's. An academic, a mechanic, and a biker—it was hard to understand what made them a group. After Frederic poured us some of that deep red wine and brought out small plates of crispy octopus and pork croquettes, I relaxed a bit, and it was then that I must have switched to German without realizing it.

"Deborah! You didn't tell us that you speak German!" Gina said. "What a shame, I would have spoken to you in German as soon as you arrived."

"Oh no, I don't really speak it," I said, "or at least, I speak it very poorly."

"Not at all," Gina said. "You speak it quite well. In fact, you should speak it more often. It would be a shame to waste it."

"You'll see," I said. "It's not really German. If I speak it long enough, you'll understand."

The biker smiled and emptied his glass. "This is a country of many dialects. You should hear me when I speak Bavarian."

"It's true." The academic nodded. "I can barely understand him."

"What is your dialect?" the mechanic asked. He hadn't talked much since we had arrived, and was still nursing the same glass of wine.

"It's really old," I said. "My family is of Franco-German ancestry, and my grandparents spoke this dialect, which they must have inherited from their parents and grandparents. I don't think it's spoken in present-day Germany anymore." Markus looked over at me then, a curious expression in his eyes. He had been busily consuming tapas as I had carried the conversation, in his typical reserved style. Now he sat with his arms folded and lips pursed in amusement, saying nothing.

"Why didn't you tell them it was Yiddish?" he asked me later, as we stumbled back to our room in the dark.

"Look," I whispered, pointing at the sky. I had suddenly noticed it then. It was as if the universe had lowered itself to us. Constellations twinkled like sequins loosely sewn onto blue velvet. The stars shimmered so brightly they seemed to run into each other, in a pulsing twisting movement, like silvery snakes squirming in a pit. It was by far the most magnificent view I had ever seen of the night sky; it made the most impressive planetarium seem puny in comparison. "Have you ever seen the stars like this before?"

Markus looked up. "It's because we're far from the city. No light pollution."

"But I live in the country and I never see them like this. They always seem so far away. Do you think it's because we're in the Alps?"

"You mean because we're higher up? Could be. It seems like the difference should be negligible, though, when you think about it."

We fell silent, and the soundlessness around us was suddenly palpable, like a thick curtain had dropped over the town, muffling all sound. Overhead, the stars continued their dance, glowing and fading in rhythm. We walked up the darkened stairway to our room.

"I guess I was afraid of their reactions," I said finally.

"I was wondering if that was it."

"There are no Jews here, Markus. Not one. I can actually feel it, like it's something in the air that's missing, a smell or a sound that I usually recognize."

"You may be right."

"That scares me for some reason."

It rained then, for three days straight. On the third day, we gave up trying to go out. We were lying in bed, and we had the windows open for air, so we could hear the drops pinging off the metal drainpipe and bouncing off the clay-pot roof. They plopped onto ferns and broad-leafed trees and splattered into the muddy driveway.

"I'll sing you something, okay?" I said to Markus, who was lying next to me with his eyes closed. "Tell me if you understand it. It's a lullaby from my childhood."

"Mmm." He nodded, relaxed.

I began to sing in Yiddish.

"Sleep my child, rest my soul / Keep your eyes closed. / A mother is holding you in her arms, / Ai li lu li lu. / And you should not fear / And you should not worry / That the sun is going down / For surely a new morning will come / Full of joy and happiness."

"*Sehr schön*," he said. "It's a nice little song."

"Wait," I said. "It's not finished."

I continued: "My child, you once had a mother / But you barely knew her / In the Auschwitz flames / They burned her. / An angry wind blew then, / A cold, wet rain, / When I found you, my child, / In the damp forest. / Both of us ran off together, / Looking for a safe place, / And we found some partisans, / And stayed there with them. / Don't worry, my child, / Sleep well. / For one day you shall grow up, / And avenge your mother's blood.

"That's my lullaby," I said, and turned to look at him. His eyes were open now, and he raised his eyebrows.

"*Ja*, that's quite intense."

"I feel like that song sums it all up, my whole childhood."

Finally, the sun came out. When we opened our eyes in the morning, we jumped out of bed and scarfed down a quick breakfast. We were anxious to take advantage of the weather and do as much as possible, as the forecast was predicting more rain later in the week.

"Where shall we go?" Markus asked once we were in the car.

"To the mountains, of course!" I'd never seen the Alps up close, or any mountain range that could compare. I was thrilled at the prospect.

It was a beautiful drive, the slopes a steady wall in front of us, never seeming to recede or shrink as we came closer the way I expected them to. We stopped at Mittenwald, the last town before the Austrian border, to catch a glimpse of the Isar River, a glacial runoff with waters the color of mint-chip ice cream, frothing around rocks and boulders, in a hurry to get somewhere. We stopped to take pictures at the riverbank, the Alps a splendid but still distant backdrop.

Then came the sheer drops and sharp turns over the border, and finally, somewhat carsick, we arrived in Innsbruck, Austria. We walked through the old town, which was packed with tourists, and purchased a picnic lunch at a supermarket. Then we headed back out toward the less populated area, to a park with ancient willows and birches on the banks of the River Inn. Across its sparkling green rush, the brightly colored homes ascended up the hills, and the snowcapped mountains soared breathtakingly above them. Spires and cupolas peeked playfully out onto the scene. We finished our lunch and climbed down some makeshift steps to the riverbank. Markus took off his shoes and socks and ventured in, and I rolled up my jeans and did the same. The water was ice cold and sped furiously around my feet.

"Would you swim in this?" I asked Markus. "It's probably dangerous because of that strong current."

"I've been watching that big branch out there in the middle, and it keeps coming back in circles. It's like there's a circular current out there, or two separate currents going in opposite directions." I followed his gaze, and sure enough, a large branch was whipping back and forth in the middle of the river, seemingly tossed between two opposing forces.

"So," Markus said, once we had our shoes back on. "Where would my Jewish princess like to go next?"

I was looking at the map. "Did you know we were so close to Italy?"

"You want to cross another border?"

"Since we are already here, it feels like such a shame not to. Who knows if I'll ever be in this part of the world again."

"How far is the drive?"

"An hour, maybe an hour and ten," I fudged.

It was closer to an hour and a half, but we got to see the Brenner Pass. We crossed the entire mountain range, stopping in Bolzano, the first real city on the Italian side. Formerly known as Bozen when it belonged to Austria, it had been heavily Italianized by Mussolini. Signs were printed in German and Italian. The temperature seemed to change drastically as soon as we started our descent. The sun shone brightly down on orchards and vineyards embedded into the verdant green slopes in neat, angular steps.

We parked in front of a big church and walked across the street, where Markus ordered some pizza from a street vendor in German. We stood at a tall table under an umbrella to eat. Sparrows began to crowd around us hoping for crumbs. Markus, after having eaten his fill, started to feed them.

"Look at this," he said. He was making the sparrows fly to his fingertips to eat the bits of bread he held out. I watched as they approached him tentatively, batting their wings as they hovered near his hand, trying to take some bread back with them. Most of the piece would crumble to the ground, and they would be left with only the crumb in their beak.

I threw some of my crust at the sparrows perched on the hedge near us.

"Don't do that," Markus scolded. "Make them come to you."

"I'd rather not. It feels wrong to make them do that just for my entertainment."

He scoffed. I watched as he continued to coax the birds to his outstretched hand, grinning triumphantly each time a sparrow flew awkwardly out to meet it. He had mentioned to me many times how much he loved animals, and I'd seen him stop for every cat and dog on the street, but this struck me as a peculiar way to express that love.

A pigeon approached and I tossed some crumbs its way, remembering how my grandmother had always left food out for the city birds on our porch.

"Ach, don't feed the pigeons!" Markus said. "They're just stupid."

"Does that mean they're less deserving of a meal? My grandmother wouldn't have made such distinctions between the birds she fed."

A crowd of pigeons descended then, and the scene quickly turned to chaos. Markus had been right in a way. I watched the pigeons stumble blindly in circles, seemingly unable to see the food in front of them. Then a sparrow flew into their midst so quickly I almost didn't see it. It left in a blur with the food in its mouth.

"See?" Markus crowed. "They're too stupid to even eat what you throw at them. The sparrows are getting everything."

My cheeks felt hot, but I didn't say anything, because I couldn't articulate to myself at the time what was bothering me.

We walked around the city for a bit after that, stopping at every gelato stand until we had stuffed ourselves silly. Then we embarked on the long drive back, stopping at Hall-in-Tirol for an aperitif and then Seefeld-in-Tirol for a very late dinner.

On the way home, I brought it up.

"You know, you may not have realized it, but that story with the birds was kind of a metaphor for the whole idea of survival of the fittest," I said. "You singled out the intelligent birds as the ones deserving of being fed, and then made them dance for their crumbs. Kind of fits with your whole *Übermensch* thing, doesn't it?"

"*Ja*, of course. I'm a Nazi after all, how can I help it?"

"I think it's funny that I'm the one who is looking out for the underdog, trying to feed the ones that can't feed themselves, and you clearly expressed with your behavior an idea that you don't necessarily agree with consciously or intellectually. What does that say about how our culture is ingrained in us? I clearly have a persecution complex after the way I was raised, but I wonder if possibly you were affected by the Nazi side of your family more than you realize?"

He shook his head impatiently. "We already agreed on this, no? That's why I'm with you, for some *Wiedergutmachung*—reparations, right?"

"I don't even feel that that's funny anymore."

"I should stop joking about it?"

"I remember reading about Katrin Himmler, who married an Israeli Jew, the son of Holocaust survivors, and she used to say that everything was great until they argued, and then she was a Nazi and he was a Jew who couldn't get over it."

Markus's face showed no expression. His hands remained on the wheel as we sped down dark roads.

"Of course I don't see you like that, as Himmler's descendant. I know you're not like that. Otherwise I wouldn't even talk to you. It's just that sometimes the voice in my head that screams *All Germans are evil*, that voice I grew up with, it just kind of takes over."

"*Genau*. Understandable."

I leaned over and kissed him, and stroked his neck. He had the most beautiful face. How could I really be so horrified by my relationship with him in these odd, random moments when my whole body seemed to thrill in his presence?

The next day I felt a bit off. It was raining again. We decided to nap after lunch. I fell asleep for thirty minutes and awoke in the midst of what felt like the peak throes of a panic attack. I had never woken up in such a state. Before I even opened my eyes, I could feel my heart racing, my body trembling from the force.

I lay paralyzed with fear and shock for a few minutes before I was able to whisper to Markus, who was lying next to me reading a book. He had not noticed I was awake.

"Markus."

"Yes, my dear?"

"Can you feel my pulse?" I asked. I didn't want to seem crazy. I assumed that I must look ordinary on the surface, as I was lying still on the bed. One couldn't see a racing heart.

"*Ja, natürlich,*" he said and took my hand, looking at his watch.

After a minute, he looked over. "Quite fast, *ja*, especially since you're lying in bed, no?"

"Markus, I, I—" I faltered. "I feel really sick."

He sat up. "What's wrong?"

"I don't know. I just woke up in the middle of what feels like a heart attack."

He looked at me with concern and immediately my anxiety let loose like a racing horse at the sound of a pistol shot. My heart was pounding even harder, and now I could feel my hands and legs getting numb. I started to hyperventilate.

He got up and came over to my side of the bed.

"I'm scared, I'm so scared," I cried as I thrashed under the sheets, trying to shake off the sensation.

"Calm down," he said, holding my arm and looking into my eyes. "What are you feeling?"

"Everything's numb. Why does it feel so bad? What's happening to me?"

"Just breathe," he said.

I followed his breathing, deep and slow, even though it didn't feel like it was helping. After about ten minutes I started to feel a bit more like myself, although still woozy. I sat up.

"You're okay?"

"Yes, I think so. I need some air."

He went back to his side of the bed and resumed his reading, as if nothing had happened.

Outside on the patio I reflected that no one had ever seen me panic like that except my ex-husband, who never understood what I was going through. No one had ever looked at me when I felt my craziest and made me feel that normal.

What had frightened me so much, I wondered? I knew only that it was time to leave. No matter how many beautiful visions I had encountered here, I was too uneasy to really enjoy them. Perhaps the fact that it was so lovely was the very thing that was disturbing me—did it have any right to be such a picturesque, fairy-tale-like region when it had been the birthplace of one of the greatest horrors in the world? As if I were looking through the lens of a Grimm brothers' tale, I wanted the forests to turn dark and gnarled, the sky to be an angry purple, the brittle leaves to cut like glass. This place, I thought, should reflect what happened. To appear so innocent and calm was a wrongdoing on its part, an unforgivable betrayal.

But the only one to feel betrayed was me. Only I didn't belong here.

We checked out the next morning and drove to Frankfurt, stopping only for lunch in a tiny town in Hesse. I had to move on to Berlin very soon, but I had decided to stay in Frankfurt for a day or two because Markus had arranged for me to meet his mother. I was curious to meet her because she had been raised by real Nazis. Although Markus had told me that she had always had a very troubled relationship with her family and their beliefs, I still wondered if I might detect any trace of her background imprinted on her character, the way mine was no doubt imprinted on me.

Ada had recently been widowed and was now living in the small apartment she had used as her private sanctuary throughout her marriage. It had a lovely garden out front and another in back with a little terrace, and that's where we sat. Young pink climbing roses were carefully tied to the railing of the terrace; the plants were immaculately tended in attractive ceramic pots. Ada had pure white hair, large pale blue eyes, and very fair skin. Her home was perfectly tidy, and pretty objects and collectibles were displayed throughout. This reminded me instantly of my grandmother, and as we made small talk on the porch, I realized for the first time just how much I missed having an older person in my life, the way I used to.

"I wanted to ask you about your parents," I said eventually, after we had licked clean a bowl of strawberries and cream. "I'm really curious what it was like being raised by them, and how you were able to turn out so differently and raise a son like Markus."

"My parents hated everyone who wasn't German, not just Jews. Even on his deathbed my father expressed no remorse. My mother could never stop talking about the time she kissed Hitler's hand. Come, I'll show you a picture of them."

We walked into her little office, and there was an old sepia photograph taped to the side of a curio, showing a surprisingly diminutive couple walking their German shepherd in the rain, smiling from underneath their shared umbrella. His face seemed to disappear under his squashy hat and large, thick-rimmed glasses, but I could detect a decidedly prominent nose. He looked like the average middle-aged Jewish man buying a bagel on the Upper West Side. She was no different, with a narrow forehead and thick, dark eyebrows.

"They look more Jewish than most Jews I know!" I said.

"Right?" Ada laughed. "And with their German shepherd, so proud of themselves. They looked nothing like the ideal Germans they had in their fantasies."

"But you do," I said before I could help myself. "You're so blond and blue-eyed. It's interesting—Markus looks nothing like that."

"Markus looks like his father." Indeed, he had a tall, broad forehead but a large nose and dark hair. His eyes were hazel, but his smile was distinctly Bavarian, the upper lip coming out slightly over the lower, which lent him a look of perpetual bemusement.

"My generation was different. Back then, everyone was rebelling against their parents, against what they had done. We didn't want to be anything like them. It didn't help that my parents were brutal to me as well. My mother used to give me electric shocks as a way of disciplining me. I tried to accuse her of it when I was an adult, and she wouldn't even discuss it with me. It was clear she knew it was sick, that she was sick and compulsive and couldn't stop herself from committing brutality."

I remembered seeing all those photos of Hitler cavorting with children, reading how Nazis would go home and hug their wives. It never occurred to me that some of them might have been as cruel to their own offspring as they were on the job.

Markus drove me around the city for a short tour. I asked him if any of his siblings had turned out anti-Semitic, wondering if these patterns were in any way genetic, skipping generations and then popping up again out of context.

"My younger brother went through a phase when he was a teenager, but I think he's mostly grown out of it."

"What do you mean by 'mostly'?"

"It's how young people do their rebellion here. You know it's against the law, and it's considered politically incorrect, so of course that's the issue that young people will pick as a way of showing they are going against the grain. It makes them cool. But it's abstract for them; it's not like they actually know any Jews. My brother is not an anti-Semite; he just makes an offensive joke once in a while."

"I would say that's an anti-Semite, Markus."

"Every teenager in Germany is an anti-Semite then, because that's what they do now, to be cool. They make politically incorrect statements, to show they don't give a fuck, and since Jews are a sore topic here, they like to pick at the wound."

"Would your brother disapprove of you being with me?"

"I don't think so," Markus said. "But it wouldn't matter anyway."

"It would matter to me."

We slept together on our last night in his narrow bed, neither of us moving from the position we fell asleep in, with his arms wrapped around me, and the humid summer air cooking us like chickens on a rotisserie. My head swam when I awoke. I had a train to catch to Berlin. He kissed me on the forehead. "Call me when you arrive," he said. I nodded.

When I arrived in Berlin, I immediately felt as if I had lost that magical sense of orientation that had guided me through most of Europe. Berlin's sights lay sprawled in every direction, and I felt dwarfed by the scope of the city, beleaguered by its complicated maps, its chaotic layout. The streets were filled with scaffolds and trenches; there was construction happening everywhere. What about those orderly arrondissements and neatly delineated quarters? Here the river was not something to skirt around via a pedestrian bridge; it was not even a body of water you could easily view in its entirety, the way you could see down the Seine in Paris. Elevated tracks crisscrossed on top of it, and buildings squatted over its narrower parts. What was missing was the sense of knowing what to expect.

In my first few days there, I was afraid to go out. Markus was gone, and it was strange to navigate my life without him, even though I had done so for years. I was staying on the edge of the old Jewish quarter, but it was only when I finally ventured out that I realized that. The old synagogue was a two-minute walk away. It had been perfectly preserved in its mostly disheveled state, with bits of still-intact marble and mosaic cordoned off. I had to go through an extensive security check and a metal detector just to get inside. On the exterior of the building was a plaque that described how the synagogue had been violated and ultimately destroyed. Underneath the description was a line in bold, enlarged letters: "Never forget it." I snapped a photo, and the security guard standing alongside it smiled as if to pose. I wanted to tell him that a smile was inappropriate, that this wasn't some tourist trap he was showing off, that this was a reminder of this country's shame, and his face should reflect that. But I stared straight ahead instead, pretending I didn't notice.

After that I descended into the subway and headed in the direction of the Holocaust memorial. It was a gray weekday morning, the stations were empty and quiet, and aboveground the wide city blocks with their cold contemporary buildings seemed forbidding. Normally I stayed away from Holocaust exhibits, as my visit to the Holocaust Museum in Washington, D.C., when I was a teenager had scared me off future attempts. I remember my class went there on a field trip, and although all of us were from survivor families, I was the only one who didn't make it halfway through before I dissolved into hysterical tears, hyperventilating in a bathroom stall for nearly an hour.

But the German museum's exhibits couldn't compare to the thoroughness of those in D.C. In Germany, memorials were brief and succinct. For someone so well versed in this particular history, I had yet to learn something new at any of the Holocaust sites. I descended into the underground chamber below the memorial, where the Holocaust was summed up for tourists and schoolchildren. I joined the procession of visitors that passed slowly along its corridors.

"It happened, therefore it can happen again; this is the core of what we have to say," read a quote by Primo Levi emblazoned on the wall behind the entrance.

I was okay, as expected, holding my coffee cup and a napkin, shuffling along behind the line of people. Even in front of that high-definition photograph of the Einsatzgruppen moving among a writhing pile of naked moon-white women, rifles cocked as they shot each one individually. The quality of the photograph was unparalleled. Although I'd seen it before, I hadn't previously noticed the visible relish on the Germans' faces, or how each woman was twisted into a grimace of anticipation or a tremor of death. It was so fantastically horrible as to be pornographic. The women were piled in the forest like slain Venuses, like raped fairies. They were stunning in their innocence. It must have been horrible to die in such a way, made to run naked into one's own grave. But from the lens of history it was those men who were immortalized in their ugliness, their sneers frozen for an eternity of analysis. The smooth white backs of those women were impeccable in their grace and dignity.

I followed the crowd into a darkened room, the floor of which had a small collection of backlit testimonials from various victims of the Holocaust, collected from postcards or journals. Afterward, it struck me, the irony, that it was writing that felled me and not a photo.

Here was a poem by Miklós Radnóti, the Hungarian Jewish poet that Zoltán had spoken of to me so fondly. It was translated into German and English. I whispered it out loud to myself.

I fell beside him and his corpse turned over,
tight already as a snapping string.

Shot in the neck—And that's how you'll end too—
I whispered to myself; lie still, no moving.
Now patience flowers in death. Then I could hear
Der Springt noch auf—above, and very near.
Blood mixed with mud was drying on my ear.
                    —*Szentkirályszabadja, October 31, 1944*

I choked on a terrible sound coming from my throat. Suddenly
I had to sit down, and the napkin wasn't enough to mop up the
mess of mascara and snot on my face. How vivid and powerful
those words were, that I felt as if I was lying right there beside him
as he died, and it was unbearable.

The other visitors stepped cautiously around me, but I was
blind and did not care. I sat in front of the poem until my chest
stopped hurting so much. I recalled the intense rage and sorrow I
had experienced the first time I had seen those images in the U.S.
Holocaust Memorial Museum. It felt just as fresh. Would this
feeling ever dissipate or dilute itself?

In the other room, the names of the victims were being read,
with descriptions of how they had lived and died. In the next room
was an explanation of the death camps. A little boy around the
age of seven sat in one of the audio booths with earphones pressed
to his head, listening to information about how Auschwitz was
operated. I looked at him in shock: he could have been my own
son, and he looked somberly into my red, swollen eyes. You
shouldn't be here, I wanted to say; you're too young. But who was
I to say that? Was this how it was done here, the Holocaust education? You started when they were young, as if to root out that
Nazi tendency before it had a chance to grow? Was there really

such a thing as a seven-year-old boy who needed to be educated about death camps in order to grow up to be a decent human being?

My son did not yet know about the Holocaust, and this made me realize that I could not recall a consciousness that did not include it. Did my awareness of my grandparents immediately coincide with my awareness of them as survivors of genocide? Was there ever a moment in which I did not align my identity so neatly and perfectly with theirs, knowing with certainty that I, too, would have been a target, and still could be if the world lost its mind again before I died?

In a room off to the side, a group of German schoolchildren clapped loudly but perfunctorily as a Holocaust survivor finished her lecture. As the students filed out of the room, their faces seemed to say, Yeah, another one.

I remembered seeing my son's head when he was born, his wet curls still gleaming blond, and thinking, Thank God, he'll pass for non-Jewish, before I collapsed back onto the pillow.

I wondered what these young students would think if they knew there was at least one person of their generation in this world who was still deeply and indelibly marked by an event they considered a relic of the ancient past. I wrote something in the guestbook then, underneath a message from a young Ukrainian student that read, "We must always remember."

"How can I describe this feeling of being at once alive and wiped out? To be descended from the living and the dead? A part of my soul has been erased. How will I ever heal this wound in my family? How will I tell my son about this?"

I signed my name underneath. I hoped someone would read it and realize it was still real.

I came at last to a photograph of Bergen-Belsen at liberation. This was the scene that first greeted the dumbfounded British troops when they arrived. They had proceeded to document everything. Here was an image of skeletal women sitting up among piles of corpses as if rising from the dead. It was some unimaginable horror: as far as one could see, a vision of a postapocalyptic wasteland. I stood transfixed before it.

My grandmother had witnessed this. She had been there that day, lying in that filth and ugliness and inhuman horror. It would never be erased from her memory. I felt that rage from earlier return like bile in my throat. I left the exhibit and raced up the stairs to disappear into those concrete pillars. Walking down the aisles in between them was spooky; here and there I'd catch the ghostly shadow of some other visitor passing fleetingly between the aisles. They were there, and then they weren't.

I stopped in between two pillars and leaned against one of them and let myself cry with the intention of drying up my tears for this trip. *Just this once, get it out, and then you'll be through. There's nothing left to cry about. None of this is new for you. Someday you're going to have to stop crying about all of this.*

That night I woke up at 3 a.m. after a bad dream.

I lay awake remembering the photograph of the Einsatzgruppen. I couldn't get over the lifelike expressions I had seen on their faces, up close. What was it about these men that made them capable of this?

I called Markus. He was awake.

"I can't sleep. Bad dreams." I told him about the photograph.

"Can you find it on Google and send it to me?"

I did.

"That's a pretty bad picture."

"I feel, for the first time in my life, that I really could murder someone. I didn't think it would make me feel that way. But now I am filled with anger, which scares me, because maybe somehow that explains what they did, and I don't want it to. It can't. But I have this conviction that we should have eliminated all of them, that it's a gene, you know, and we didn't eradicate it, and it will spring up again."

"You are racist," he said.

"I'm racist against murderers."

He was silent.

"When I'm angry, you're a Nazi. When everything is fine, you're just a person."

"*Genau*. But I gladly pay my reparations, if it makes you happy."

"I just remembered something a good friend of mine once told me. She's Jewish, too, with a grandmother who survived the camps. She's from California, very liberal, a lesbian who married a non-Jewish woman. She said she could confront her family with anything; they were so open-minded. But that the one thing she could never do was bring home a German. It's like this line we know not to cross."

I wondered if, in the act of crossing every line that had ever been drawn in front of me, I had somehow failed to draw any of my own.

The next day I signed up for a tour of Sachsenhausen, the model concentration camp just outside Berlin. On the trip there I met a Jewish couple from Park Slope in Brooklyn. The woman was a daughter of Ukrainian survivors. She told me about how she and her mother had gone back to their little Ukrainian village and had been chased out by an angry, drunken mob.

"How could you let them do that to you, in this day and age? How could you bear to let them get away with it?" I asked.

"What was there to do? It's Ukraine."

"I would have done something. I wouldn't have let them treat me that way. The world isn't like that anymore. They can't do that to us."

She fell silent, her head bowed toward her lap.

"Do you think there is any place in the world where we can go and not experience anti-Semitism?" I wondered out loud. I told her about the conductor slamming the door on me in Rosenheim.

"You've got to be careful of what you speak about in front of the Germans," she whispered, nodding toward the other passengers. "They're very sensitive about these things."

"They goddamn well should be. I'm not going to censor myself!"

"You're a guest in their country," she said. "You can't just go around talking like that."

"Like my grandmother was a guest in their concentration camps?"

"Why are you here?" she asked.

"I'm trying to deal with this part of my identity, to put it behind me."

"That's impossible," she said. "You'll never put it behind you. I've tried my whole life."

"I think I'm doing okay," I said. "I believe I can achieve some measure of closure. Most of why I feel so bound up in it is all the secrecy I grew up with. I knew about the Holocaust, but no one ever discussed the details of their experiences. It was as if life before America had been a collective experience, summed up by one word. I need to feel like I know the individual stories; I think that will bring me peace. I don't want my grandmother's story to be diminished by a broad category."

There was a beautiful blond man in our tour group. He was Swiss-German, very tall, with a chiseled jawline and hollows under his cheeks. His eyes were cool blue marbles under a golden brow. He didn't talk much. I invited him out for a drink later; we were staying in the same neighborhood.

"Why did you decide to visit a concentration camp while in Berlin?" I asked, wondering what someone so clearly non-Jewish and so young and normal-looking would be doing on a tour like that.

"Don't you think it's important," he asked, "to learn about those things?"

"It happened to my family. What's your relationship to it?"

He cleared his throat and pushed his drink away. "It's obvious to you, no?"

"Was your family involved somehow?"

"No, they were not, but in some way I think we all feel connected to this event, from both sides. We all participated in a way, even just by being bystanders."

I remembered meeting a German man in my coffee shop back home. Peter was his name; he had been born shortly after the war. "Every German has a story," he had told me, "of being refused service, or of a door slamming in their face, or of a hand left dangling during an introduction. We take it for granted. But when I was a child in school, history stopped at the First World War. The education about the Holocaust didn't start until recently, until people felt they could sufficiently separate themselves from the actions of the Nazis."

I walked back through the streets of the Scheunenviertel, the old Jewish neighborhood, in the late afternoon. There were some lovely, quiet side streets, with neat rows of beautifully restored homes once occupied by working-class Jewish families, now gentrified by skinny jeans–wearing residents. I approached a beautiful gated park, and then noticed the haunting sculpture at the entrance. This was once the Jewish cemetery, I read. Since the stones had been completely destroyed by the Nazis, it was now a public park. I saw a young mother and her toddler in there, and the little girl was running down the garden path on chubby legs, squealing happily. My heart skipped a beat at the sight. Did that mother know her daughter was running over the desecrated graves of Jews, that their violated bones lay just beneath her innocent soles? What kind of reality is this, to raise children on the very streets on which so much blood was spilled, and so much havoc wrought? Did that young woman ever stop to think about it? Wouldn't she eventually have to explain it to her child, once she grew old enough to read the words on that sculpture for herself?

I burned with the desire to ask them this but remained silent, watching. It was difficult to admit that I had come here wanting the satisfaction of knowing that this earth was somehow permanently scorched, that it couldn't sustain a replete life anymore. But here were children frolicking among the ghosts, as if none of it had occurred. To my right, a group of artists were working on a colorful mosaic on the wall of the apartment building next to the cemetery. It was a happy mosaic of dolphins and butterflies. The banner beside it read, "The Peace Wall Project."

Finally, on the way back, I saw my first *Stolpersteine*, those stumbling stones I had searched for so fervently in Salzburg. I noticed it by accident, embedded in front of an elegant home, four of them grouped together, a name on each one. They were for a family that had lived there. The stones gave the date of their deportation as well as of their death. Yet from above they seemed so innocent, a part of the touristy decor. How chilling it was to think of the people who walked over these stones nonchalantly every day. Even more haunting to think of the people who now built their lives in the apartments that had been systematically freed up for "true" Germans. Did this generation not have to worry about guilt anymore? Could they simply blame it all on their ancestors and say those were crazy times and we had nothing to do with it? Even so, how could one stand to be around all of these reminders? I could never live in Germany, I thought, not when I risked running into memorials around every corner.

Odd's wife, Turid, called unexpectedly. She and her daughters were staying in their apartment nearby. They took me out to lunch, which was comforting. Alone in Berlin, I had felt disoriented and uneasy, and it was nice to sit with people I knew for an hour and recoup my sense of self.

"We're heading back to Norway tomorrow," Turid said as we paid the check. "Why don't you come visit us before you leave for the States?"

Germany had positively exhausted me, and I was only too happy to agree. On my last night in Berlin, I dreamed that a war had broken out while I was still abroad, and the airline canceled my ticket. The only way home that remained was through a German airport, but it had already been occupied by Nazis. "That's okay," Markus said. "We'll smuggle you out." But his friend Wolfgang gave me up to the authorities just before I awoke.

The next day I caught a train to Denmark, where I would take a ferry across the Skagerrak to the seaside village where Odd lived. I sat next to a divorced single father and his seven-year-old daughter, and as the ride was quite long, we started to converse. I asked what it was like, learning about the Holocaust as a child.

"I must have been seven years old when my class visited Auschwitz on a field trip," he told me.

"How did you feel?" I asked, almost dreading the answer. I couldn't even imagine a child that age, a child like his daughter sitting across from us clinging to her doll, being shown such a horrific place.

"To be honest, I felt nothing," he said. "I was simply too young to even process what was happening, I think, so my brain simply rejected the whole experience. I think it was only when I was older that I was able to read about it and deal with the information."

"Do you think it's wrong, that the educational system allows for the exposure to this kind of information at such a young age?" I asked.

"What can you do? It happened. We have to educate the kids about it, otherwise how are we going to stop it from happening again?"

"Surely, you don't believe that eliminating the possibility of another Holocaust rests wholly on the education of young Germans? That would be like saying there was something genetically or culturally built into them that has to be eradicated."

"But it was the Germans who did it, after all, not anybody else. What does that say? Is it not dangerous to ignore that basic fact?"

At that point in our conversation, his daughter began to resent not being the focus of her father's attention and tugged on his sleeve as he was explaining his views to me. He brushed her off a few times before getting frustrated and reaching over to force her back into her seat on the other side of the table. She began to cry loudly, and her tears soon escalated into a full-on tantrum.

"Her mother spoils her so much," the man said. "I'm the only one who provides any discipline." Then he proceeded to grab his daughter by the shoulders and shake her, quite hard, while ordering her to stop her antics. Her high-pitched wails became shrieks that filled the entire train car. Bystanders watched uncomfortably. The old woman sitting next to us looked extremely distressed; I could tell she was thinking of intervening. I cringed as I watched the situation worsen; the daughter's shrieks were positively terrifying at this point, and her father was growing angrier and angrier.

Eventually her tears subsided into whimpers, and she spent the rest of the ride huddled against the window, clutching her doll. As they left the train, her father handed me his card. "Call me next time you're passing through," he said.

I felt a quiet joy wash over me when I first caught a glimpse of Odd's estate; already I knew that my stay here would smooth over all the knots and bumps in my spirit that had formed on my trip. The property featured a small complex of buildings painted brick red and arranged around a lovely courtyard filled with haunting sculptures—a small Viking boat, a maternal angel. But what immediately drew the eye was the vast sea beyond, with its Neolithic rock formations scattered out into the horizon like a treacherous series of steps. Between the sea and the home, flowers grew wild and tall, in many different colors. Somewhere out on a rock was a sculpture of a man meditating peacefully while facing the water. I had the sense of being outside of time.

Over a dinner of freshly caught salmon and a salad of herbs and nettles just picked from the garden, Odd and I drank a crisp white wine that put us both in a talkative mood before the meal was halfway through.

I told him a little bit about my trip. He was impressed with how much ground I'd managed to cover in so little time.

"Deborah, what is it about the Jews that makes them so smart?" he asked. "I think it's because they've had to be so vigilant! Did I ever tell you the story about the lobsters?"

I shook my head no.

"Those lobsters that we have here in Norway are lucky enough to live in calm waters, where they don't have to fear many predators. A few years ago an experiment was conducted in which a boatload of Scandinavian lobsters was transplanted into the sea outside Shanghai. Do you know what they have in the waters in Shanghai, Deborah?" Odd looked at me with a twinkle in his eye.

"I don't believe I do. Please go on," I said.

"Sharks. Lots and lots of sharks. Do you know what those scientists found when they went to check on those lobsters three years later?"

"What did they find?" I looked over at Aftur and Minden; they were smiling as if they'd heard this story before.

"Those little lobster brains had swelled to three times their original size!" Odd roared. "You see, Deborah? They had to become vigilant! This made them very smart. I believe that's why the Jews are such an exceptional people. They are always living in foreign places, and have to ward off predators. They've got bigger brains!"

"I guess that's a possibility," I said, amused. But inside, I was wondering: Was smarter necessarily better? How had having giant new brains helped those poor little lobsters, wrenched from their peaceful life in the North Sea?

It did not get dark there in the summertime, even at night. Turid and the girls and I ventured out on the rocks at around ten o'clock in the evening, when they had their nightly swim in the freezing sea. They tried to get me to join them. I managed to get in up to my waist, but it was too cold for a real swim, in my opinion. Aftur found a purple sea star and put it on my leg. She pointed out the pulsing jellyfish that swam near the rocks, all of them poisonous, one a translucent purple color, the other bright pink. I had never seen one outside an aquarium before. When I withdrew from the water into the chilly night air, I could feel my skin throbbing and stinging from the high salt content. I was promptly bitten by three *klegger*, or Norwegian horseflies, and my calves swelled and turned red.

We dressed and joined Odd in the Fire Room, where a blaze was already roaring in the hearth. Turid sat down on the floor directly in front of it. Odd was nursing a tumbler full of cognac in his easy chair. I curled up on a sofa next to Börk.

Odd seemed to want to talk about Jews again. When he was little, he said, the only people who ever noticed his talent were Jews. A Jewish woman in his town gave him art books and encouraged his drawing. He longed to be around Jews today, but there weren't many who crossed his path anymore, at least not in Norway.

"Aftur told me you were born on the border, during the war, while your mother was trying to escape, is that right?"

"Yes. And then when I was fifty, I found out my father wasn't my real father after all."

I hadn't heard about this before.

"My mother wouldn't tell me who my real father was. She has refused, no matter how many times I've asked her. For this reason I hate her. I have tried to find out myself, to do research. Right away I realized that if she was so ashamed, and kept it a secret for so long, that it must have been a Nazi. There were many Nazis in Norway at that time, and they fathered quite a few children, and after the war those children suffered like hell in Norway."

"Who do you think your father is?"

"Himmler."

I couldn't tell if he was being serious. I made a shocked face.

"Look, I'll show you something." He played a clip from the movie *Downfall* on his little tablet computer. It was a scene where Hitler had gathered all his nearest and dearest and said good-bye to them as they prepared to leave Berlin for safer territory. As Hitler left the room after parting with Himmler, just as the scene was about to end, one could see the twitch of Himmler's head meeting his shoulder, the same Tourette's tic shared by Odd and his son Ode.

"We have exactly the same tic. Himmler and my mother were in the same place right around the time I was conceived. I have often pondered this. But she will not even have this discussion with me."

"My God, to even wonder such a thing. I cannot imagine it."

"Apparently Himmler fathered many children," Odd said.

During the day I watched Odd paint in the enormous barnlike structure he had designed for that purpose, the sloping ceiling fading into dim light, the sun pouring weakly in from the open door. He was working on several large canvases at the time—all of them scenes of desolation or barrenness in some way; a family clinging to each other in an arctic wasteland, a community in postapocalyptic mourning for lost land and home. In one painting, parents stood in the ocean while their child stared straight at the viewer; it was the face of Minden, Odd's daughter. Even in the scenes of intimacy, the eyes told stories of enormous bereavement and violation.

As Odd touched a brush to a cheek or an eye, adding imperceptible glimmers of light that made bones seem to pop under their skin, Börk and Ode stood around with various apparatuses designed to direct light one way or another; students painted on small easels in the corners; Aftur and Minden watched from the sidelines. All was quiet and focused. When Odd sat down to drink a glass of water and rest for a moment, he turned to where I was sitting, reading one of his books, and said, "I live under a black cloud, Deborah."

"What do you mean?"

"My whole life I have lived under it and fought against it, and it is always trying to overtake me."

"You mean the one we all struggle against to create something."

"It's a terrible thing to labor under."

I could see from the expression on his face that despite the life he had created, and the family that rallied around him like ramparts, he truly did live in the prison of that black cloud, just like every artistic creature I'd ever met. Even though he'd established all the things he thought he needed for security and happiness, his internal alienation could never be rectified. Just like I was beginning to discover, a home did not guarantee peace or security, success did not mean self-validation, and most important, other people thinking they knew who you were did not give you an identity.

This is how it is for us, and how it will always be for us, Odd, Richard, myself—though we have been recognized by the public, we now know just how deep the chasm is that lies between ourselves and the personas of us that are out in the world. Certainly we will never be finished with the struggle to know ourselves.

Odd came to say good-bye to me the morning I left for the airport. He seemed sad.

"I do so love the company of Jews, Deborah," he said. "If only more of them came through here." He hugged me and kissed my cheek, and I wished I could find the words to tell him how comforting it had been to see his world from the inside, that learning of his alienation had made my own seem somehow less lonely. But as I looked at his face, I could see that he already knew; it was as if we spoke a secret language.

I didn't know how many more opportunities I'd get to see him; it seemed I was always drawing inspiration from the old, who were bound to leave this world sooner than I would have liked, leaving me to fend for myself when I might not be ready yet.

At the airport, I called Markus. We had not spoken in a while. I had been distracted.

"I was wondering if you'd call," he said. "I thought that with our not being together, maybe you felt your passions ease up a bit."

"Is that the case with you?"

"If anything, my passions have increased."

"Then why assume that it's different for me?"

"I guess we are always afraid."

"Do you remember that part in *Pride and Prejudice* where Darcy tells Elizabeth he loves her against his better judgment, despite the inferiority of her connections, and she's so insulted?"

"Mmmm," he said.

"I guess I love you against my better judgment. Against the part of me that says you live too far away and you're descended from Nazis, against it's too damn hard to make this work. I can't believe I let this happen."

"I guess you could say that I love you too, against the odds, I believe I do, yes," he said, as if he was checking internally to make sure.

I felt my stomach sinking. "What are we going to do? This can't possibly work out."

"I'm coming to visit you in September," he said. "Let's see how it goes."

"Okay," I whispered. "I have to get on the plane now."

"Call me when you get home."

"I will."

I settled into my seat and peered out the window, remembering a time a few years back when I left New Orleans, feeling in every bone of my body the pain of separation from Conor. But there was no pain now. I was older, and loss and endings in my life no longer felt like the end of me. Whether or not this worked didn't have such high stakes for me anymore. I had stopped being a survivor who couldn't handle disappointment and had started being a person like any other, secure enough in myself and my life to deal with the buffeting of external forces.

VIII

גלגול

reincarnation

Isaac and I flew to California on my twenty-seventh birthday to visit Justine, with whom I had stayed three years earlier on my first trip to the West Coast before driving cross-country. I spent the day scared and anxious. Twenty-seven! Why was that such a big number for me? It had been five years since I'd left, since the first birthday when I had started the ritual of measuring my progress. I had acknowledged that the transition years would be difficult. I had allowed myself a few miserable years; I had not been naïve about what to expect. And I found myself at my birthday each year thereafter assessing how far I'd come, internally and externally, from the last. And as my external world had shaped itself so exquisitely from year to year, I lamented at my slow-to-catch-up internal self, which still felt displaced and depersonalized.

I was twenty-seven. I had built the life I thought would bring me security and peace of mind. When I had stayed with Justine in her beautiful home in Moss Beach a few years ago and looked at her life, I'd thought, This is what I need! A home. And I had built it. Yet if there was something I had to face about this birthday in order to move on, it was this: There was nothing I could point to, externally, that would ever bring this transition period to a close and propel me into the future, which I had sacrificed everything to achieve. What had to happen on this birthday was an end to the ritual of measuring, of being hard on myself, of giving myself a time frame in which to achieve the impossible. I was right then, when I thought I needed to build a home, but I found the wrong place to build it: outside myself.

I knew then that I would not be charting my path anymore. It wasn't a race or a contest. I would need to learn to be okay with a little uncertainty in my life, a few blurry edges around my personality.

We drove down into the wilderness of the peninsula en route to Santa Cruz to take Isaac to the beach. On the way there we stopped on a cliff to take a closer look at a slender strip of fog that remained out on the ocean, the rest having burned away. It was bent at one end, like a refracted beam of light; it was reflected in the water as a silvery slash amid the brilliant blue. Two enormous red-tailed hawks cried out above us, and I looked up to see them flying in a circle around a nearly full moon. "You're almost finished," they seemed to say to me. "Just hang on a little while longer."

My phone rang. It was Isaac's dad.

"Yes?"

"Are you okay? Is Isaac okay?"

"Yes, of course. Why do you ask?"

"Someone started a rumor that you committed suicide. I freaked out."

"That's ridiculous. No, we're fine. We're on our way to the beach."

It wasn't until I ended the call that I noticed all the messages on my phone. I checked in on social media and saw that indeed the rumor was thriving. On Facebook, my friends were tagging me in posts that read "Homicide or suicide?" or "Is it really that hard to leave?"

I tweeted a photo of Isaac and myself. "We're having fun at the beach."

As I put my phone away and took a last look at the splendid, glittering ocean, I reflected on the irony. Why would anyone believe I could be at the moment of despair now, when I had put those dreadful years of wandering behind me, when I finally knew who I was in my very bones, and my life had just started to feel real? I had left, and it had been worth it, and I had come to cherish my freedom to build a sense of self that was authentic. I was no longer a ghost, threatened with obliteration.

In September, Markus and his mother came to visit. Isaac had already started second grade, and the leaves had begun to curl by the time they arrived. The weather was glorious, with brilliant blue skies that showcased clean, clear sunsets, like a ball dropping on New Year's Eve. We rowed across the deserted lake in the evening, the summer crowds having returned to the city after Labor Day, and crunched leaves underfoot as we explored picturesque New England towns.

I drove them into Manhattan one day, just to show Markus's mother the city. It was her first visit to the United States, and her first time traveling without her husband. She seemed tremulous throughout, trying to recapture the joy she had always felt while traveling, but which is never the same without your traveling companion.

We walked through Central Park, tasted gelato in the shadow of the Flatiron Building, and narrowly avoided a collision with a truck driver in the East Village. We drove over the Williamsburg Bridge and I offered to drive them through my old community. It was Sukkos, so the streets would be dead, but the Hasids would be out in full regalia. I pointed out the little wooden huts in people's front yards, porches, and fire escapes; the holiday was based on the ancient biblical celebration of the harvest, when people slept out-side in makeshift huts to watch their crops.

Ada gazed out the window, transfixed. I drove past the double brownstone I had grown up in. It looked silent and implacable, its window blinds tightly drawn, its heavy metal doors indifferent. In the next house, an old woman sat under the shade of her doorway and stared at me as I drove by. I bent my head to avoid being rec-ognized. At the red light, we paused, and across the street a family of Hasidic Jews crowded on the corner, young girls cooing at their nieces and nephews in strollers, a young couple standing shyly, removed from each other by the mandatory four feet.

"It's impossible for me to imagine you here," Markus said. "I look at you, and I look at them, and I just can't make the connection."

I thought, *I can't either at this point. It doesn't feel like my past, not when I look at it up close. My life is too different now to accommodate that story. But if this isn't my past, then what is?*

I drove down Kent Avenue and we parked at the waterfront. We walked down toward the little beach, from which you could see the entire Manhattan skyline. A Hasidic man had wandered over, no doubt trying to find a temporary escape, and he sat on a log with his black hat and coat neatly folded alongside him. He looked away as we approached.

"Careful," I told Markus. "Don't forget that they can understand German."

"Right," he said. "The last thing we would want is for them to figure out you're a former Jew dating a Nazi."

"Actually I was thinking more in terms of your own safety—they just don't like Germans, period."

We posed for a picture then, against the spendid, glittering backdrop. Ada held the bulky camera awkwardly, trying to figure out how to use it, and I froze my smile in patient expectation. But as the flash finally went off, Markus leaned in suddenly to kiss me on the mouth. Later, over a seafood dinner in an outdoor beer garden, I looked at the photo on the camera's small screen and thought it odd that the surprise and unease I had felt in that moment weren't at all apparent in the image.

At night we rolled toward the center of the bed, latching on to each other as if to avoid falling. He, who had never been able to sleep in the same bed with someone, and I, who had lain awake on those nights I spent with Conor, the weight of his arm heavy on my chest.

It's crazy how well we fit together, he whispered. Indeed I felt like an oddly shaped key that had finally found the right lock.

I took them to the local farmers' market on Saturday.

"How can this be?" he said as we drove past the exquisite views I had already become accustomed to. "It's exactly like the postcards! They don't even have to Photoshop the images."

His mother was positively gleeful when we arrived at the market. A bluegrass band strummed in the gazebo, and shoppers milled about in the autumn sunshine. "Just like in the movies," she whispered, enthralled.

We ran into various people I knew around town, and so I introduced them. There were my friends Dan and Debbie, Jewish lawyers from New York City, and Anita and Harvey, more Jewish lawyers from New York City. When we returned to the car, loaded up with fresh tomatoes and cheese and jam, Ada's face had suddenly gone white, and she appeared tired and withdrawn.

"What's wrong?" I asked her in German, but I couldn't quite make out her mumbled reply. I nudged Markus. "Ask her what's going on," I whispered.

He turned to his mother. They had a rapid exchange in German.

"Ah, she's never met any Jews in real life before," he said to me. "She's feeling a bit overwhelmed—actually she feels guilty." His tone was, as usual, neutral, almost amused.

"Guilty? Why would she feel guilty?" I asked, incredulous.

"Because of what her father did. It's her first time encountering the actual people who were persecuted by him. I think it just hit her."

"But I'm Jewish! She wasn't traumatized when she met me."

"True. But I think she's just starting to process what it means, you know. She never dealt with it before because it didn't come up."

Later, in my living room, I could see her try to recoup. She told us about her memories of her father, about how he had beaten her older brother when he came home talking of a Holocaust film his teacher had shown him. Ada's father had then visited the teacher in his home and threatened him with violence if he ever showed such filth in his classroom.

"I was so young I didn't really understand what was going on," she said. "But my brother did. Yet we never talked about it as adults. I'm sure he knew much more about our parents than I ever did."

"I don't care about what your parents did," I said. "I want to live in the present. I want my life to be filled with love and understanding and forgiveness. I don't want to get stuck with those old grudges and prejudices like the way I grew up. I want to get past it."

"Yes, but it's easier for you, perhaps," she said. "Only the forgiving can speak this way. The guilty cannot simply say that they want to get past it."

We were walking along the lake the next afternoon, Markus and I, and a gentle breeze was ruffling the leaves on the trees and creating small ripples in the ponds and streams that collected the lake runoff. I had a sudden memory of my childhood: It was summer, in the Catskills, and I was standing at the edge of an enormous open field of uncut grass. I started to run, and I sprinted across the entire field, my movements like a cat's, my whole body like a well-oiled machine. The wind picked up my hair and brushed across my cheeks. I had felt gloriously boundless in that precious stolen moment.

I broke out into a run then, to recapture that feeling that I had forgotten about. I ran the length of the road and then doubled back to meet Markus.

"You have good form," he said. "I expected you to run like a girl, knees out, slapping the ground—but you're a real runner. And you looked so happy and free, with your hair flying out behind you."

"I'm not a runner, though. No one has ever told me I can run."

"If you run like that without any training, then you're definitely a runner. You should try it, see what happens."

Later he played soccer with Isaac, teaching him to kick, to dribble, to pass. I sat on the lawn and watched. The late-afternoon sun glowed brightly from across the lake, blurring their outlines until they became shifting shadows against the light, as if they had disappeared into another world, another dimension. I was stuck as if behind a glass, viewing.

This feeling, of fitting together in a way that felt suspiciously part of some grand design, some greater story I couldn't quite recall but that filtered into my dreams as if from a past life, scared me for precisely that reason. Such a feeling was dangerous; its power did not promise happiness, but rather the opposite. There was love that nourished you, I thought, and then there was this kind of love, that grew independently like a tumor on your soul, starving your spirit until it disappeared. The feeling was too big for me.

I drove them both back to the airport that evening, feeling

numb. I couldn't imagine how I'd feel once he was gone. At the drop-off point, Markus looked at me and said, "It's like going sky-diving. You know you have a parachute strapped to your back, but it still feels like falling to your death. That's what it feels like to be leaving you right now." He laughed weakly, his eyes tired. I saw in his face the same exhaustion I had felt earlier. The feeling was too strong, too intense—there was no way he wasn't feeling knocked off his balance like I was.

"We'll be fine," I said briskly. "The parachute will open. We'll go back to our routines."

"I don't know," he said. "Maybe." He watched me drive off from the curb, holding his backpack with both hands. In the rear-view mirror I glanced back at his forlorn face, just once. I was still numb then, and stayed that way for the whole way home, and slept that way, too, turned away from where his body had been the night before, like some inexhaustible furnace to which I had been drawn for warmth.

I went down to the lake later that week, to watch the sunset. We had sat there a few days before and picked flowers, and I had cried.

"I'm scared to keep going," I had said. "Won't it hurt less if we stop now?"

"Why do you have to cut the rope already?" he had asked.

Because that's all I'm good at.

Now I watched as a heron skimmed the still waters for fish. The lake was silent. There were no boats, and most of the houses that fronted it were empty of their summertime residents. This time of year the lake began to feel like my private property.

I thought about distance, then, about my pattern of forming attachments to people who lived farther and farther away that had formed itself over the last few years. I wondered if it was as simple as perpetuating my own alienation, or if somehow I understood that by moving the goalpost ever farther, I was galvanizing myself to travel as far from my roots as possible.

In my life, I have expended so much effort in order to put distance between myself and the place I come from, and yet there still seems to be this chasm lying ahead of me, reminding me how far I truly have to go before I sleep, as Frost put it. Yet I wonder now if it is fair to say that I was pushing myself toward my dreams all along, instead of alienating them, in this process of assigning myself such long journeys.

These people that come from far away to breathe newness into my life; they move me. It is as if I am a playing piece on some enormous chessboard, inching along to victory in the grip of a shrewd mastermind intent on taking the long view. The strategy seems unfathomable at times, but I cannot deny that I am still on the board, advancing in the direction of an end goal. Though what awaits me on the other side I cannot guess, what a marvelous thrill it is, at times—contemplating that unknown shore toward which my inner compass invariably strains.

I find my young self now—sinking into my consciousness suddenly and heavily like quicksilver—twelve years old, sitting outside the principal's office. Even at that age, I'm getting into trouble for things I can't quite understand.

This time I know the rabbi will call my grandfather, my grandfather will call my aunt, and I'll get weeks of lectures and intense supervision because of something I said, or wore, or did in school without noticing. I'm sitting on the hard wooden bench swinging my legs, and my shoulders are hunched and I'm looking at the scuffed floor, and I can feel my eyes stinging, because I'm sad and weary, and I feel it's unfair.

I start to pray. I have one prayer, Psalm 13, which I say over and over when I find myself in difficult situations. I've memorized it by now. I whisper it now to myself, in Hebrew:

How long, O Lord, wilt thou forget me forever? How long wilt thou hide thy face from me? How long shall I take counsel in my soul, having sorrow in my heart by day? How long shall my enemy be exalted over me? Behold Thou, and answer me, O Lord my God; lighten mine eyes, lest I sleep the sleep of death; lest mine enemy say: "I have prevailed against him"; lest mine adversaries rejoice when I am moved. But as for me, in Thy mercy do I trust; my heart shall rejoice in Thy salvation. I will sing unto the Lord, because He hath dealt bountifully with me.

And then, sometime after the twenty-seventh or twenty-eighth iteration, the door to the office opens, and it's the secretary, saying the principal is too busy to see me today, and I should head back to class.

Oh the joy I experienced on that short walk back to the classroom, knowing I had been saved from certain punishment! How to describe the wonder in fathoming that with my prayer I might have reached over some looming wall to something powerful and magical on the other side that could save me! Still today I search within myself for that spirit, rendered lost and aimless by my subsequent alienation from all things familiar, clinging to the belief that somewhere in there is still the ability to manifest the impossible, see the invisible, touch another dimension.

In March of 2013, I attended the annual Poets & Writers fundraising dinner, where it was a long-standing tradition for each table to have its own writer as a host. At the beginning of the event, an MC announced each writer, asking us to stand up and be introduced to the audience, and I watched as brilliant and acclaimed authors rose from their seats, one by one, to be applauded. My name was called between Erica Jong's and Siri Hustvedt's, and as I stood up between the two of them and realized suddenly what my standing meant, my knees buckled and I had to hold on to the table to stay upright. I was standing beside writers I had worshipped and adored as a reader for so many years. I had never actually stopped to consider that I was a writer now too, that it was real, and I had made the transition into that community, giving back to the world with my words, with my voice.

And I went back to the little girl in the purple dress then, and asked her with a smile, "Did you ever think this is where we'd be?"

And I know, for a fact, that she never did. In that moment I gave her my hand to hold, and together we sat there on the stoop, looking out onto the empty street of our past. We were finally reunited, she and I, and everything was fine, just like I had promised.

acknowledgments

First I must thank my agent, Patricia Van der Leun. I can't believe we've worked on two books together now; it seems just yesterday that we met in that café on 74th. When I am too stuck in my own story to see things clearly, you light my way through the fog. I don't know if I would have the fortitude to continue along this path without that kind of support.

I would also like to extend my sincere, heartfelt gratitude to my publisher, David Rosenthal. You met me at my most naïve and vulnerable and somehow sniffed out an ember of potential, which you fanned into a flame. I won't say the process has been entirely painless, but I feel privileged to be under your eye and wing. I hope to continue to learn from you in the years to come.

Thank you so much, Sarah Hochman, for your consistent and unparalleled faith in my voice, for helping me find my narrative direction through much trial and error, and for your shrewd literary judgment. Liz Stein, thanks above all for making me laugh—and for making this book that much more fun to write! You were such an asset to the creative process. I hope we can work together again.

A very special thanks is owed to all the wonderful people at Blue Rider Press who had a hand in making this book the best it could be in every way. Aileen Boyle and Brian Ulicky are people I've been lucky to know for quite some time, and I must say it's awfully nice to work with them on such a personal level. I'm so grateful for all the efforts of this most excellent publicity department. I'm also really appreciative of Phoebe Pickering and Rebecca Harris for handling the everyday back-and-forth with such aplomb—it really does make the business of being a writer that much more appealing when you have such dedicated people on your side. Thanks to Marie Finamore for her keen eye, Meighan Cavanaugh for the beautiful design, and Linda Cowen for making the whole legal thing the opposite of a nightmare. For the marvelous cover, kudos is owed to Gregg Kulick.

I feel so lucky to have fellow travelers in my wanderings: Richard, who never ceases to inspire me; Odd and his family, who beckon like a welcoming lighthouse on distant shores for myself and many others; Kat and Scotty, for showing me that even the unconventional can find a sense of home and belonging; Milena and Audrey, those glamorous Jewish denizens of Paris—you've expanded my sense of what's possible, and my sense of self as well; Esther Munkacsi, a kindred spirit I met in Budapest—who, despite her Jewish-sounding name, did not actually need to be Jewish to show me the kind of solidarity and understanding the likes of which I have rarely come across—I want to commend your capacity for empathy despite seemingly intransigent limitations; Zoltán Janosi, Gabi Losonczi, and Farkas Bacsi—those few days I spent with you all in Nyíregyháza were some of the most poignant and transformative of my life. I will never be able to repay your immense generosity and kindness.

An additional thanks is owed to the lovely community of people who have made returning home after my wanderings a truly wonderful and welcoming experience. This is certainly new for me. Thank you, Dan and Debbie Sternberg, for your wise words, for your patience . . . and for turning my tears into laughter. Carol and Carlo Huber, I owe you a debt for generously inviting Isaac and me into your home and heart, and for broadening our cultural horizons in the process. Thanks to Julie and

ACKNOWLEDGMENTS

Mike Zahn for being so supportive and helpful and for hosting sleepovers and playdates when I couldn't find a sitter. To all the people at my son's school who have helped us both feel at home and among family, I am truly grateful.

Per, thank you for helping me translate that file, even though it was written in old Swedish. Gina, those few days that you hosted us in Murnau were transcendent. Thank you for opening up your home and your heart to total strangers. I feel I must also thank my various babysitters, on both sides of the ocean, who made it possible for me to juggle my parenting responsibilities while writing this book. And of course, my gratitude to every coffee shop and library across the world—by making yourself a haven with free WiFi, soothing ambience, and brain-jolting caffeine, you are a boon to writers temporarily displaced from home. I have been so fortunate to find anonymous yet heartfelt kindness in unexpected corners, and will try to pay that kindness forward to the next traveler I meet.

about the author

Deborah Feldman was raised in the Satmar Hasidic community in the Williamsburg section of Brooklyn, New York. Her first memoir, *Unorthodox*, was a *New York Times* bestseller. She is twenty-seven years old and lives in New England with her son, where she is currently working on her next book.